Fortune's Always Hiding

Fortune's Always Hiding

From Stratford to Seville

Paul Brand

First published by Pitch Publishing, 2023

Pitch Publishing
9 Donnington Park,
85 Birdham Road,
Chichester,
West Sussex,
PO20 7AJ
www.pitchpublishing.co.uk
info@pitchpublishing.co.uk

A CIP catalogue record is available for this book
from the British Library.

ISBN 978 1 80150 416 4

Typesetting and origination by Pitch Publishing

Printed and bound TJ Books Ltd.

Contents

Foreword

I HOPED to call this book *Finding Fortune* but, alas, Lady Luck remains elusive. It's not the West Ham fan's lot in life to prove victorious. I sometimes think how different things would be if I'd chosen to be a Manchester United fan. I mean, it would have made me a c***, and an embittered one at that come middle age, but at least my teenage years would have been happier.

For proper fans, their fortunes are intertwined with the fate of their football club. It's impossible to be truly joyful when your team is in the doldrums, and vice versa. My own symbiosis seems to have extended to my life path. I left Stratford at the exact point West Ham were preparing to move in, semi-reluctantly departing for the north-west of England on the final day of the London Olympics, having hitherto spent my life in the Hammers heartlands of Havering and Newham. Both relocations were supposed to represent fresh starts, a move on up, yet things rarely go to plan do they? Before my team even made their comparatively small move across the borough, I found myself hospitalised and unemployed at the same time I was supposed to be providing for a growing family.

It's frequently noted that football clubs act as surrogate families. West Ham thus became my umbilical cord, a source of nourishment connecting me to my roots and feeding me the motivation to keep going, because something better must be lurking around the corner. Our impending rebirth as West Ham–London (E20) gave me something to hold tight to, which might explain my relatively unswerving positivity towards Stratford. Navigating fatherhood for the first time also brought paternal empathy – leaving the Boleyn felt a little bit like kissing goodbye to my reckless youth, while the new stadium represented the weight of expectation that comes with being a grown-up and having to deal with more complex business.

Initially conceived as a blog, my scribblings were always contrary to the aims and objectives of the World Wide Web in that I never really sought an audience, deterred partly by the fact that my own kin were at loggerheads over our relocation. A brief foray into the volatile Twittersphere confirmed that I'm too introverted to be an online influencer, no matter that there was an obvious vacancy for a spokesperson on the more rational branch of the supporters' club. Instead, my writing fulfilled the traditional role of a journal, preserving my sanity by acting as a release valve for the myriad of frustrations that come with caring far too much about 11 men kicking a ball about and the ridiculous hoopla that surrounds it.

Hindsight is a wonderful thing, as is the ability to learn from one's mistakes, and revisiting my words it was astonishing both how many hit the target, Cassandra-like, and how many missed the proverbial barn door, Mido-like. This book is intended as a time capsule, so my thoughts are unexpurgated, exposed for your merriment. Everything within is my personal opinion, so if you disagree then either write a book of your own or feel free to debate the details over a pint, which is how generations of football fans have vented their frustrations and why Twitter will never be as good as the pub.

Will I ever find fortune? Well, I suppose I can consider myself fortunate if my thoughts finally find an appreciative audience. But just so you know, I'd bin you all off in a heartbeat for one gleaming Carabao Cup.

Year Zero – 2015/16

Splitting Heirs

18 September 2015

Aside from the inevitable prelude of death, an inheritance carries largely positive connotations of treasured belongings and new-found riches. But inheriting an affection for a football team is more often a curse, carrying failure, disappointment and heartache. And it's tantamount to child cruelty, inflicting a life sentence of supporting West Ham on to an unknowing infant.

I was born in late 1980 so am yet to see us lift a trophy, save the widely ridiculed Intertoto Cup (I'm also discounting play-off wins because, as jubilatory as winning the richest match in football might be, they're essentially second-tier bronze-medal matches). That Gerrard equaliser in injury time of the 2006 FA Cup Final remains the most painful moment of my life, and I happened to need airlifting to hospital earlier this year! I'd like to be able to blame my father for 30-plus years of suffering but, beyond encouraging an interest in football, he's not the one responsible. It was my own choice. At least to an extent it was; neither as a foetus nor as a toddler did I have much say in picking a house on the Essex–East

London borders. You see, as far as I'm concerned, there are only two valid reasons for supporting a sports team: the first, familial allegiance, was in my case overridden by the second, geography. When I asked at the age of seven who our local team was, and Dad answered 'West Ham', a seed was sown.

Things could have been different. He might have said Dagenham & Redbridge. Or Hornchurch, depending on how low down the football pyramid he was prepared to go. But he stuck to teams with league status and, of my own volition, I became a West Ham fan. In doing so I deviated from family tradition, for I'm descended from a clan of masochists who have had it even worse than me by backing Fulham. The words 'West Ham' must have stuck in my father's throat, for Alan Taylor is his Steven Gerrard, ruining Cup Final Day in 1975. He's suffered 60-plus years *sans* success, and my two grandfathers, who were also Fulham fans, even longer, albeit alleviated by that Irons-engineered World Cup victory in '66.

The thorny issue of family bonds versus geographical proximity rears its head again now that my own son approaches his first birthday. Should I buy him a little West Ham replica kit? Obviously I'd like him to follow West Ham. Misery loves company. But having relocated to Chester, they're not his local team as they were mine. Do I guide him towards the Olympic Stadium, or allow him to veer off in his own direction as I did? I was allowed to stray. Until Dad took me to Craven Cottage (post-visiting Upton Park) I thought Fulham was just the name of the push-along toy dog that I'd long outgrown and had been banished to the loft along with other things we no longer had any use for. This shaggy metaphor probably captures the old man's feelings towards Fulham FC as they languished unloved in the old Fourth Division. We all want our children to be happy, and West Ham represented a much greater shot at happiness, fresh off our highest-ever league finish.

But even with the promise of a bright future ahead in Stratford, looking instead towards Salford would surely gift my boy the greatest chance of tasting success. Of course this might be wrongly equating glory-hunting with happiness. Already one senses a hollowness to Manchester City's victories as hope has morphed into expectation. For most sets of supporters, a League Cup run is like the search for the Holy Grail, and actually getting your hands on it would spark wild celebrations, the memory of which would be cherished forever. The big boys, meanwhile, treat it as a mere consolation prize.

Our location in the north-west offers a choice of so-called big clubs, equidistant as we are between Manchester and Liverpool. The red half of Merseyside might be seen as offering the best of both worlds since my wife is a Scouse lass with Anfield-going relatives, although she herself is pretty much disinterested in the 'beautiful game' and would probably declare herself a Hammerette thanks to my influence. Opting for Liverpool would be quite apt, a deliverance of karma and the sins of the father being visited back upon him following those torturous cup finals of 1975 and 2006.

An alternative that would broach no complaint from me is choosing to support Chester. As the Boleyn was from my previous home, the Deva Stadium is within walking distance of our home now. Emotional investment could be rewarded with a return to the Football League or an

FA Cup giant-killing (knowing us, against the mighty Hammers!), which would measure as high on the Richter scale as winning the competition would for us. I'm a strong believer that supporting smaller clubs bequeaths a certain romance, not to mention mental fortitude.

I suppose the ideal course is that my offspring's loyalty to West Ham is taken as given, never questioned but not forced on to him either. The process of good old-fashioned indoctrination has already been started by his grandmother (my mother), who bought him West Ham coats and bibs. She always endorsed my own support for West Ham, I think out of spite to my father for devoting a bit too much time to sport in general, if not Fulham. And that was pre-Sky Sports, so I might want to rein in my own consumption so as not to be on shaky ground with the missus! Buying him the kit won't imprint the Irons on his soul but it's a start in forging a bond. I'm not going to go as far as prising his eyes open *Clockwork Orange*-style and making him watch *Upton Park's 100 Greatest Goals* on repeat, although that might be fitting revenge for the past 12 months of sleep deprivation!

Hopefully he'll be a happy Hammer and we'll get to enjoy successes together rather than endure relegations. But whatever club he chooses, even if he shuns football entirely, I'll find solace in the thought that it could be worse: rather than moving a couple of hundred miles, I might have moved just a couple of miles north and thus presented him with the legitimate option of being a Spurs fan.

MC 1-2 WTF

20 September 2015

[Man City 1–2 West Ham]

Team	P	GD	Pts	Form
Man City	6	10	**15**	WWWWL
West Ham	6	6	**12**	LLWWW
Leicester	6	4	**12**	WDDWD
Man Utd	5	3	**10**	WWDLW
Arsenal	6	0	**10**	WDWWL
Everton	6	3	**9**	WLDWD

Did anyone actually enjoy the match yesterday? I mean, from the 94th minute on it was absolutely brilliant, but the preceding 60 minutes felt like a heart attack waiting to happen! Maybe I'm just a particularly nervous spectator, and it was certainly exhilarating even if it didn't quite meet my definition of enjoyable.

One thought that had been running through my head in the early stages of this season and that I now feel compelled to share is the bold prediction that there will be an interloper in the top four come May. I refrained from writing this last night lest I be accused of intoxication (I did indeed have a stiff whisky to celebrate/calm my nerves!), and I may well be suffering from vertigo, but beating the champions-elect encouraged the belief that it could *possibly* be West Ham.

Let's be clear, this isn't a roar of 'Champions League here we come'. Past false dawns have taught me to be pessimistic and I'd still be delighted with a top-half finish and an exciting cup run.

Improvements in the middle echelons of the Premier League, notably the strengthened squads of Stoke, Palace and ourselves, have been well documented elsewhere and the league is expected to be more condensed than ever before. And as Slaven Bilić's Claret-and-Blue Army have spectacularly proven, the big boys are beatable, even on their own turf.

With their unrivalled investment (the starting XI we overcame was the most expensive ever assembled) and an otherwise bright start to the domestic season, I fully expect City to recover from the bloodied nose we dealt them and I wouldn't be surprised to see them stay atop the Premier League summit all season. Chelsea should be pushing them close and the sole downside of yesterday's result is that we've done the Darker Shade of Blues a favour in reducing their arrears. Conversely, had we maintained our dismal home form and lost to Newcastle on Monday night [2-0], the consolation I had prepared was that Chelsea would have plummeted into the relegation zone, which indicates how far off the pace they are. However, it would still be pie-in-the-sky thinking to suggest we have any chance of finishing above them.

Arsenal were my other title contenders at the start of the season but we quickly exposed their old frailties [Arsenal 0-2 West Ham]. Wenger was quoted on Friday as saying, 'You have to score the perfect goal to beat Čech,' which will come as news to Kouyaté and Zárate! But if it's same old, same old for Arsenal, then it goes without saying that they'll finish third.

That leaves one space to be filled in the top four. Manchester United seem the obvious contenders but they also appear immensely fallible these days. As with Big Fat Sam at the Boleyn, Van Gaal isn't on the same wavelength as the Old Trafford crowd and there are bust-ups simmering that could derail their campaign. Of the other usual suspects, Liverpool and Spurs are locked in a state of perpetual transition that they look incapable of moving on from. If I were a betting man then I might back Everton for that final Champions League spot – a solid, settled team with some strength in depth and an eminently sensible manager.

Once can be dismissed as lucky, twice as fortunate, but three remarkable away wins [see also Liverpool 0-3 West Ham] … Naturally they've raised hopes that we might enjoy a glorious season but, as Bilić wisely instructed in light of the Arsenal and Europa League matches, we shouldn't get too high after positive results or too low after negative ones. A fiver on us exiting the Capital One Cup at the hands of fellow high-flyers Leicester appears a safe bet right now.

[Leicester 2-1 West Ham, League Cup third round]

Have Boots, Will Travel

24 September 2015

The breaking news that Carlton Cole is set to sign for Scottish champions Celtic (presumably to play football and not to run their social media, despite providing far more entertainment on Twitter than on the pitch in recent years) begs the question, far more pressing than how the game north of the border has reached such a perilous state: just how far north would I have to move to make it as a top-level footballer?

I cling forlornly to the belief that I always could have made it, if only I'd been spotted at the right age. Unfortunately I had the competitive disadvantage of coming from a hotbed of talent. In my school year, playing in my local league were John Terry, Ledley King, Bobby Zamora, Jlloyd Samuel, Paul Konchesky and Fitz Hall. And they all played for the same team, Senrab. And, believe it or not, Comet were better! In hindsight, those 13-0 thumpings that had ten-year-old me on the verge of tears over Sunday lunch probably represented the highlight of my footballing career, an opportunity to share the pitch with players who would one day fulfil every schoolboy's dream of pulling on an England shirt and gracing the turf of Wembley. Maybe if I'd grown up in Stirling I'd have stood a better chance of standing out and being talent-spotted.

So, besides learning earlier than most what an irritant JT could be, my youth was lost to thrashings that damaged my football prospects but encouraged me instead to concentrate on the academic side of things, leading to the University of Warwick. There I learned just how bad most boffins are at sport, making me look like Zidane in comparison as I averaged two goals a game in the halls league and comfortably won a Sciences six-a-side tournament with the Sugar Daddies, diligently named after the nightclub at which we imbibed Vodka Red Bulls at 50p a shot the night before. Confidence boosted, the realisation that I was no longer eligible for England U21s brought with it a pang of remorse. Maybe if I'd attended the University of St Andrews I might have been papped dumping Prince William on his arse during a kickabout and the professional clubs would have wondered who this whizz they'd overlooked was …

Rags to riches tales such as Jamie Vardy's and our own Michail Antonio's, slowly working his way up from playing non-league with Tooting & Mitcham, mean that hope springs eternal but, at the age of 34 and having not kicked a ball in nine months, I think I'm ready to concede that it's never gonna happen. But if Kevin Nolan pitches up playing Champions League for Zenit St Petersburg or any other team higher up the lines of latitude, then I'm relocating to Greenland to resurrect my own dreams of footballing glory.

Job Description: Carefully Handle 50,000+ Dreams on a Weekly Basis

25 September 2015

Once upon a time I believed that managers made little or no difference to their team's fortunes. Then along came Glenn Roeder and Avram Grant who, in the harshest manner imaginable, taught me the error of my ways. I continue to believe that the manager's influence is often overstated, particularly by the national media, which caricatures the Premier League's protagonists as 'the special one' or 'the wally with the brolly', when the truth is undoubtedly more nuanced. But, especially in the wake of Big Sam, I'm willing to concede that the manager's role is an important one. So, here's my attempt at answering the $64,000 question: what makes a good manager, and have we found one in Slaven Bilić?

In fairness to Roeder and Grant, both seemed thoroughly decent people who perhaps weren't suited to the cut-throat world of football management, in which it sometimes seems that you have to be a tyrant, like Fergie, or an intolerable prick, like Mourinho, if you want to prosper. Nice guys finish last, although Eddie Howe, Garry Monk and Roberto Martínez are among a few gallantly working to dispel this myth, even if they remain some way off finishing first.

If we're to accept that statistics show Mourinho to be the best, does that mean he'd be welcome at any club?

Hand on my heart, I can say that I wouldn't want him at West Ham. At least not the latest model of Mourinho. When he first arrived at Stamford Bridge a decade ago, he was already big-headed, dubbing himself 'the special one' before the tabloids got there, but he did so with a knowing smirk that made his outlandish arrogance bearable to most neutrals, even us West Ham fans, who are naturally disinclined towards anyone calling SW6 home. Even when being rude or obstinate, his actions would reach the height of farce, such as when he was allegedly smuggled into the Champions League quarter-final tie with Bayern in a laundry basket in order to beat his self-inflicted touchline ban, which made it impossible to think of him as 'an enemy of football'.

But since returning to English football in 2013, admittedly after even more success in Italy and Spain, he seems to have bought into his own myth, with his second spell at Chelsea characterised by the petulance that helped bring a premature end to his first. Like it or not, in this media-saturated age, a manager's job goes beyond tactics and team talks; a manager is its club's public figurehead. Abramovich reportedly doesn't take kindly to his frontman abusing the medical staff but Mourinho will be indulged his outbursts and myopic viewpoints on *Match of the Day* as long as he's able to haul his team back into title contention.

Personally, I'd prefer the club's spokesperson to be more judicious, and therefore appreciate that Slaven is more eloquent than most, even in his second language. As spokesperson, it's also imperative that a manager understands the ethos of the club he represents, which is where Bilić has a big head start on Allardyce. I'm not a Big Sam hater. Whatever our most vocal fans might shout, he's a good pragmatic manager with a strong track record and was probably exactly what we needed at the time. We took our medicine but it would have been easier to swallow if he hadn't so forcefully denigrated the 'West Ham Way'.

For Sam and Sir Alex and anyone else who proclaims not to understand what this is, I'll attempt to explain in the simplest terms: passing football, with an emphasis on entertainment. The vast majority of West Ham fans know that trophies are out of reach, although it goes without saying that we'd still like to have a damn good go at winning them and we'll accept any league finish that doesn't result in the tears of relegation, as long as we're entertained along the way. Then there's the academy and the long-held tenet that homegrown youth deserves a chance. Handing 16-year-old Reece Oxford his league debut, away to Arsenal no less, was Bilić underlining that he knows all about our club, having of course served as a player under Harry Redknapp. 'Arry, for all his faults, would have tutored him well, having been a product of the academy himself. Although out of fashion, I like the idea of appointing from within because it breeds a consistent philosophy and I see it as a point of pride that the club has had just 15 full-time managers in its long history.

The point being made, rather long-windedly, is that the blend of club and manager, not to mention players, is far more important than anything one individual can bring. For all his love of Opta data and talk of maximising performance, when Big Sam was unable to understand the basic concept behind the club, it always made me question whether he could ever really be much of a tactical genius. And in the words of the late great Brian Clough, whose antics put Mourinho to shame, 'There's so much crap talked about tactics.' Even if a manager does possess genuinely revolutionary ideas, good luck trying to explain them to John Terry or Ashley Cole!

In short, I'm happy with the appointment of Slaven and what I've seen since he's taken charge further convinces me that he and West Ham will be a good fit. It's a shame that he wasn't regarded as the automatic choice when we parted ways with Allardyce; I can see the appeal of some of the other contenders and our supposed first choice was undoubtedly a big name, hence his final destination, but in terms of his footballing philosophy Rafael Benítez is basically Sam on steroids.

Back to the bigger question: what makes a good manager? In conclusion, I'm buggered if I know, but not as buggered as Football League chairmen, who on average pay for a new one every 14 months.

Ignoble Omission

2 October 2015

Poor Mark Noble. Every international break, when the likes of Darren Randolph, Joey O'Brien and James Collins desert club for country, he remains rooted in Chadwell Heath. He couldn't be blamed for taking the well-trodden path of the average (in more than one sense of the word) Premier League player and opting to play for the Republic of Ireland, based on ancestral ties, regardless of whether or not he's ever actually set foot on the Emerald Isle. But I'd like to think he's better than that, both in terms of quality and in treating international representation as a sacred birthright rather than a matter of convenience.

There's a section of the Irons support that's started to slander Noble recently, mainly in the belief that he doesn't merit automatic selection if we hope to move to the next level and be competing for a European place. But in any team aiming to play at a high level, no one warrants an unchallenged place. His Canning Town roots have even been used as a stick to beat him with – 'He's only been made captain coz he's a local lad!' With some people you're damned either way.

The sloppy cross-field pass that gifted Robbie Brady Norwich's first goal last weekend [West Ham 2-2 Norwich] provided ammunition for his detractors, but it was uncharacteristic of his fine early-season form. Even following that error, two Sky Sports pundits (not the greatest purveyors of wisdom and rationality, I know) included him in their team of the season so far and he's regularly found towards the top of the statistical league tables for passing, tackling and distance covered. I wouldn't disagree with some of the claims being made for Winston Reid to be club captain instead but Noble embodies a lot of what's good about our club and you can't go too far wrong with Mr Reliable, producing 7.5/8 out of 10 performances every week, even if he's rarely the star man.

Personally I wouldn't swap Noble for one of our old boys who appears to have re-established his place in the national squad. He might not match Michael Carrick for range of passing but Carrick somehow manages to disguise floating about in front of the back four without ever putting his foot in as elegant positional play. Noble is a more complete midfielder who operated in the channels and then went box-to-box before improving immeasurably as a defensive shield after a couple of seasons spent with Scotty Parker. Perhaps Noble's big problem, and the reason that England recognition continues to elude him, is that he's a jack of all trades, master of none.

Still, when you look at some of the other capped midfielders in recent years, he has a right to feel aggrieved at not receiving the call: Leon Osman (a similarly tidy footballer who should be Noble's role model for not losing hope), Jonjo Shelvey, Jake Livermore, Tom Huddlestone ... then we come to Ryan Mason, who elbowed his way into the squad on the basis of half a season's good performances, and now Dele Alli gets promoted above him based on three bright shows! Not that Alli doesn't display great potential, but isn't the under-21 team designed for nurturing youthful promise and the senior squad reserved for proven performers?

It's common practice for members of early-season surprise packages to earn that England call, hence Ryan Bertrand and Nathaniel Clyne of Southampton breaking into the squad this time last year. We're third, and ... nothing! Upton Park ought to be a regular destination for Roy Hodgson this season to check on the form of Cresswell, Jenkinson, Tomkins and a fit-again Carroll, as well as Noble. Then again, based on current form, maybe he's best sticking to our away matches.

As news of the latest England squad broke yesterday, Nobes could be forgiven for wearing an even more perplexed look than he did after being farcically sent off against Liverpool. But, in consolation, he's keeping good company with Billy Bonds, another Hammers captain who was unfairly overlooked for international duty. If he manages to attain Bonzo's legendary status then he can retire content, regardless of whether or not he ever gets to wear the Three Lions.

England Squad – Euro 2016 Qualifiers: Estonia (H), Lithuania (A)

Goalkeepers Jack Butland (Stoke City), Joe Hart (Manchester City), Tom Heaton (Burnley)

Defenders Ryan Bertrand (Southampton), Gary Cahill (Chelsea), Nathaniel Clyne (Liverpool), Kieran Gibbs (Arsenal), Phil Jagielka (Everton), Phil Jones (Manchester United), Chris Smalling (Manchester United), John Stones (Everton)

Midfielders Dele Alli (Tottenham Hotspur), Ross Barkley (Everton), Michael Carrick (Manchester United), Adam Lallana (Liverpool), James Milner (Liverpool), Alex Oxlade-Chamberlain (Arsenal), Jonjo Shelvey (Swansea City), Raheem Sterling (Manchester City)

Forwards Danny Ings (Liverpool), Harry Kane (Tottenham Hotspur), Wayne Rooney (Manchester United), Jamie Vardy (Leicester City), Theo Walcott (Arsenal)

The Sick Note Blues

5 October 2015

I'm crocked. Have been since January when my scooter came off worse in a high-speed altercation with a Land Rover, which is presumably why sportsmen seem to be contractually obliged to drive heavy-duty vehicles and are banned from two wheels, although former Fulham right-back Moritz Volz endeared himself to many a London commuter and no doubt gave manager Roy Hodgson palpitations by cycling to home matches. In my motoring mishap I managed to break multiple bones but not the notorious metatarsal, which is where my half-baked analogy with football's walking wounded begins …

The metatarsal, of course, shot to fame on the eve of the 2002 World Cup thanks to David Beckham and has since enjoyed reprise appearances in the careers of Gary Neville, Wayne Rooney, John Terry, Michael Owen and Ledley King, although in the case of the latter two it was very much a cameo, with the hamstrings and knees the headline injuries. This English curse of the metatarsal is striking in two respects. First, the innocuousness of its occurrences, far closer (at least to the untrained eye) to having your toe trod on than the horrific collisions that caused David Busst or Luke Shaw's leg-breaks. Second, the injury's complete abstention from the world of soccer until the noughties; one wonders whether the metatarsal is a product of Darwinian evolution, an anatomical mutation designed to improve free-kick taking that lay undiscovered until Beckham brought it to everyone's attention.

Perhaps because of its diminutive dimensions, perhaps because of its association with sarong-wearing Mr Spice, a fractured metatarsal fails to attract too much compassion from the average spectator. A break to the more prominent tibia or fibula, on the other hand, perhaps also because it's more inconveniently incapacitating in everyday life, is a valid reason for commiseration. Here I have some sympathy for the metatarsal: size isn't everything. The filthy-minded among you can stifle your laughs. I'm referring to the tympanic membrane, which does admittedly sound a bit pervy. Indeed, the only serious ongoing ill-effect I'm feeling from my accident is due to the perversion of this teeny inner ear tissue after it was shunted out of place. In the aftermath of my own impairment, I'm more sympathetic towards 'smaller', less conventional injuries that don't carry noticeably visible scars.

Which brings me on to our most prominent 'sick note', Andy Carroll. Most fans seem to have run out of patience with the big guy, or see him as a superfluous throwback to the playing style of Big Sam. Without desiring the return of long-ball, I do wish to mount a defence of our record signing. To begin with, he's not helped by that £15m price tag. It's funny how fans' perspectives on an injury alter according to the player; Dean Ashton's wrecked ankles were a matter for mourning, whereas Carroll's have almost become a source of mirth, gallows humour masking the drain on the club's finances. Perception is probably skewed by the belief that we'd unearthed a relative bargain in Ashton, a player in the ascendancy who was destined for greatness, whereas Carroll had already failed to live up to one astronomical transfer fee. Another way of seeing things is that Carroll is now the same age Ashton was when he was cruelly forced to retire but has already scaled greater peaks, having played and scored at Euro 2012 and having produced performances that persuaded Kenny Dalglish (a four-time league-winning manager not known for his route-one tactics) to part with £35m. Still, both Carroll and Ashton would no doubt contest that they've been denied the opportunity to fulfil their true potential, even if it's not yet too late for one of them.

Many will claim that Carroll's career has been in decline since he swapped Tyneside for Merseyside to join a team that didn't play to his obvious strengths. This underestimates his impact. Just as Ashton came close to etching his name into history in the 2006 FA Cup Final, only to be outdone by Scouse Steven to the extent that it's now agonisingly known as the Gerrard Final, the much-maligned Carroll very nearly defined the 2012 final. Despite scoring the semi-final winner in a derby against Everton, he had to wait until the 54th minute of the final against Chelsea before being introduced as a substitute, by which time Liverpool were 2-0 down. The term 'unplayable' is overused, but for the remainder of the match he was absolutely unplayable, scoring one and having another late effort spectacularly saved by Čech, with replays needed to confirm whether or not the ball had crossed the line. A couple of centimetres might have dramatically altered his career trajectory. Which makes it sound as if he's been on a downward spiral ever since, when in fact we've been the beneficiaries of some similarly devastating performances, perhaps most memorably against Swansea [West Ham 3-1 Swansea, 2014/15]. We've not seen as much of this as we'd have liked, and I therefore empathise with fans' frustrations, but consider how frustrating this must be for the man himself.

The critics will argue that picking up a weekly pay cheque of £80,000 for lying on the treatment table will significantly ease any mental anguish. I now know that, yes, a degree of financial security does lessen the burden, although it would be amusing if millionaire footballers were forced to survive on statutory sick pay. I also know how defunct you can be made to feel when incapable of doing the job you trained for, especially with aspersions being cast; when I've visited my workplace – a local secondary school – I know full well that some of the glances from students say, 'He looks alright, must be milking it,' which is nothing compared to the abuse dished out to footballers on the terraces and internet forums! And it's probably fair to say that professional footballers, having dedicated endless hours of their youthful leisure time to have forged a career in such a competitive industry, are more addicted to their vocation than I am to teaching.

A further black mark against Carroll is the stream of Instagram and Twitter selfies snuggling up to *TOWIE*'s Billi Mucklow on nights out, which don't do much to evoke sympathy. Rather than reminding us that he's a human being with a family and social life beyond his football career, this increased visibility (not available to Ashton less than a decade earlier) awards him the status of celebrity rather than working man, which serves to irritate fans denied the chance to see him demonstrate the skills for which he became famous in the first place. Many footballers (or their agents) take to social media under the misapprehension that it brings them closer to fans when in fact it tends to have the opposite effect by highlighting the ever-widening social divide. This affliction, rather than being unique to Carroll, is symptomatic of the modern game.

And why is it that injuries are more widespread? Gone are the days of 85/86, when we flourished with a squad of just 18, five of whom started fewer than two matches, with a grand total of 17 substitutions made all season! Those players were battle-hardened men who earned our respect. Many of us will fondly recall the 'magic sponge', which cured all ills but is now nowhere to be seen, replaced by state-of-the-art medical technology. Cars are supposedly safer than they've ever been, offering greater protection as the technology has evolved, so why has science not helped to protect footballers' precious feet? Football boots is a misnomer when players' footwear these days is more akin to slippers, offering lightness and flexibility but very little in the way of protection, which is another possible explanation for the emergence of the metatarsal into the public consciousness. According to a brand statement, Carroll wears Nike Hypervenom Phantom II soccer cleats, which sound dangerous, but the threat is presumably not meant to be to the player's own ankles. Had I gone driving in a beanie hat rather than a motorcycle helmet then it goes without saying that my injuries would have been rather more severe!

So, to some extent, the injury woes of 21st-century footballers are self-inflicted and sympathy for a pricey millionaire playboy is always going to be in short supply. But let's not lose sight of why our owners paid £15m for Carroll in the first place. Footballers who can change the direction of a game are in as short supply as our sympathy and, although dominant in aerial duels, Carroll is more than a long-ball merchant. Obviously, as long as he's crocked he's essentially worthless to the club, but he should be exceptionally motivated to prove his worth upon his comeback, which will hopefully last longer than his previous ones. We need to accept that he'll be rusty and won't look like a £15m player straight away, but just as I hope to get my teaching career back on track before long, let's hope that Carroll can recapture the form that's so far fetched an aggregated £50m in transfer fees. That way, even if he doesn't suit Bilić's preferred formation and playing style, we can either recoup some of our losses or we'll have one hell of a Plan B!

Schadenfreude: Mourinho's New German Signing

9 November 2015

[Stoke City 1-0 Chelsea]

Pos		Team	P	GD	Pts
15	▲	Norwich	12	-7	**12**
16	▼	Chelsea	12	-7	**11**
17	▲	Newcastle	12	-9	**10**
18	▼	Bournemouth	12	-13	**8**
19	▶	Sunderland	12	-13	**6**
20	▶	Aston Villa	12	-10	**5**

I find it amazing that the English language doesn't have an equivalent of the German word schadenfreude. The sheer notion of taking pleasure in another's misfortune seems more suited to the English psyche than that of perennial winners Deutschland (two World Wars and one World Cup aside of course).

Just how much we relish schadenfreude was rammed home by the weekend's football. Despite being 200 miles removed from London and without access to Sky Sports, I witnessed the rivalry of the North London derby played out minute by minute across Twitter, Facebook and WhatsApp. What was clear was that neither set of fans wanted to win for the sake of the three points that are on offer every match and for what they'd do to the club's own league position; success was instead defined by denying the opposition gratification. Honours even was the ideal result for all concerned: Arsenal were kept off the top spot, and Spurs kept at arm's reach from the coveted top four.

But many Spuds still derived satisfaction from leapfrogging West Ham, having been in the unusual position of looking up at the East End upstarts for much of this season. For a few hours at least, fifth became the new fourth, with local bragging rights over a position that bestows entry to the dreaded Europa League and heartache at coming so close to the riches of the Champions League. And if things were to remain as they are for the next 26 matches, it can be guaranteed that West Ham fans would derive more pleasure in seeing Spurs fall agonisingly short of the Promised Land yet again than we would from our second-highest-ever Premier League finish and the prospect of Thursday night European football in our new home.

Schadenfreude is stamped all over derby matches. West Ham vs Spurs isn't even really a local rivalry, but in the absence of Millwall, Leyton Orient and Charlton from the top flight (ha, ha, ha!), it's the best the Hammers have. And the best of these fixtures in recent years must surely be the 2006 lasagne-gate, when a 2-1 victory, aided by ten Tottenham players being struck down by food poisoning, denied our neighbours a Champions League place. Far more valuable than the three points that sealed mid-table mediocrity was the pain etched on the faces of our opposition's fans. And you can be sure Arsenal fans took almost as much pleasure from the fact that Spurs didn't get the fourth Champions League spot than the fact that they did. Gifting fourth spot to Spurs' biggest rivals was also the cheese on top of the lasagne for Hammers fans because Arsenal, by virtue of being a few miles further west, aren't such fierce foes. That said, it's still pleasurable to see their Premier League and Champions League hopes quashed each year.

Then again, Chelsea are even further west, and we hate them with a passion. But most people hate Chelsea, that's the price paid for success. When there are only three domestic trophies to be won annually and they're typically divvied out between a small cartel of clubs, it follows that fans of clubs outside this cartel, denied the chance to actually celebrate success, will be forced into celebrating the failure of others. So schadenfreude isn't just the product of intense local enmities, it's woven into the fabric of being a football fan. The season's end is a case in point: it doesn't matter that we've been through it umpteen times ourselves, empathy goes flying out of the window and a gleeful sociopath emerges at the sight of grown men weeping because their team have tumbled into the Championship. Which brings us back to Chelsea … regardless of how our own teams perform, an awful lot of fans would consider this to be the greatest season of all time if the Blues' rotten form was to continue and we got to see their fans crying over relegation!

So here's an attempt to coin an English equivalent to schadenfreude, albeit with a distinctly Portuguese flavour. Inspired by the joy of the masses at the sour-faced failings of Chelsea's manager this season, I propose *Mourinhumour* as a new entry in the Oxford English Dictionary.

In Defence of the Davids

13 November 2015

A porn pedlar would, you might think, face some difficulty in passing a 'fit and proper person' test, but this risible piece of legislation wouldn't bar Hitler, Stalin, Pol Pot or even Massimo Cellino from running a football club. However, I put it to you that Messrs Gold and Sullivan are in fact among the most fit and proper persons around today.

The best of luck to Leeds fans in wrestling ownership of their club away from the nutty Italian who's currently running it into the ground. It's heartening to see so many fan consortiums seeking to take back control of their clubs but they're almost invariably formed in the face of adversity, a desperate last resort once negligent chairmen have already taken hundred-year-old institutions to the brink of annihilation. We, on the other hand, are fortunate to already have fans in charge. They're not without their faults and, as the controversial Olympic Stadium move proves, not all fans will agree with them all of the time, but Gold (on our books as a schoolboy in the '50s) and Sullivan (wishes he'd been on the books) undoubtedly have the club's best interests at heart and, despite the earlier Hitler quip, dictatorships do actually hold some key advantages over decision-making by committee. At the same time, Gold and Sullivan are astute businessmen who I trust not to do a Ridsdale, reaching beyond our means in pursuit of glory at the risk of devastating consequences.

David Sullivan was mocked a couple of weeks ago for saying that the aim was to finish in the top four and that we could even do the double. A dire defeat to Watford in the next match [Watford 2-0 West Ham], followed by an injury to the team's creative hub, Dimitri Payet, would make a mockery of any such claim, but anyone who bothered to read beyond the headlines would see that this wasn't the grandstanding braggadocio that most media outlets made it out to be, rather a touchingly sweet statement along the lines of 'what's the point of being involved in sport if you can't even dream of glory?'

The same week we had David Gold inviting ridicule for re-tweeting a missing persons plea accompanied by an image of underused deadline day signing Michail Antonio. This after he'd tweeted news of Pedro Obiang's signing accompanied by a photo of Angelo Ogbonna, with many wags joking that we only signed the latter to cover the chairman's blushes. Such are the perils of the baby boomer generation taking to social media. Best leave it to youngsters such as Jack Sullivan, he's far less likely to put his foot in … oh dear. Such embarrassing errors rightly receive a degree of criticism but, in the age of super-rich owners hiding behind hedge funds, I find our owners' clumsy attempts at transparency to be endearingly humanising.

Among the other charges levelled at the Davids is their reliance on Karren Brady, another outspoken presence who doesn't always endear herself to fans but in my view is admirably bolshy. Complaints about her, unfortunately, can't escape the whiff of misogyny. Then there's the time spent at Birmingham, with Brummies having been vocal critics of their regime. Surely in retrospect they can appreciate that Gold and Sullivan brought some good times to St Andrew's – the best in my memory. I remember the optimism when Carson Yeung took over, not dissimilar to when Eggert Magnússon arrived at Upton Park. Oh how misguided that was, on both counts. Both clubs have a lot to thank Gold and Sullivan for.

I've heard it said that the move to Stratford, which for right or wrong was masterfully engineered, will attract new owners who can take us to another level. I think the moral to be taken from the tales of Yeung, Magnússon and countless others is that the grass isn't always greener and I for one hope our current owners stick around to ensure the turf is smooth in E20.

What Is Love?

4 December 2015

Cards on the table time, I have to admit that I don't attend quite as many matches as a true fan ought to. I could count on the fingers of one hand the number of matches I took in during Big Sam's tenure. I'd like to be able to say this was a stylistic choice, or I could fall back on the fact that I now live far away from the Boleyn, but the truth is that even when I lived down the road I was an infrequent visitor.

Popular wisdom has it that you can't put a price on love but in football terms I think you can, and I think I discovered on Tuesday that this price, for me at least, is £65. That was the cost of a Band 1 ticket to the Southampton match in December. I'd earmarked this match at the start of the season as being potentially my final pilgrimage to Upton Park, conveniently coinciding with coming home for Christmas. I avidly watched availability while club members and bond holders could purchase tickets and waited patiently for tickets to go on general sale on 1 December. And as I logged in to the website at 9am it was like Black Friday all over again. I didn't object to being put in a queue due to 'heavy demand' between 9 and 10am, but when I tried again for the umpteenth time between 9 and 10pm, having been continually logged out, timed out and thwarted every which way possible in between times, it started to get even more dispiriting than the second half of the West Brom match [West Ham 1-1 West Brom].

The crux is, had I opted for a Band 1 ticket on the first of the two occasions that I actually got as far as picking seats in our online box office, then I may well have a ticket. But no, I was drawn first to the Bobby Moore Stand – the best atmosphere is always behind the goal – where availability seemed to be nil, despite the stadium graphic suggesting otherwise, and when my first choice was unobtainable I went for the Band 2 or 3 cheap(er) seats to save myself a tenner, but these were snapped up before I managed to proceed as far as payment.

So had I not been pound-pinching, I might well be going to see my beloved Hammers during the Christmas break. Of course that would have been the best outcome. But as it is, with the £65 resting in the bank to be spent instead on other Yuletide festivities, I'm not overly disappointed. I can also see the bigger picture and if demand is that great to see us take on fellow mid-table mediocrities then we shouldn't have a problem filling the 54,000-seat Olympic Stadium, which is good news for all concerned, especially the casual fans being squeezed out of the Boleyn.

Those who've already secured their seats for next season at a cost upwards of £499 will no doubt find my laid-back attitude towards supporting from the stands heretical. I respect their devotion. Even if money and distance were no object, I'm still not entirely sure I'd want to own a season ticket ... it's one hell of a commitment! It's okay if you're guaranteed a good time – sexy football and three points à la Manchester City. But supporting a club of West Ham's stature is more often a marriage of convenience – we tolerate inadequacies and accept that we're stuck with one another, through the good times and the bad.

That's not to say that we don't love our club. But how do you define love? Is it just about being present? To continue the marriage analogy, some of those that were ever-present took on the role of wife abusers during Allardyce's time. I'm not saying they were in the wrong (although wife abuse obviously is!) but did paying their money to hurl invective towards the touchline make them better fans than those who cheered the team on from afar?

In a global society, we can't all be in East London every week, although I'm aware that there are diehards who commute from every corner of the globe. I can only wonder what's going on in their family and professional lives to allow for this! We can add this to the West Ham-related thoughts running through my head, because my second admission is that I spend more time than is healthy thinking about football, our boys in claret and blue in particular. My wife would be shocked if she knew how much time I spend in bed thinking about Manuel Lanzini, Dimitri Payet and the rest. It's not like I don't have more important things to occupy my thoughts: airstrikes in Syria, finding a new job, Christmas shopping. But when I switch off from the strains and stresses of everyday life, my brain's default recourse is to West Ham. It's like an advanced version of Championship Manager is playing in my neurons, which pulse away with meditations on the make-up of the squad. Who would I sell? Who would I buy? Who should be promoted from the development squad? Best formation and line-up for our next match?

I sincerely hope that this is standard behaviour for football fans. Maybe if I were a regular attendee at Upton Park, I'd know from terrace talk that it's perfectly normal. And maybe if I spent more time among other fans it would provide a degree of relief to my one-track thought-pattern. Or maybe it would make things even worse. Either way, I present this confession as proof that I do love the Hammers. It's my serenade to the club. In Elvis's words, 'You were always on my mind.' It's been a long time since we were actually in each other's company and I also hold my hand up to infidelities such as slumming it at Meadow Lane to watch Notts County vs Fleetwood Town, but all the while I was thinking about how West Ham were getting on against Spurs [West Ham 0-1 Tottenham, 2014/15]. If any further evidence were required of my dedication, I'll be putting myself through the agonising rigmarole of attempting to buy tickets again on Tuesday when the Liverpool match goes on general sale, and will keep doing so until I've secured my last visit to the place where I first fell in love with live football.

A West Ham Christmas Wish List

19 December 2015

Dear Santa

I can't promise that we've all been good this year but I can vouch for the fans I know and they've mostly been alright, so on behalf of thousands of Hammers around the world I'd like to ask for …

1. A fit Dimitri Payet.
2. Three points from at least one of our festive fixtures (ideally Liverpool because I'll be in attendance).
3. Favourable home draws in the FA Cup. I know you can't get us the trophy because it's a bit out of season for you, but a little help along the way would be nice.
4. Some memorable performances that see us leave Upton Park on a high.
5. Chelsea to appoint Avram Grant – he has form in a relegation battle.

As you can see, we don't ask for too much, certainly nothing fantastical like the Spurs fans wanting to finish top four, and I think we deserve extra credit for thinking of our neighbours Chelsea in their time of need.

Yours sincerely,

Hopeful Hammers Everywhere

P.S. A little of whatever you got Leicester last year wouldn't go amiss either!

Boring Boring West Ham

21 December 2015

[Man Utd 0-0 West Ham]

[West Ham 0-0 Stoke City]

[Swansea 0-0 West Ham]

A hat-trick of nil-nils. When we ousted Big Sam this wasn't what we had in mind as the alternative. But I'm reasonably content with these goalless bore draws, and here's why ...

First, we're hard to beat. The unfortunate White Hart Lane defeat aside [4-1], we've put up a fight in every match. You could perhaps count Watford away as another off day but that was decided only by a couple of individual errors, which the Hornets' subsequent fine form has put into perspective. Such defensive solidity was something that Allardyce staked his reputation on, regularly trotting out the line that first and foremost we should keep it tight and not lose, yet tame submissions occurred more regularly in the past two seasons, with FA Cup capitulations to Nottingham Forest [5-0, 2014 third round] and West Brom [4-0, 2015 fourth round] springing most painfully to mind.

Even this time last year when we were riding spectacularly high, we'd suffered the same number of defeats as experienced so far this term.

Recent possession stats might look like a return to the dark days but the fundamental difference is that we've been happy to concede the ball to the opposition in certain areas, restrict them in others and looked to counter with purpose, whereas in the recent past we always had less of the ball simply because we hoofed it away too easily. I've yet to see yesterday's match with Swansea – annoyingly a rare televised fixture clashed with the community Nativity, which is even rarer and therefore couldn't be argued against – but highlights of the previous two suggested that we created the better chances against teams who, on paper at least, should pose a formidable attacking threat.

Don't get me wrong, I don't enjoy not having a goal to celebrate for weeks on end and, across the season, one point per match is flirting with relegation form but, under present circumstances, it's keeping us ticking along nicely.

Any team stripped of its most creative offensive talent will be rendered a tad impotent and yesterday we were missing the entirety of what seems to be Bilić's first-choice front four, plus our record signing. And at the other end we're missing our most reliable centre-back, so to have remained above Liverpool and Everton (who are still being talked of as Champions League contenders) rather than plummeting into the bottom half of the table counts as an accomplishment.

With a stretched squad demonstrating a new-found fortitude, I'm hopeful that the only way is up in 2016 with the return to fitness of Payet, Sakho, Lanzini and Moses, not to mention Carroll, Valencia and Reid. And let's add to the Christmas wish list a vacant treatment table.

Bye Bye Boleyn. You Were ... Forbidding

9 January 2016

[West Ham 2-0 Liverpool]

First of all, thank you to Michail Antonio and Andy Carroll for scoring the goals that ensured I returned to the north-west happier than Jürgen Klopp and co. last Saturday. I didn't share in the general consensus that it was a great performance; on the day I thought we were the better of two poor teams, so special thanks to Liverpool for gifting us victory on what will no doubt be my final trip to Upton Park. It was memorable in that it's the first league double we've done over them since 1963/64, a season even more notable for a triumphant trip to Wembley and, with our latest FA Cup venture beginning at home to Wolves today, a similar repeat would be very welcome.

Although the turn of the year saw the club's 'Farewell Boleyn' promotional campaign kick up a gear, I know I'm ahead of the crowd in saying a definitive goodbye to the old ground. I've taken time to reflect before composing this and, truth is, it wasn't as emotional as I was expecting. Come 7 May I'll join in from afar with the mass outpouring of emotion as the gates are closed for the last time and I'll snap up the inevitable commemorative DVD, but I'm not among the hordes who will still be in mourning come August.

Having read the viewpoints of other fans and shared in their fond memories of the place in the *Over Land and Sea* fanzine and elsewhere online, it's evident that the surrounding area and the pre- and post-match rituals play as big a part in many supporters' matchday experience as what happens within the bricks and mortar of the Boleyn and on the pitch in the middle. But what struck me on reading most of these accounts of supporting West Ham is that the Upton Park described exists only in the mind.

This isn't to diminish the obvious emotional attachment that many fans have with the stands along Barking Road and Priory Road in particular, but the word 'stands' is itself something of a misnomer; watching clips of yesteryear on the big screen from the corner of the Betway Stand and then glancing left and right to the East Stand and the Bobby Moore Stand rammed home the realisation that the Chicken Run is already confined to the past. And the stand that I was in (formerly known as the West Stand or the Dr Martens Stand or the Rio Ferdinand Stand after his sale to Leeds in 2000 helped fund its development) might have substantially increased our capacity but it left the ground feeling lopsided, and if the Taylor Report hadn't already gone a long way to killing off the claustrophobic and intimidating atmosphere in top-level football, its faux-turret façade helped finish the job.

As for the general environment, *newsflash*: Newham is grim, and that comes from someone with a big enough soft spot for the place that I spent my twenties living there, as opposed to the Essex tourists who probably only set foot in the borough for the football and latterly perhaps for the shopping at Westfield. I'm glad that Newham remains our home because I'd hate to do a Wimbledon or Woolwich Arsenal and stray too far from our roots, so I consider it fortuitous that we're decamping to the greenest, most pleasant spot the area has to offer at the heart of the Queen Elizabeth Park. I've written before about how I deviated from the family tradition of supporting Fulham because, as a boy, West Ham were my local team; I recall on my first visit being enthralled by the size of the crowd, but the scale of Craven Cottage's 3,000-strong support probably would have been equally awe-inspiring to eight-year-old me, and if I'd been taken on the amiable stroll from Putney Bridge before experiencing the slightly daunting otherworldliness of Green Street, then my allegiances could well have swung another way. I know that in comparison with Green Street some supporters will find the new milieu overly sanitised, and patches of it are, but if you explore the streets of Stratford in one direction and Bow in the other there are still a few classic East End watering holes within walking distance that we can make our own.

The other prevalent fear about the new home is lack of atmosphere. While some stadium structures lend themselves towards generating a feverish atmosphere and others don't, having attended a few events at the Olympic Stadium I believe it's leaning towards the first camp. My worry is that the club will over-commercialise an already iconic stadium that comes to us weighted with national history. Come August 2016 the onus will be on us to stamp our character on it and create many more Super Saturdays of our own.

Que Será, Será

10 January 2016

We might have somewhat laboured to victory over Wolves yesterday [1-0, FA Cup third round], but a win's a win, especially when it puts your name in the draw for the next round and especially given our record against lower-league opposition – the first FA Cup match I attended saw us draw with Farnborough, which was better than the next, which ended with seats being ripped up after we lost to Wrexham!

What was perhaps more heartening than the performance was the line-up, a strong indication from Bilić that he takes the competition seriously. Indeed, he's made the point in the press that there would be no better way to sign off a historic season than with cup glory. He includes in that finishing in a Champions League place, and I must say it's refreshing to have a manager willing to go against the grain by prioritising cup over league. I agree fully with his logic that a cup win confers tangible silverware and would live longer in the memory than the prize of playing a few extra matches the following season, as demonstrated by our forgettable foray into Europe this season.

Bilić's comments were one of a few of interest to Hammers in a *Times* article yesterday, titled 'What the FA Cup means to me'. Here are some of the best soundbites:

Slaven Bilić *West Ham United manager*

> I would like to win the FA Cup – win the Cup, and I can hold it up. Get in the Champions League and I have to buy a magazine to show everyone the league table, shouting, 'Look where we are, look where we are.'

Alan Pardew *Crystal Palace manager*

> You look at the chances of actually winning a trophy as a manager, for me it is the trophy with the utmost importance. I got to the final at West Ham and we were close to winning. My favourite Cup moments are etched in my

memory. I can reel them all off. To be part of that folklore of winning is something that has just missed me on two occasions.

Kim Montague *Corporate administration manager at West Ham United*

Our 1980 FA Cup triumph felt extra special as I went to school with Paul Allen, and I started working at the club in the preceding August. More than 36 years later, I am the longest-serving employee. I had been going to matches since the age of five with my family, but the other half of my family supported Arsenal. That night after we won, Ray Stewart brought the trophy to our staff party at The Savoy hotel and it felt amazing to touch and lift it. I've stayed in touch with the players from that era and I'm the only person at the club to experience this. I've so many good memories of Upton Park and we realise today's match with Wolves could be the last Cup tie here. It would be great to leave on a high.

Window Watch

30 January 2016

The transfer window slams shut again on Monday. Strange that it always slams and is never gently fastened. One senses that most managers, aside perhaps from Redknapp in his pomp, can't wait for it to close. Fans, on the other hand, relish the Sky Sports sideshow. That's probably because it allows us to play Fantasy Football Manager; few of us are truly capable of delivering an effective team talk or dissecting the opposition's tactics but we all like to believe we could splash the cash and enjoy speculating on how we should spend our club's budget.

From a Hammers perspective, it's been a fruitful window. Not a busy one but a fruitful one, nonetheless. Accepted wisdom is that, unlike on the high street, there are few bargains to be found in the January sales, coming as they do mid-season when a premium has to be paid to prise star players away from settled squads. Usually, extortionate fees are paid out of a sense of panic, so it's a sign of a stress-free campaign that Gold and Sullivan aren't having to wield the chequebook as Mike Ashley is. And for once the sharks aren't circling around our best performers. Indeed, since Winston Reid did an about-turn and signed his contract extension, West Ham has felt like a club that players want to be a part of, with the lure of the Olympic Stadium undoubtedly playing its part.

Our sole first-team signing, Sam Byram, looks an outstanding prospect. Right-back has been an area of weakness, exacerbated by the injury to Carl Jenkinson, who's failed to hit the heights of last season and didn't seem to be a long-term candidate for the role anyway. Whereas Byram, handed an earlier-than-expected opportunity to do so in the Manchester City match [West Ham 2-2 Man City], could make the position his own for the next decade. From his very first touch, bringing down a high ball and then spraying it back out to the wing, he showed class and composure against high-calibre opponents. Much is made of the step up from Championship (or indeed from just about anywhere, including La Liga, the Bundesliga and Serie A) to Premier League level but Hammer of the Year Aaron Cresswell made a mockery of that last season.

If Byram is able to follow his example, then we'll have our best pair of full-backs since Breacker and Dicks were patrolling the channels. The Terminator's such a West Ham idol that it's easy to forget that our current first-team coach was also originally plucked from the relative obscurity of the division below.

The club's readiness to hunt for gems outside of Europe's top flights is gratifying, especially when it results in the likes of Manuel Lanzini arriving from the UAE Arabian Gulf League. This trend continues with our only other notable incoming thus far, the young but highly regarded Bermudian goalkeeper Nathan Trott. We probably won't see his name on the team sheet for some time yet, if ever, but for a taste of what the last days of the window might hold there was also David Sullivan's cryptic hint at a striker signing from a 'very strange league'! This is generally assumed to be Emmanuel Emenike, a Nigerian currently plying his trade in the United Arab Emirates while on loan to Al Ain from Fenerbahçe. I know nothing about the fella beyond what I've read of the transfer gossip; why a team playing in the Europa League would send a player of any quality out on loan remains a mystery but he's familiar to our manager from his time in Turkey so, excuse the use of the horribly hackneyed phrase, in Bilić we trust.

I felt the same when he brought in Jelavić on the last deadline day, familiar as a Croatian compatriot and who, despite terrace criticism about his lack of pace and overall effectiveness, has manfully filled the thankless role of fourth-choice striker in a team that typically plays one centre-forward. Without him, we might not be in the fourth round of the Cup today and for that alone he's earned my thanks before his mooted move to China.

And our other departee, Zárate, has generally flattered to deceive, the occasional moment of magic failing to mask a questionable work rate and team ethic. Again, he's been a valuable squad player, chipping in with five goals, but his comments on joining Fiorentina suggest he might have suffered delusions of grandeur and not been content playing second fiddle to Payet.

Should the speculation about Emenike prove correct, a man who's been shipped out to the desert for the first half of the season should hopefully have no qualms about being a benchwarmer and occasional go-to guy. Of course, not knowing much about him, I might be underestimating Emenike. He seems like a makeshift solution designed to flesh out the squad. Right now, it's about fine-tuning rather than overhauling and even in the summer I don't see much need for any more than that. The average age of the squad is low and we're now well catered for in most positions. Quality not quantity should be the watchword as it's difficult to breed a positive team spirit in an overly bloated squad. If we buy one Payet-level player per season, that will more than do.

Money MADE the World Go Round

20 February 2016

From the nouveau riche Chinese Super League to the maximum cost of a matchday ticket, money – as it so often seems to – has dominated the footballing agenda lately.

Against a backdrop of £, € and ¥, the prospect of little Leicester City lifting the Premier League crown is truly the stuff of fairy tales. To put it into perspective, the team that humbled Manchester City [1-3] cost less than half a Kevin De Bruyne. That makes David versus Goliath look like an even contest. As will hopefully be proven at Shrewsbury Town [vs Man Utd] rather than Ewood Park over the weekend, the FA Cup is still capable of bridging even greater inequalities, but whereas the minnows are occasional victors in cup battles, Leicester are on the verge of winning the war. Even should they be toppled from the summit before the season's end, they still look dead certs to break up the Champions League cartel, and that in itself could significantly alter the Premier League landscape. One of the big guns missing out, coupled with the increased broadcasting revenues for all, will redress the balance sheets and create a more level playing field but, even more importantly than that, Leicester's escapades have shown others outside of the elite that they should dare to dream and that money isn't the be-all and end-all.

Leicester provide further ironic evidence that wealth doesn't guarantee success in the shape of club-record signing Andrej Kramarić. Bought for £9m in January 2015, his arrival coincides neatly with their ascension from bottom to top but this seems to be purely coincidental given that he's only played 15 times in total, just twice this season when he's been comprehensively outshone by non-league recruit Jamie Vardy, and shipped out on loan within a year of signing. West Ham can relate. Our one-time £9m record signing Savio Nsereko was an unmitigated disaster.

On a similar note, Spurs exceeded this by squandering €90m from the sale of Gareth Bale. It goes without saying that it was a pleasure to watch the travails of £26m mishap Roberto Soldado. A redeeming feature in our three decades of underachievement has been the frequency with which Spurs fans have seen their own dreams fade and die. But, and I can't quite believe I'm going to say this ... should Leicester fall short in their title ambitions then, of the other realistic contenders, I'd like to see Tottenham win the league, for many of the same reasons that every neutral in the country is currently throwing their weight behind the Foxes. In Manchester, Louis van Gaal and Manuel Pellegrini have been lavished with extravagant transfer kitties, making it more remarkable that Mauricio Pochettino has outperformed them while recouping more in transfer fees than has been spent during his time in charge at White Hart Lane. Demonstrating that thriftiness can be fruitful, arguably the two best performers in a streamlined Spurs squad have been plucked from their academy and from the Championship and, as with Ranieri's charges, they're showing what can be accomplished through astute leadership, a strong team ethos and a fair sprinkling of quality.

On the other side of North London, Arsène Wenger's frugality is also admirable, if only for the amount it frustrates the bawling Arsenal supporters! I generally feel less enmity towards the Gooners than the Spuds but I don't have any sympathy over their 12-year barren stretch in terms of league titles when they still have the buzz of being there or thereabouts each year and can console themselves in having not lost an FA Cup tie for three years, not to mention the upcoming visit of the brilliant Barcelona and the return leg at Camp Nou, which would be the most thrilling awayday imaginable for the average supporter.

Here's hoping that 2016 really is a new dawn and that, in the years to come, the galácticos of European football will be visiting the East Midlands, East London and a variety of other places instead.

Welcome Back BFS

26 February 2016

I've stated previously that I never belonged to the Big Sam Out brigade. By the end of last season his tenure had run its course but I wouldn't advocate ousting a manager unless there's an obviously better candidate ready to replace him. When we brought Allardyce in, he was obviously better suited to steadying the ship and steering us back to the Premier League than the outgoing Avram Grant. If it hadn't been for his appointment then I strongly suspect we'd still be languishing in the lower divisions like Leeds, Sheffield Wednesday, Nottingham Forest, etc. Therefore I think it's right that Sullivan and Bilić have both gone on record this week thanking him for his service to the club and imploring the fans to be respectful when he returns to the East End this weekend.

On the other hand, I *really* want to see Sunderland get relegated. Nothing against the Mackems, I'm pretty ambivalent towards them on the whole. I mean, Lee Cattermole is a Sunday league player living the dream, Adam Johnson is a talented player with a tenuous grasp on the moral and legal ramifications of dating a schoolgirl, and Defoe is a rat, but much water has passed under the bridge since he deserted us. Like Villa, they've also been flirting with relegation for a few seasons and deserve to get caught out eventually, but the chief reason I have for wanting them to be relegated is our friend Sam.

More specifically, I long for their demotion to disprove the popular theory that the likes of Allardyce and Tony Pulis, with their safety-first, joyless brand of football, are immune from relegation. Most Hammers fans can sympathise with the Baggies, having been constantly castigated for wanting something better with the sanctimonious reproach 'be careful what you wish for'. One senses that the self-anointed 'Allardici' is often guilty of believing his own hype, hence the occasionally befuddled look he's worn as Sunderland have continued to struggle under his command while we go from strength to strength without him. Given how big he is on statistics, it's worth pointing out that combining the first half of the 2013/14 season with the second half of 2014/15 we'd muster a paltry 34 points, which wouldn't have been enough to keep us up in 15 of the 20 seasons since the Premier League was reduced to 20 teams (the class of 2002/03 retain the unwelcome record of being relegated with the most points – a relatively whopping 42).

So Sam, welcome back, and thank you for all you did but, without wishing you the sack (because Sunderland probably were in greater disarray without you), I don't want to see you again next season. I don't care whether we win while playing free-flowing football or we beat you at your own game, as long as we nudge Sunderland closer towards the trap door and dispel the smug belief that certain managers are invulnerable.

[West Ham 1-0 Sunderland]

ReF Off!!

11 April 2016

[Man Utd 1-1 West Ham (FA Cup quarter-final)]

[Chelsea 2-2 West Ham]

[West Ham 2-2 Crystal Palace]

[West Ham 3-3 Arsenal]

I've always subscribed to the belief that borderline or dubious refereeing decisions that prove to be either particularly felicitous or particularly calamitous will largely even themselves out across the course of a season. Following recent events, I'm tempted to cancel my subscription.

Let's begin at the end. And we know that football fans are notoriously myopic so I'm going to do my best to be fair and even-handed. Still, we *should* have beaten Arsenal. That modal verb is based not on a sense of injustice stemming from critically poor officiating but on the conviction that we were better than them. Not by a mile (in the grand scheme of things a draw was fair enough) but by small margins, which, as we're witnessing, have the potential to make a world of difference. Given that Arsenal have been on a different footballing planet to us for most of Wenger's reign, those long-held feelings of inferiority at least make parity with them on Saturday an awful lot easier to swallow, whatever the score *could* have been.

The match was also such a thrilling incident-packed advert for football as it should be played that it would be curmudgeonly to come away from it moaning about a few seconds of action. Nevertheless, there's cause for complaint. Goals change matches, as was dramatically proven when Carroll pulled the first back in the 44th minute, so who knows what would have transpired had we scored first, as we legitimately should have in the first 15 minutes. Let's not beat about the bush, assistant referee Darren Cann was clearly wrong to flag Lanzini offside. However, I think there's always room for sympathy for those making split-second decisions when defenders are running out, attackers running in and there's a cluster of players obscuring their line of vision. Unlike the sanctimonious television pundits, it must also be remembered that matchday officials make decisions without the benefit of endless replays (use of technology is a whole other can of worms that I won't open up right now except to say that, handled sensibly, I don't think there are many in the game who wouldn't welcome its introduction). What rubs salt into the wounds in this instance is that Özil benefited from a borderline (albeit correct) onside call so soon after; swap Cann with his competent counterpart Lee Betts (who's no doubt made his fair share of errors on other occasions) and the 0-1 scoreline might have been reversed.

We're entering the heady realm of what ifs and maybes so I can hear the gnashing teeth of Gunners who contend that hat-trick hero Carroll should have been sent off. Personally I think that his early tackle on Laurent Koscielny was worse than Cheikhou's on Dwight Gayle, if only because it contained a little bit of malice, which the FA's review panel failed to detect in Kouyaté's marginally mistimed challenge and therefore correctly rescinded his red card. This doesn't make Carroll's a red card offence though. It was what I'd call a proper yellow card, one that might have brought about a caution in the '70s or '80s, before all it took to have centre-backs rolling on the ground in mock agony was a powder-puff brush. The physicality of Carroll's duel with Koscielny and Gabriel, who gave as good as they got, was an aspect of the match to be relished. If we're to decree that the second Carroll flashpoint, when a raised arm brushed Gabriel with no intent whatsoever, should have warranted a second yellow card then football may as well cease to be a contact sport, which for this onlooker at least would make it a far less entertaining spectacle.

Taking things back a week to Kouyaté's dismissal against Palace, it was a shocking decision made all the more galling by Clattenburg's tendency to flourish cards with theatrical glee. However, as opposed to offside and penalty decisions that can result in a change to the scoreline within seconds, being reduced to ten men only indirectly contributes to the outcome. This is not to minimise the hardship of being a man light but I prefer to view the last half-hour against the Eagles as a test of our credentials, our ability to hold on in a backs-to-the-wall scenario. Where we've been so impressive in overcoming the odds for much of the season, on this occasion we failed. The very top teams, in contrast, are so good as to make dubious refereeing almost irrelevant.

Which brings us on to Chelsea, themselves victims of an FA conspiracy to … I'm not sure what exactly! Some have espoused the theory that West Ham aren't wanted in the Champions League as the powers-that-be dread what untested quantities such as ourselves and Leicester would do to the Premier League's UEFA coefficient and to BT Sport's viewing figures next season. I refuse to buy into any conspiracy simply because such things always sound ridiculously far-fetched when coming from other quarters; it's nice to see Bilić adopt a placatory tone and to be graciously accepting of this run of misfortune, and I'd cringe if he followed Mourinho's path of blaming everything under the sun for the team's failings.

Again though, there are genuine grounds for consternation, with Fàbregas deciding the position of a free kick and then Loftus-Cheek tripping over himself just outside the penalty area. Admittedly my grievances are mitigated by the manner in which they were administered.

Had I been watching in real time (but with the benefit of slow-motion replays, naturally) then I'd have been livid with the outcome. As it was, my tactic of avoiding all screens on a Saturday afternoon so as to watch *Match of the Day* as if it were live was scuppered by a friend who said 'You must be sick,' before I stopped him in his tracks. Expecting the worst, a draw was the best possible outcome. Not that that stopped me from raging at the TV when the man in black pointed to the penalty spot!

And so to where our run of bad luck began, with Bastian Schweinsteiger unceremoniously body-checking Darren Randolph into the back of the Old Trafford net, leaving an unguarded goal for Anthony Martial to tap into. While it would be foolhardy to refuse a quarter-final victory away to Manchester United, my preferred result beforehand was a draw, simply so that there could be one more memorable FA Cup match at Upton Park, taking it for granted that we will dump the Mancs out back at our place. And I still believe this to be the case, save any more harmful refereeing decisions. In fact, given my karmic belief in the judgement of match officials, we're now owed a few, and if the decisions start to turn our way, taking us to a written-in-the-stars May day victory at Wembley, then I'll merrily pass the woe-are-we whinges to fans of Everton and Watford or Palace.

[Semi-final draw: Crystal Palace vs Watford; Everton vs West Ham or Man Utd]

The Fantastic Mr Foxes

16 April 2016

After Wednesday night [West Ham 1-2 Man Utd, FA Cup quarter-final replay] left me feeling nauseous, this weekend's match is that rare and welcome beast: a win-win situation. Win and it helps banish the FA Cup blues, plus another three points takes us a step closer towards our highest-ever Premier League points total and keeps alive faint hopes of a Champions League place. Lose and football generally wins as the Leicester fairy tale of being crowned unlikeliest champions ever edges closer. Jamie Vardy's having a party and we're all invited. A draw is probably the worst-case scenario as it's of reduced benefit on both fronts.

Bar a few fans of their closest competitors – Spurs, Arsenal and the Manchester clubs – I've yet to encounter anyone who would begrudge Leicester the realisation of their wildest dream. Even as part of the chasing pack, with the heroics of a 'littler' club overshadowing our own, I sense no resentment whatsoever from the West Ham faithful. Like fans of most clubs, we're watching with fascinated admiration and vicarious pleasure as our Midlands counterparts live the dream, while revelling in the unravelling of the hateful big club/little club hierarchy that we too have been doing our best to dismantle.

At the other end of the spectrum, Aston Villa fans have probably been left too comatose by their own team's long, slow, miserable fall from grace to feel any enmity towards the East Midlands upstarts at the opposite end of the table. As with London derbies, there are degrees of rivalry, so West Midland clashes with Birmingham and West Brom are more heated than the Leicester–Villa match that bridges the East–West divide. Nevertheless, all derbies are imbued with extra meaning and their meeting in early autumn was undoubtedly a pivotal moment in both teams' seasons. As the Jamie Vardy story goes into production this summer, the match at the King Power Stadium that day was essentially a footballing rerun of another Hollywood tale about the capriciousness of fate, *Sliding Doors*.

Hard as it is to believe in hindsight, on 13 September 2015 a 'dominant' (source: BBC match report) Aston Villa led 2-0 away to Leicester with more than 70 minutes played. The final score was Leicester City 3-2 Aston Villa, Nathan Dyer (on loan from Swansea) scoring a rather untidy 89th-minute winner for the hosts. The incumbent Villa manager, Tim Sherwood, bemoaned how his team conceded momentum in the second half. He didn't know the half of it! Granted, the season was still in its infancy, but a Villa win would have left them on seven points and Leicester on eight. In a parallel universe, Leicester and Villa are now nestled together in mid-table mediocrity.

Many will claim to have seen Villa's demise coming but the Foxes' remarkable ascent almost defies sensible analysis. Anyway, here's my attempt, many aspects of which could probably be branded insensible …

Had the unsung Dyer not bravely stooped to win the header that garnered three points and, even more importantly, the subsequent momentum and surge in confidence, then all of this would be moot. I honestly believe that confidence has been more important than pretty much anything, with Villa amply demonstrating what a lack of it can do for you. Would Vardy have had the temerity to try to volley in against Liverpool from 30 yards if he hadn't already broken scoring records? Success breeds success. By contrast, I've not seen a Villa player attempt anything remotely audacious all season. The poisonous atmosphere that necessitated cancelling the end-of-season awards ceremony won't have helped, although long-suffering fans certainly can't be blamed for taking out their frustrations on the underperforming, overpaid players on the pitch.

How else then do we account for the inclusion of Jamie Vardy, Riyad Mahrez and N'Golo Kanté – three players who, pre-season, would have been described as 'decent' at best – on the PFA Player of the Year shortlist? Like Villa, I think Leicester would be well-advised to cancel their own player of the year award based on the impossibility of being able to pick one! Schmeichel, Fuchs, Morgan, Huth, Drinkwater and Albrighton have all consistently performed at their peak and any other year would be deserving recipients of an individual award. As is often the case, the goalscorers get most of the glory, but Leicester's is a triumph of the collective.

Whatever the final weeks bring, the man responsible for the collective, Claudio Ranieri, surely can't fail to win the Manager of the Year accolade. Even if pipped by Pochettino's Spurs, turning relegation candidates into title contenders is unprecedented in the Premier League era. However, somewhat obtusely, I'm going to claim that Ranieri has performed miracles by doing not very much. His team is well organised and keeps its shape but tactically there's nothing revolutionary. The Tinkerman hasn't tinkered.

It might be said that Ranieri wisely recognised that the seeds of success had already been planted following the remarkable run of victories that secured safety under the leadership of Nigel Pearson and that his biggest contribution has been to not rock the boat. That, though, ignores the loss of last season's star player, Esteban

Cambiasso, and the inactivity of his relatively high-profile replacement, Swiss captain Gökhan Inler. At the risk of sounding trite, luck has undoubtedly played its part. Inler has been kept out of the team by the undroppable form of understudies Drinkwater and Kanté, who also, luckily enough for such combative midfielders, have avoided injury and suspension. The winning formula seems to have been stumbled upon almost by accident but credit still to Ranieri for maintaining a strong team spirit and for not tinkering, as his erstwhile nickname suggested he would.

When the previously divisive and controversial owner Vichai Srivaddhanaprabha appointed the seasoned Italian, he presumably did so because he was a big name with an impressive track record. Cynics may have argued that he was yesterday's man, only returning to the Premier League for a final payday. After all, only a fool would have suggested that he could fully rehabilitate his nearly-man image and usurp the achievements – runners-up in league and cup – managed with Chelsea. Conversely, having a manager without the urgency to stamp his personality on the club, maybe even adopting a laissez-faire approach in order to play down the Tinkerman reputation, has worked in everybody's favour, for the players have stepped up and filled the power vacuum normally occupied by dictatorial managers such as Mourinho and Van Gaal, who browbeat modern-day footballers into mindless automatons. Ranieri's charges are disciplined and hard-working but, crucially, they don't look tactically straitjacketed; rather than over-complicating the game, rejects from Stoke, Newcastle and (oh, the irony!) Aston Villa have mastered the basics and thrived in the trust and responsibility given to them. Maybe keeping it simple is a revolutionary idea.

So, Leicester have got lucky with their manager, with injuries, with timely winning goals. And yet the average fan doesn't hold it against them because they've shown that when all the ingredients come together, average players can make an extraordinary team capable of overcoming star-studded squads managed by tactical masterminds. Leicester's story is truly Spielbergian. Villa's, on the other hand, would need to be directed by the Midlands' master of kitchen-sink trauma and misery, Shane Meadows.

Murphy's Law Added to FIFA Rule Book

18 April 2016

[Leicester 2-2 West Ham]

Sod's law, isn't it. Declare a match win-win and it's destined to end in a draw that feels like a defeat.

Regardless of what happens in the remaining few matches, fans shouldn't lose sight of what a scintillating season both West Ham and Leicester have treated us to. It was devastating to be knocked out of the FA Cup when it was there for the taking, and I probably speak for more than a handful of Hammers and countless other fans around the country in saying we'll be equally devastated if Spurs (or any other team) overhaul the Foxes. Fretful fans must keep in mind, however, that there are only three domestic trophies up for grabs each season so a top six or seven finish and a bevy of hugely entertaining and memorable matches shouldn't equate to failure.

So it might have been accompanied by that inevitable tinge of disappointment and frustration but it's worth remembering that yesterday's match was another cracker. The quality may have been patchy but both teams put their heart and soul into it, and what more can we ask for? A heckler might at this juncture respond, 'A decent referee.'

Professional sportswriters are supposed to be insightful and articulate but evidently a bit too much of the *Daily Mail*'s incandescent rage and intolerance has rubbed off on Martin Samuels when he saw fit to describe yesterday's ref, Jonathan Moss, as 'inconsistent' ... 'flaky' ... 'thoroughly unsatisfactory' and to state that he deserved removing from the pitch by 'a big shepherd's crook, or the clang of a talent-night gong'. It's all too easy to take umbrage with refereeing decisions so let's have a look at Samuels' take on events versus mine:

57 mins – Jamie Vardy sent off

Samuels opines that it was 'exceedingly hard to call on first sight, and after several replays many were still not sure'. Rather than using this inconclusive reading of the incident to defend the referee from 30,000 baying fans in the stadium and millions more at home, he instead berates Moss for daring to give Vardy his marching orders when it wasn't entirely clear-cut. My gut instinct in real time was that it was a dive and my feeling is that replays show this quite conclusively. The general consensus appears to be that Vardy was at best trying to 'buy' a penalty by wrapping his legs around Ogbonna's and dramatically hurling himself to ground. To most minds this is cheating and I, for one, applaud Moss for having the kahunas to send off a home favourite despite what it might mean to the title bid of everybody's second-favourite team.

Others have averred that Vardy's first yellow card was harsh. Here I have a degree of sympathy (Samuels makes no mention of it), but it came at a time when the referee was trying to cool things down, having admirably attempted to let a well-contested match flow for the first half-hour. Vardy's 'soft' booking was followed by similarly innocuous ones for Reid, Noble and Payet, but it could have been preceded by several more if Moss had been as card-happy as most referees are from the outset.

84 mins – penalty awarded for Morgan foul on Reid

'That was the point when Moss decided to take a stand, just the once. Holding, wrestling, body-checking – even headlocks – could be spotted in the penalty area yesterday. Yet this was the only time Moss felt moved to act,' writes Samuels. Well, you're damned if you do and damned if you don't! It's widely accepted that referees need eyes in the back of their heads to spot all that goes on in the penalty area from dead-ball situations, and there's a case for awarding a penalty practically every time the ball comes in. Yet on the rare occasions they're given they tend to be labelled 'soft' penalties, and when they're not given commentators moan about the preponderance of pushing and shoving. In fairness to Moss, as with the yellow cards, he'd let a lot go but he clearly gave Morgan and Huth – undoubtedly the worst offenders – a verbal warning and they were eventually punished for continual grappling. It's unfortunate from West Ham's viewpoint that this wasn't dealt with straight away as we could have been awarded a penalty for Huth checking Reid in the 17th minute, but instead the ball ended up safely in the hands of Schmeichel and before Reid could get back in position it was at the feet of Vardy and from there the back of our net.

90 mins – no penalty for Ogbonna challenge on Huth

Samuels concedes that granting West Ham a penalty was the correct decision. 'Yet why wasn't it also the right decision when Ogbonna did it, very obviously, in the first half? Why wasn't it the right decision when Ogbonna did it, again, on Robert Huth minutes later?' I and the Sky cameras must have missed the 'very obvious' example of man-handling from Ogbonna in the first half, although, as already detailed, such challenges are ridiculously commonplace. The reason Leicester were penalised was an accumulation of indistinct transgressions. To penalise the West Ham defenders – who hadn't received a prior warning as Leicester's had, although what was the penalty award if not a warning to all players on the pitch to stop the wrestling – would have been grossly unfair.

93 minutes – penalty awarded for Carroll foul on Schlupp

And so it makes sense that Moss pointed to the penalty spot moments later; it was that accumulation of 50/50s. Some you get, some you don't. In isolation I'd call this a terrible decision; Carroll didn't even fully commit to a challenge. As Samuels describes it, 'Schlupp and Carroll came together, no more. They are both big lads, and Schlupp fell over. Moss needed no further invitation.' In essence we're in agreement but where I spy a logic, however flawed, in Moss's decision-making, Samuels sees only 'one final travesty'.

For all his bluster and a sizeable frame that suggests he rarely participates in sport, Samuels is a respected journalist and a West Ham supporter, which is why I still sometimes read his opinions, despite his transfer from *The Times* to a right-wing rag. What our varying interpretations demonstrate, along with the 700-plus vitriolic comments from his readers, is that it's not easy being a referee. Nor is video technology the panacea that we all imagine it to be; it would help, but yesterday was a perfect example of just how subjective officialdom can be. That at least is good news for sportswriters and TV pundits who are paid to speculate on decision-making without the pressure of having to make any hard-and-fast decisions of their own.

As Samuels admits, 'In the end, the draw was the fair result,' and Moss played a thankless role in justice being served, although it wasn't as simple as 'Leicester scored, referee Jonathan Moss equalised for West Ham. Then West Ham went ahead, and Moss pulled one back on Leicester's behalf'. Fans in attendance are often made to see red by the man or woman in black (or yellow as the case may be these days) and need little encouragement to suggest that those responsible for controlling on-pitch affairs are prone to indulge in self-pleasure. What's become more widespread since the advent of Sky Sports and the forensic analysis of every moment that they put the whistle to their lips is for everyone else to jump on the ref's back too: armchair supporters, press, tweeters, bloggers and managers, which is why I'm joining Bilić and Ranieri in bucking the trend despite the magnitude of the result, Bilić expressing sympathy with Moss in post-match interviews and Ranieri at least maintaining a dignified silence.

Even in allowing that I'd have been as unusually content with a Leicester win as I'd be delighted with a West Ham one, yesterday still failed to bring the result I wanted and by the 95th minute I felt mightily aggrieved. But isn't the beauty of football the fact that it stirs the emotions so, even when you're lulled into thinking you can remain ambivalent. Rather than howling in protest and blowing hot air against the wind, let's all calm down and reflect appreciatively on 95 minutes of high drama that encapsulated a breathtaking season.

And Now, the End Is Near ...

10 May 2016

So here we are. The morning of the last-ever match at the Boleyn. The end of an era. Readers will know that I'm all in favour of the move to Stratford. The end of an era isn't the end of the world, rather the start of an exciting new epoch. Which isn't to say that I'm glad to see the back of Upton Park. Like any Hammer who's ever attended a home match, my experience of supporting West Ham is indelibly linked to the place and, despite the shortcomings of both the ground and the generations of teams to have graced it, I harbour fond memories that the club's relocation can never erase.

Being 200 miles away inevitably makes me a more detached observer. Even as a resident of West Ham and then Canning Town, financial restrictions prevented me from ever being a season ticket holder or from attending even a small proportion of the matches that I'd have liked to. However, just as the 35,000 who are fortunate enough to be taking their seats in the Boleyn for the last time ever tonight will be savouring their pre- and post-match rituals for one final time, were I back in the vicinity of E13 there are certain things that I'd do to partake in the occasion beyond sitting in my replica shirt watching Sky with my little one's bubble gun. These are the things that I'll miss most about visiting the Boleyn:

– Pie and mash, not from Nathan's (the quality didn't warrant the queuing time, although the snaking lines of punters were testament to its popularity) but from BJ's Pie House further down Barking Road, where you could usually be assured of a seat, even on matchdays. Having only opened in the past decade, BJ's lacks the tradition and the prime positioning of Nathan's but my preference for it acts as a reminder that pie and mash isn't the sole preserve of Nathan and I'll be flabbergasted if there's no pie, mash or jellied eels to be found within a stone's throw of the new ground. Given the forecast loss of revenue to Upton Park traders and their centrality to the current matchday experience, it seems poor form of the club not to have offered Nathan's a new outlet within the Queen Elizabeth Olympic Park.

– A pint at The Central. Without wishing to flaunt my anomalous routine, I'd always swerve The Boleyn or The Queens to go somewhere with an outside chance of being served before kick-off/closing time. There were plenty of other public houses further afield where waiting time would have reduced along with atmosphere so it's about achieving that balance and there are plenty of sources of refreshment around the Olympic Park that Hammers can appropriate depending upon their route. That said, I can't imagine gastropub The Cow on the Westfield boulevard becoming a hotspot for football fans. Maybe the ground itself will prove a more spacious, welcoming and cost-effective place for refreshment and The Boleyn/The Queens can be kept alive through regular pilgrimages.

– The history. We're rather fortunate to be moving into a new build with ready-made historical import thanks to Team GB's 2012 heroics. But I'll miss reminders of our own glory days, epitomised by the statue of our World Cup winners. I made sure to get a commemorative snap of this before I left London and it's right that it remains on the junction of Barking Road and Green Street as a monument to the greats who called Upton Park home. The once-mooted idea of uprooting it and taking it to Stratford was nonsensical as Moore, Hurst and Peters didn't ply their trade there and a new group of players need to write their own chapter of history in E20. In my humble opinion the club seems to have struck a good balance between modernity and history with the digital wraparound representing the former and the recycling of the John Lyall Gates representing the latter. Similarly, the giant claret-and-blue shirts that adorn the concourse bear the names of both legends such as Bonds and present luminaries such as Payet.

– Old-school East London. The most cherished memory of my final trip to the Boleyn in January wasn't Antonio stooping to head us in front against Liverpool or Payet nonchalantly nutmegging players on his return from injury; it was a bunch of Cockney urchins trying to catch some of the action from atop a garage on Priory Road. This struck a chord because I once considered buying a high-rise flat on that road for the very same reason. New stadiums such as the Etihad and the Emirates don't have neighbouring council blocks offering such vantage points and it's safe to say that gaining a sneak peek from the ArcelorMittal Orbit won't carry the same quaint charm.

There's no place like home. I can't pretend to have the same emotional investment as someone who's been more than a hundred times or who's occupied the same seat for years on end; for me, tonight's like saying goodbye to an old friend, for others it's like letting go of a soulmate. But home is also where the heart is, and the heart of any football club is the fans, not bricks and mortar. Given that the average Brit is said to move house eight times in their life, the disconcerting sensation of going from the familiar to unfamiliar is unlikely to be wholly new to anyone and it's imperative that we make ourselves at home in Stratford as quickly as possible. But for now, let's give the old place a send-off to remember. As sorrowful as some of us may feel, let's make tonight a celebration, not a wake.

Postscript

11 May 2016

[West Ham 3-2 Man Utd]

Sad to say, the ugly scenes before the match tarnished the evening. Shame on the 'fans' involved. One thing I won't miss is the notoriety of Green Street; I find it distasteful that unofficial Farewell Boleyn merchandise has included ICF-emblazoned T-shirts and I sincerely hope that the move provides a break from any remaining hooligan elements who won't fit in quite so well at the Olympic Park. Media coverage has been dominated by the smashed-up Manchester United coach and it's regrettable that this has overshadowed the occasion, in the national (and international) consciousness at least. Will top transfer targets be drawn to the East End by these images? And would parents want to subject the next generation of supporters to such sights? I have my doubts.

Obviously throwing bottles can never be condoned, even at Rooney and co., but, on the other hand, what were Manchester United doing arriving so late? They have form for this, having done the same at Tottenham just a few weeks ago. One would assume that traffic congestion is unheard of in Manchester but I can assure you this isn't the case. The lack of foresight beggars belief. Primary school teachers are required to conduct a thorough risk assessment every time they cross the road with kids, so you'd think a business transporting hundreds of millions of pounds worth of assets through a disreputable area on a night when passions were running predictably high would have taken the necessary precautions such as arriving before the crowds were at their peak. Jesse Lingard's quickly leaked amateur horror movie showing the coach passengers cowering in the aisles with smirks on their faces further dissipates any sympathy that might have been due to the Red Devils.

Anyway, on to the football, and the 90 minutes couldn't have been much better scripted. A blistering start was rewarded with an early lead and the fans couldn't have been in better voice. We should have been 3-0 up by half-time but, naturally, that wouldn't have been dramatic enough. Understandably, the intensity of both players and crowd dropped in the second half and the Mancs predictably took advantage, turning the match on its head, with both teams reverting to type: the United in red grinding out a result and the United in claret and blue threatening to dash our hopes once more. But we lifted the tempo again, reaching a crescendo in the five minutes between Antonio's equaliser and Reid's winner. If 35,000 fans can create an atmosphere that seeped through the TV screens and shook the old ground to its foundations, imagine what 60,000 vociferous fans backing a rejuvenated team full of commitment and flair can generate …

After that near-perfect finish, the grand send-off awkwardly orchestrated by Ben Shephard all felt a little bit superfluous. Credit to the club for laying on a knees-up, but it wouldn't have been the worst thing if ManUre's tardiness had led to a heavily truncated version of events. Applauding club legends such as Brooking and Di Canio made for a fitting finale but Sébastien Schemmel and Matty Etherington being wheeled out in taxis was a tad underwhelming.

Ultimately, if we'd just let the football do all the talking, it would have truly been a night to savour.

Will We Be Forever Blowing Bubbles?

13 May 2016

N.B. When this idea was initially conceived, the intention was purely satirical. In gestation, however, I'm unsure whether it's become sacrilegious or serious, so I'll leave it for fellow fans to decide …

Theme tunes are designed to capture the essence of whatever it is they soundtrack. To communicate personality, ambience and values. So, what does our signature tune say about us?

> I'm forever blowing bubbles
> Pretty bubbles in the air
> They fly so high
> Nearly reach the sky
> Then like my dreams
> They fade and die
> Fortune's always hiding

I've looked everywhere
I'm forever blowing bubbles
Pretty bubbles in the air

[Music: John Kellette Lyrics: James Kendis, James Brockman, Nat Vincent
© Sony/ATV Music Publishing LLC, Universal Music Publishing Group,
Warner Chappell Music, Inc]

Sounds about right. Aspirational, dreamy, head in the sky, looking to the stars but forever braced for a fall. Bubbles symbolise the West Ham Way – pretty and effervescent but at the same time fragile and insubstantial. The closing repetition of the opening couplet says that we won't give up, hope springs eternal, even though we're destined to always fall short. 'Bubbles' condemns us to failure, its brutality hidden by a mellow melody.

A reminder of how we got saddled with this anthem of doomed ambition: it started life as an American music hall ditty in 1918 before being adopted by the terraces in the late 1920s in tribute to trialist Billy J. 'Bubbles' Murray. Inappropriately enough it was a school headmaster, Cornelius Beal, who first sang about blowing Billy. Beal was friends with Irons manager Charlie Paynter, who obviously liked the tune but didn't give much thought to the lyrics as it was at his request that a house band was hired to play it before matches. As an origin story it's not up to much; the song's attachment to the club is highly tenuous, largely lost in the mists of time but simultaneously strengthened by time and tradition, with the team's failings making it ever more apt. Even in a final season at the Boleyn that's exceeded expectations, the curse of 'Bubbles' has struck, our hopes and dreams of FA Cup glory, Champions League football and possibly even Europa League qualification reaching a peak before being cruelly burst.

Nevertheless, 'Bubbles' is special. I can't possibly advocate never pursing our lips and blowing again; the prospect of not blowing any bubbles is far worse than having them popped in our faces. But is there a third way? A new verse perhaps, in which at least one bubble reaches the stratosphere. Since my musical talents don't stretch to composition (I'm ever grateful to those sat around me for drowning out my tuneless renditions), I instead got to thinking about potential alternatives. New stadium, new song.

First, I want to make clear that what I'm about to propose hasn't been drawn from my personal collection; I most definitely don't own Disney's *Aladdin* OST on vinyl, nor can Peter Andre or Katie Price be located anywhere in my iTunes library. Disturbed yet? Bear with me, all will be explained, for I'm recommending 'A Whole New World' as our anthem for a bright new era.

> A whole new world
> A new fantastic point of view
> No one to tell us no
> Or where to go
> Or say we're only dreaming

[Music: Alan Menken Lyrics: Tim Rice
© Universal Music Publishing Group]

Goodbye fatalism, hello optimism. 'A whole new world', hopefully with 'a new fantastic point of view', perfectly sums up our situation right now. The Cockney Rejects might have tried to inject the spirit of punk into 'Bubbles' but it still can't compare to the f*** you attitude of 'No one to tell us no'. What's more, it shares the weightless dreaminess of 'Bubbles', its association with Aladdin conjuring up images of magic carpet rides.

Worried that we'll sound a bit sissy crooning the tune that Andre and Price butchered in honour of their undying love that subsequently corpsed? Well, 'Bubbles' isn't exactly overflowing with street cred, and its only serious rival for number one terrace anthem, 'You'll Never Walk Alone', comes from a Rodgers and Hammerstein musical. Thousands of baritones joined in harmony imbue these songs with a whole new dimension.

So let's give it a go, eh? If I manage to get hold of a ticket for the landmark visit of Juventus, I promise I'll start up if you join in.

'A whole new world …'

That Was the Season That Was

16 May 2016

Perhaps the most surreal season ever has come to an end. As if saying farewell to the Boleyn wasn't going to feel weird enough, we've had to contend with such abnormalities as finishing above Chelsea and Liverpool but below champions Leicester (that still sounds strange!), maintaining a positive goal difference throughout, and supporting our conquerors Manchester United in the FA Cup Final if we want to christen the Olympic Stadium with European football (which some do, some don't).

Overall, it's been a pulsating season in which most of the players have done us proud most of the time. Now, I'm not a fan of player ratings; they're both subjective and reductive. However, the final league standings (save for Manchester Utd versus Bournemouth – will they ever kick off when they're meant to?!) mark the customary time to appraise performance, so please indulge the teacher in me who's written end-of-season reports for each squad member.

1 Darren Randolph B

Better than expected. Bournemouth are evidently his bête noire. After conceding 12 to the Cherries while playing for Birmingham in the Championship last season, he shipped another four against them on his Upton Park league debut, leaving many fans praying that Adrián would henceforth remain injury and suspension free. However, several fine performances as an integral figure in the FA Cup run dispelled any ideas that he'd only been purchased as a freebie based on the board's Brum connections and he now looks a safe, competent deputy who will hopefully do himself proud with Éire at the Euros.

2 Winston Reid B-

Delivered A+ performances in the stellar early wins at Arsenal, Liverpool and Manchester City, and then struggled to play more than three matches in a row for the remainder of the season. Although he isn't captain and his presence doesn't skew the statistics quite as much in our favour, he is to all intents and purposes our Vincent Kompany, and the defence would benefit immensely if the man who's surely the greatest Kiwi soccer player of all time could be an ever-present next season.

3 Aaron Cresswell B+

Mr Dependable. His native Liverpool are worryingly sniffing around for a reported fee of £15m. I'd rate him higher than that. Has the quality to chip in with a few more goals and assists, which would surely make it impossible for the England manager to ignore him any longer.

4 Alexandre Song D-

What went wrong? The thoroughbred that ran midfield for the first half of last season appears to have turned into a donkey. Having erroneously believed that securing his re-signing from Barcelona was more significant than any other summer addition, he's instead been relegated to squad member and a little used and ineffective one at that. It's a shame to see talent squandered but, on his reported wages, Song looks set to resume his inactivity in Catalonia next season.

5 James Tomkins B

A bit like mum's cabbage, I know I should like him because he's homegrown. His deployment at right-back also felt like the healthy option that would keep us in shape. But there's no escaping that there are tastier options! Nevertheless, he grew into the right-back role, beginning to exhibit more attacking threat than hitherto shown, and the versatility displayed this season ensures that he remains a valuable squad member.

8 Cheikhou Kouyaté B+

The midfield engine, when he purrs the whole team seems to click but, on those increasingly rare occasions when he splutters, we suffer a breakdown. It's a big plus point that he and Noble have added goals from deep midfield positions but, to become the complete midfielder, he's in urgent need of shooting practice!

9 Andy Carroll B

Adjusting for inflation, he's finally starting to look like a £15m player. I've defended him before on the basis that he's the world's best Plan B but if he can stay fit for a full season he could still form part of a mean Plan A.

10 Mauro Zárate B-

Unlike Lanzini, was unwilling to sacrifice personal glory to the team ethos and Bilić promptly dumped him on Fiorentina, where he's continued to blow hot and cold. It's a shame his selfishness couldn't be curtailed because he demonstrated in the opening months of the season that he posed an effective attacking threat. Belongs at a mid-level club with a manager willing to indulge him.

11 Enner Valencia C-

Besides the brace against Bournemouth I'm struggling to recall what else he's contributed. I do believe the endeavour's there but he seems to be the latest casualty of headless chicken syndrome, constantly out of position and running down blind alleys. The rumoured interest from Chelsea always flattered him but if they or Mourinho, wherever he winds up, are still interested then please make us an offer.

12 Carl Jenkinson D

When your most memorable contributions to the season have been the losses to Leicester and Bournemouth, giving away a penalty against Man City and brazenly hitting on *X Factor* winner Louisa Johnson, you know you've had an *annus horribilis*. Good luck to Jenko in his pursuit of both Louisa and a first-team place back at Arsenal.

On last season's evidence he's capable of pushing for an England place, on this season's evidence he's more likely to whittle away his career among relegation fodder such as Sunderland or Watford.

13 Adrián B

A proper old-school goalkeeper: idiosyncratic and unpredictable or, in other words, mad as a box of frogs and prone to the occasional rush of blood to the head. I love how he's embraced the club, and the fans have in turn taken him to their hearts. However, howlers can prove as costly as saves can precious. Part of me still sees him as an excellent back-up and thinks we need Mr Consistency to take us to the next level. But for Mr Consistency read Mr Boring and perhaps the greatest proponent of this, Petr Čech, has himself committed some uncharacteristic misdemeanours this season, starting with the misjudgements that gifted us three points.

14 Pedro Obiang D

Maybe I've just watched the wrong matches but I've yet to see him have a noticeably positive impact. As a defensive shield he appears to lack mobility and speed, and his passing is restricted to sideways and simple. He possesses the pedigree (Spain U21 caps and impressive enough performances in Serie A for us to pay about £5m for his services) to suggest that there's more to come but, even with Song on the way out, with Nordtveit on the way in, how many more chances will he get?

15 Diafra Sakho C

Has endured a campaign blighted by injury, car accidents, relationship issues and Twitter outbursts. All these distractions have prevented him from building on an excellent first season but he still looks the best bet to be a 20-goal-a-season man from the current squad.

16 Mark Noble A

Captain Fantastic, he's not been faultless but he's been better than the consistently good that we've taken for granted down the years. Hodgson is a numpty to have not even given him a chance on the international stage. His leadership skills have been praised by the squad and we couldn't wish for a better embodiment of the West Ham Way to induct newcomers. He's a fan on the pitch and would receive an A even if his sole contribution had been hauling Ander Herrera off it!

17 Joey O'Brien C

Can't be faulted for effort when called upon; a solid but limited full-back whose best days are behind him; it's time to be reacquainted with his mentor, Big Sam.

19 James Collins A

Ginge has always excelled in physical and particularly aerial battles but is susceptible to nimble, craftier forwards. Bilić fairly declared him fourth-choice centre-back at the start of the season but, credit to Collins, he stuck in and, when needed, produced several man-of-the-match performances that cemented his cult-hero status.

20 Victor Moses C

A promising start was halted by injury and he was never again as effective, his displacement by Antonio and the prospect of having to find yet another club to call home perhaps knocking his confidence.

21 Angelo Ogbonna B-

Surprisingly for an Italian international defender who's been a Champions League finalist, he doesn't always appear the most cultured but he's certainly adapted to the demands of the Premier League better than the likes of £32m Eliaquim Mangala and £18m Mamadou Sakho. That extra-time injury-time winner against Liverpool [FA Cup fourth-round replay] was arguably the most euphoric moment of the season and he's put his head in and his body on the line on countless less notable occasions down the other end. Formed a mean partnership with Ginge, although Ogbonna–Reid looks to be the first-choice central-defensive pairing that it's to be hoped will be even stronger for a year's experience.

22 Sam Byram C

Highly rated by Leeds fans and with a lengthy list of Premier League suitors, but hard to judge thus far. Looked an excellent prospect when Jenkinson's injury forced him into the fray early against then title favourites Manchester City. The fact that he more than held his own makes it a pity that a combination of injury, suspension, being cup-tied and Bilić's bizarre reluctance to play him have restricted his progress since. The selection of Antonio and Tomkins ahead of him is hopefully due to the gaffer letting the youngster find his feet, as he did Antonio at the start of the season, before unleashing him next term.

25 Doneil Henry C-

Unfortunate to make his bow in the ignominious away defeat to Astra Vauxhall FC, which saw us eliminated from the Europa League before the competition proper had even begun. Also had another loan spell with Blackburn cut short by injury, having made a stunning impact in a very short space of time there last year. Did at least contribute to the development squad's moment of glory. His imperious stature being his greatest attribute, I'd anticipated Collins's possible departure affording him more first-team opportunities. As it is, I can't foresee him making his second Hammers appearance any time soon.

26 Nikica Jelavić C+

Poached a couple of vital goals; what more can you ask of a fourth-choice striker? Would have loved him in his prime but now lacks the sharpness to cut it in a top league. Good luck to him topping up his pension pot in China.

27 Dimitri Payet A

We've got Payet and I think the whole world now understands. Payet provides that magic sprinkle that the fans craved during the Allardyce years and some of those free kicks simply defy belief. The gripes from national manager Didier Deschamps are due to a lack of consistency and there are still matches when he's merely average, hence not awarding an A+. Finishing his report with a clichéd 'room for improvement' should make scary reading for opposition defences!

28 Manuel Lanzini B+

The 'Little Jewel' has been a valuable addition, easing the creative burden that might otherwise have fallen on Payet alone. Perhaps his greatest asset is that he couples the tricks and flicks with a work-ethic that means Bilić trusts him in a midfield role as well as an attacking one. The classic Argentinian blend of tricky and tough, deceptively so in both cases.

29 Emmanuel Emenike C

Showed against Blackburn that he'd be an ace Championship player but looks a little out of his depth in the Premier League. Has skills and is capable of the sublime but more frequently delivers the ridiculous.

30 Michail Antonio A

Once the Invisible Man finally got a look in, it's been one of the season's pleasures to see his talents revealed. Fast, muscular, direct, he's a highly conspicuous action man who somehow contrives to weave his way into positions through sheer determination, so not always elegant but frequently effective; has all the attributes to be a powerhouse winger. Not the greatest full-back or wing-back, but befitting a character who's worked his way up through the leagues he gives it his best without complaint and, although every one of us urges Bilić to play him further forward, his (occasionally torrid) experiences at right-back are a learning curve that should help him to add a little more guile and élan to his game.

33 Stephen Hendrie C

Has put in some strong performances and even scored some crucial goals for the development squad, earning him a place in a few first-team matchday squads. Unfortunate that the ever-present, ever-reliable Cresswell blocks his path, but he's an intriguing understudy who I'm keen to see more of.

34 Raphael Spiegel B

His penalty heroics in the U21 Premier League Cup Final gave him a moment in the spotlight, well-deserved for someone who seems to have been part of the development squad for aeons. Only an injury crisis will give him a chance at West Ham so it would be nice to see his credentials tested in the Championship.

35 Reece Oxford B

Gave a lesson to Mesut Özil and was given one by Romelu Lukaku; that pinch-yourself debut at the Emirates perhaps led fans to expect too much from a young man who's by no means the finished article. From this auspicious start it's a shame that he hasn't been granted more opportunities to impress but he's consistently been in the squad and that matchday experience hopefully augurs well in his development into a composed ball-playing centre-half. Bulking up will also help him to deal with the likes of Lukaku.

39 Josh Cullen B

Belatedly joined Reece Burke on loan at Bradford, where he made an impressive impact despite the difficulties of integrating part-way through the season. Looks a neat footballer in the West Ham tradition.

40 Djair Parfitt-Williams B

Enjoyed a moment in the limelight scoring the 90th-minute winner in the first leg of the U21 final and didn't look totally out of place in Europa League qualifying; one to watch, although potential is hard to judge against Andorran and Maltese outfits.

I believe that covers everybody who was given a squad number and made an appearance. Special mention must also go to Reece Burke, since Payet's not our only player of the year, 19-year-old Burke also picking up that accolade on loan at Bradford City. Following a year of steady development he's more than earned a chance to prove his worth at West Ham, but even if he fails to make the grade with us he's proven that he already belongs at a higher level than League One. Of the other loanees, Martin Samuelson also caught the eye, running West Brom ragged in their televised cup tie against Peterborough and scoring a wonder goal that went viral on social media.

As for the man in charge, the players' achievements speak for him. He was without doubt the right man to guide us through an emotional final season at the Boleyn and to lead us onwards and upwards into the Olympic Stadium.

The dust is yet to settle, the contents of the Boleyn are still to be auctioned off and we're still to find out whether we're playing in Europe next year but, having secured my maiden visit to our new home for the Betway Cup against Juventus, I already say bring on 2016/17!

We Get Around

31 May 2016

If the world has learned one thing from our selling out the 52,000 season ticket allocation at the Olympic Stadium, it's that it contains more Irons devotees than many suspected. Even our own board appeared to underestimate the size of the fanbase, hence the questionable decision to allow existing season ticket holders to snap them up on behalf of friends and family before members could get a look in. With tens of thousands allegedly remaining on the waiting list, this looks in hindsight like a rash rush to put bums on seats, but wherever these thousands of 'new' fans have crawled out from, no one can begrudge them a seat if they turn up and sing their hearts out week after week.

But never mind the excluded locals, those fortunate enough to be able to attend regularly should spare a thought for the claret-and-blue diaspora for whom taking in a live match requires a foreign holiday. I bemoan being 200 miles away, especially on momentous nights like 10 May, but at least I'm only over land and not sea. More importantly, I'm not alone (in body, that is, for no true football fanatic is ever alone in spirit).

In the Cheshire enclaves I've encountered numerous other Hammers, often identifying themselves through scarves in cars. The Hammers crest is always a conversation starter, as I found when I took the little one to church in his West Ham tracksuit top (not the traditional Sunday best, but then we're relaxed churchgoers and I'm still in the process of indoctrinating him). Making polite chit-chat about our children's developing walking abilities with the only other new-ish parent in attendance, she suddenly grew more animated and declared, 'Is that a West Ham coat?' Turns out the boy's playmate was another first-generation Chester Hammer, his dad having also been lured away from the East End. The Anglican Church at first seemed a highly unusual place for supporters' meetings but, on reflection, a place of prayer and worship is quite apt; I think on the day in question I'd been praying for Modibo Maïga to find a new club. And my prayer was duly answered. There is a God. He just moves in mysterious ways, which is why I'm still waiting for the trophy I've been pestering Him about for a quarter of a century now.

As well as the provincial supporters' groups, we also have off-shoots in New Zealand, Australia, Brazil, Malaysia, Thailand, Dubai, Bulgaria, the Balkans, Finland and Malta, to name just a few that I'm aware of. Which begs the question: where's the strangest place you've encountered your West Ham brethren?

To paraphrase the Beach Boys, whose sun-kissed melodies don't typically match the mood of the average West Ham fan, we get around. So, wherever you're going on your summer holidays, keep an eye out. I'll be lying on a beach somewhere on my West Ham towel.

England Till I Die (Of Boredom)

9 June 2016

Who else is nostalgic for Italia '90? Maybe it's a generational thing but international tournaments don't seem to be as exciting as they once were. Nothing now kindles the fire in my heart like 'Nessun Dorma' or the bumper Orbis sticker album did. Naturally it ended in tear-jerking circumstances but at least England's failure could be described as gloriously valiant, as opposed to the more routine tepid disappointments that we've become oh-so accustomed to. Euro '96 memorably restored patriotic pride but other tournaments tend to blur into one another, distinguished only by cataclysmic lows such as Graham

'Turnip-Head' Taylor substituting Gary Lineker, one goal shy of being his nation's leading marksman, when we most needed a goal against hosts Sweden in Euro '92. Still, at least we made it to those finals, which in fairness contained only eight teams as opposed to the 24 preparing for the bloated Euro 2016.

The 30 years of hurt immortalised by Baddiel, Skinner and the Lightning Seeds have now stretched to 50. In that time several friends have turned their backs on England, disillusioned by the cycle of hype, hope, struggle and sorrow. The ill-fated Golden Generation was the tipping point for many, who were bewildered by the regular sight of world-class talent such as Steven Gerrard performing more like Carlton Palmer on the international stage. In the ensuing club versus country rows, Manchester United, Chelsea and Liverpool supporters defended their own, for they were delivering Premier League and/or European titles. With the neutrality of a West Ham fan, I could never abandon a national team that represented a better shot at triumph than anything we've offered domestically. Right now I'd say that both my teams are decent outside bets to land silverware but confidence certainly doesn't extend to the luxury of putting all my eggs in one basket so my loyalties remain fiercely each-way.

However, bracing myself for the Three Lions' biannual knockout embarrassment, I'm adopting a third team for the coming weeks. There's scant chance of them outperforming the standard respectability of a quarter-final berth (although stranger things have happened; step forward Denmark and Greece) but they should provide the fun and the *je ne sais quoi* typically lacking in Roy Hodgson's men. Wales are my ones to watch this June.

It's common practice for the English to have a soft spot for the other home nations, which our neighbours duly find condescending. My affinity goes beyond this. Chester's stadium famously bestrides England and Wales but my allegiance is based on joy rather than geography. As primary evidence may I present to you *C'mon Wales: Our Euro 2016 Singalong*, aired last night on BBC Two Wales and well worth checking out on iPlayer for its gleeful patriotic atmosphere, as if Last Night of the Proms had been transplanted into a tight-knit mining community. The Manic Street Preachers' 'Together Stronger' is a good old-fashioned anthem that recalls the halcyon days of New Order's 'World in Motion'; sadly Hal Robson-Kanu wasn't invited to rap on it, but the title (ignoring the 'C'mon Wales' appendage that underscores the chorus) bestows upon it the added bonus of being reusable as the Remain campaign's anthem for the EU referendum. Then there's the ever-eccentric Super Furry Animals being inspired to record their first new music in seven years, unofficial anthem 'Bing Bong', the inexplicable equivalent to Fat Les's 'Vindaloo'.

Meanwhile, the English FA no longer bothers commissioning an official tournament song and the best anyone else from these shores can muster is Shaun Ryder's 'We Are England', despite his admittance that he knows 'absolutely nothing about football' and wants to consign football talk to Room 101. Contrast this with Wales's musical embracement of the occasion and it's clear to see who's more excited about the whole affair. With reason. We complain about our 50 years of hurt; they've had to wait 58 years just to receive an invite to the party. So while we're playing it cool, pretending not to care too much, the Welsh are going to throw themselves in head first regardless of results, and I want part of the debauchery!

Other reasons, as if they were needed, to lend your heart to Wales: in Gareth Bale they have one of the world's most exciting players, capable of raising pulses and bringing football fans of all persuasions to their feet, and they also have the Ginger Pelé – that's greater Hammers representation than there is to be found in the England squad. Being pitted against England in Group B shouldn't be a barrier to supporting them. If anything it guards against disappointment; with three teams going through from four of the six groups, it's surely unthinkable for both England and Wales to be knocked out at the preliminary stage.

Having regenerated a bit of enthusiasm in international goings-on, I'm almost tempted to go and buy myself the Euro 2016 Panini album. Swap you Sterling for Bale …

Oi Barça, Leave Payet Alone

15 June 2016

My last entry expressed nostalgia for tournament football free of world-weary pessimism. At the risk of sounding like an 'in the good old days' bore, I've since become wistful for a golden era when transfer speculation didn't surround every other player.

It was around the dawn of the new millennium that a switch in emphasis from playing for pride to playing for a lucrative new contract could be detected, and we've now reached an age where Zlatan Ibrahimović seeks permission to leave Sweden's training camp to sign a contract with Manchester United reportedly worth in excess of £300,000 a week, revealing abundantly clearly where his priorities lie. Some might say that if he was jetting off to London to sign for the Hammers then my attitude would be different but I can assure you that it wouldn't; Zlatan is a legend but I only want players arriving this summer whose focus is on the challenge right in front of them.

Transfer hijinks are a sign of the times but they're also a media construction. Granted, the major tournaments have always been a shop window for foreign talent, with the hitherto barely known Karel Poborský and Patrik Berger coming to the fore at Euro '96 and securing profitable moves to Manchester United and Liverpool, respectively. Even with the expanded format of Euro 2016 encompassing 552 players representing 24 different nations, there's barely a baller in France right now – maybe the odd Albanian and Icelander here or there – who hasn't at some point been linked with a Premier League club. And between them they've taken up reams of column inches before a ball has even been kicked. Correction: 'column inches' is an obsolete term because it's largely the need to feed a 24-hour media that fuels much of the online gossip that spreads like a rash across social networks; perhaps 'cyberspace storage' would be a more accurate description.

And the player who's used up the most megabytes in recent days is our own Dimitri Payet. As always, I'm looking forward to watching the maestro conduct the play against Albania again tonight, and if he puts in a performance anywhere near as good as the one against Romania then we're in for a treat. I just wish we could enjoy it without commentators opining that he's added another £10m to his transfer value or that another wonder goal will have Florentino Pérez reaching for his chequebook. Real Madrid and Barcelona dazzle all before them and the *Daily Telegraph*'s chief football writer, Sam Wallace, wrote recently of how the stars of international tournaments can be plotted by who Real have signed, going back to Luís Figo (wrestled away from Barcelona ironically enough) in 2000. Figo might have thought the move worth the Catalan vitriol and having a pig's head tossed in his direction but the steadily increasing marginalisation of James Rodríguez (Madrid's latest post-World Cup galáctico) offers a cautionary tale even more compelling.

Only this morning *The Sun* claimed that Manchester City have joined Chelsea and Paris Saint-Germain in 'the race' to sign West Ham's wizard. A race has to have a winner so his departure from West Ham is presented as a foregone conclusion, ignoring the fact that Chelsea aren't even in the Europa League and he'd spent several seasons under the nose of Paris Saint-Germain without them giving him a sniff. It's rare that an agent can be portrayed as the good guy but it was refreshing to hear Mark McKay play down transfer talk around his client, stating, 'As far as I am concerned, he's been happy at West Ham and it's down to West Ham that he's in the position that he is in.' Payet's tears as he was substituted to a standing ovation weren't at the thought of a £200,000 weekly pay packet from Real Madrid; he was genuinely overcome by how he'd gone from being an outcast to being embraced by a whole nation, and no one has or will show him more love than he's received this past year in East London, where he's so much more than just another brick in the wall.

McKay stopped short of saying Payet's not for sale – 'You've got to be talking ridiculous money. But football is football, so you never know,' but hey ho, we're not in 1966 anymore. Imagine the circus that would surround Hurst, Moore and Peters today. As it was, the World Cup-winning hat-trick hero went home, washed the car, mowed the lawn and happily got on with life with the Hammers earning a few quid a week. Those were the days …

Iceberg Ahead

27 June 2016

England dominated all three group matches, won one and drew two. Iceland were dominated in all three group matches, won one and drew two. So tonight's fixture looks quite evenly matched to me.

The benefits of this tournament's extended format are dubious at best but the undoubted highlight of the group stages was the jubilation with which some of the minnows greeted progress to the next round. And the minnows don't come any bigger, or should that be smaller, than Iceland: population 333,000, about the same size as Coventry. One report claimed that one-fifth of those 333,000 would be decamping to France to partake in Euro 2016. Another stated that the viewing figures for their final group match against Austria reached an audience share of 99.8 per cent. We think the Three Lions are followed in large numbers but, to put the ratio into perspective, it's the equivalent of 10.6 million crossing the Channel draped in the St George and all but 84,800 of the 42.4 million left behind subjecting themselves to England versus Slovakia.

Iceland's underdog status will no doubt attract the support of neutrals across the continent, especially in light of the Brexit debacle, conveniently ignoring that the Land of Fire and Ice is a member of the European Free

Trade Association but not a fully fledged member of the political union.

West Ham fans could be forgiven for not thinking too kindly of their Icelandic counterparts following the ownership fiasco presided over by biscuit baron Eggert Magnússon and banking tycoon Björgólfur Gudmundsson, our own Boris Johnson and Michael Gove, whose Promised Land was in fact a road leading to meltdown, but (last political parallel) let's not do a Trump and taint a whole race of people according to the actions of a few.

Iceland is an otherworldly place unlike anywhere else I've ever been, where glaciers rub up against volcanoes on a preternatural terrain. Until recently football wasn't a big part of the landscape but FA reforms now give them an unprecedented number of coaches per capita. They deserve the success they've enjoyed so far and that's united the nation. However, much as I admire Iceland both culturally and geographically and sincerely hope to revisit one day, I want the flames doused this evening and for their ardent fans to be left cold, with no further eruptions in either of our countries.

[England 1-2 Iceland, round of 16]

Year One – 2016/17

Dunce Caps Awarded to Wazza & Co.

5 July 2016

In a twist of irony, the English FA must for once be grateful for a messy departure from Europe, as the recriminations from the EU referendum have largely overshadowed the shameful exit from Euro 2016. There's still been enough opprobrium though, and my own favourite diatribe has to be Dietmar Hamann's, whose reasoning for our nation's latest turgid showing pretty much amounted to the players being thick! Similar accusations have been levelled against our electorate but, as a teacher, I must reject this slur against the whole education system, which in Hamann's humble opinion our professional footballers would be advised to engage with a little more.

Didi wasn't suggesting that you need a first-class degree in quantum physics or even a 2:2 in the offside law to flourish on the football pitch. His point was that a more rounded education will produce more rounded individuals who would perhaps be better attuned to the hothouse environment of a month-long tournament on foreign soil. Speaking from his experience as manager of Stockport County, Hamann bemoaned the sight of 13-

and 14-year-olds taking to the field at times when they should have been sat behind desks. In Premier League academies (that word's etymology is another irony) the ratio between playing and learning is skewed to an even greater extent; the teenager's insatiable appetite and dedication to improving his ability to strike a ball on the half-volley at the cost of all else is regarded as a positive, and then we're surprised when the same boy, by his early-20s, has either burned out or failed to mature.

In British academies it's a requirement for the under-18 age group to receive just nine hours of tutelage each week, as opposed to 34 hours of compulsory education for under-19s in Germany. Similarly, Spain's Juan Mata, who didn't play first-team football before the age of 19, possesses degrees in marketing and sports science. And to think we used to hold David James up as a paradigm of perspicacity based on the fact that he packed a couple of books to take to the World Cup! Far more stereotypical of our national sport's mindset is the story attributed to Icelandic defender Kári Árnason of Harry Kane having to ask the ref if defeat meant England would be going home. It sounds like an urban myth but it doesn't defy belief that the meaning of knockout football would be lost on one of our bright young things.

This lack of cultivation, combined with astronomical wages and their status as demi-Gods among devoted fans at club level, wraps players in a bubble. Club football is the comfort zone and stepping outside of it instils fear and induces paralysis. It seems to be a uniquely English ailment, so why are the Welsh, who've predominantly graduated from the same academy system, seemingly immune? It can't be argued that Gareth Bale is a *Brains of Britain* contender, and he probably leads a more stellar existence in Madrid than any of Spurs' sorry superstars do in North London. Crucially, donning the red of Wales rather than the famous white of Madrid allows him to escape the bubble. Players and fans alike had to wait 58 years to grace an international tournament, which, rather than ramping up the expectation and pressure, created a symbiotic relationship in which they've fed off each other's passion, giving all the players, regardless of their stature, a Herculean hunger and resilience. Compare this to the alienation between England's players and followers, with the apocryphal slander of Kane's intellectual capacity lapped up by disenchanted fans.

For a player of any nationality, our gaffer is quite the Renaissance man: a rock musician with a law degree who identifies himself as a socialist and is fluent in four languages. Yet as his brief stint as the nation's most popular pundit proved, he also retains the common touch, which is essential when dealing with youngsters coming from an array of backgrounds. Despite being one of the flavours of the month, he's rightly distancing himself from the clamour that surrounds the England managerial vacancy. The present generation already looks damaged beyond repair. Who would seriously want to be our King Canute, battling against a tide of ignorance? However, if Bilić can produce a culture in which West Ham's future waves of talent, led by Reece Oxford, can replicate Bobby Moore and thrive for country as well as club, then he'll deserve a bloody knighthood.

And Cheerio Tonks

I recently opined that it would take crazy money for us to part with James Tomkins in this transfer window. What

I failed to take into account is that a good centre-back in the prime of his career doesn't necessarily want to be third/fourth choice or a makeshift right-back, even if he does love the club. Cheers for the good times James, you could always be relied on to give your best. However, it's only fair that we let you move on for what's a very fair price. Having advocated sending Oxford and Burke out on loan, your exit perhaps indicates that Slaven is instead ready to place his trust in the young Reeces over the loyal Jameses.

The Famous Five

12 July 2016

Pig-gate; the Bedroom Tax; leaving his daughter in the pub after one too many bevvies; dangerous games of brinkmanship with BoJo exposing the UK to potential meltdown ... our outgoing PM's various misdemeanours stretch on. For many football fans, however, his greatest gaffe remains inexplicably forgetting which team he supports, confusing the Hammers with his 'beloved' Villans. It was always suspected that David Cameron's allegiance to Aston Villa might just be a sycophantic nod to Prince William's support, the beginnings of a new Bullingdon Club, blue blood quaffing claret in the VIP lounge of the Doug Ellis Stand. And who else might be present in this ghastly scenario? The only other famous Villa fan I could think of is classical violinist Nigel Kennedy, the bit of rough in a hoity-toity trio. It's not a club that I'd want to join but I wouldn't mind being a fly on the wall for one meet-up. Which got me thinking about our own celebrity contingent and playing a twist on the classic parlour game of which historical figures dead or alive you'd invite to a dinner party or, in East End parlance, take down the boozer. Which five of our famous fans would I want to have a pint with?

My first choice isn't everybody's cup of tea but, before any accusations of nepotism à la Frank Lampard Jnr, despite the shared family name and Essex roots, we're not, to the best of my knowledge, in any way related. By way of proof, my bald pate versus his shock of hair suggests we definitely weren't sired from the same stock. I must, though, confess an affection for the dandyish ways of Russell Brand. My opinionated namesake is perhaps the closest thing this generation has to an Oscar Wilde and he therefore merits a place at the head of the table from whence to animatedly emit his trademark wit and wisdom. I don't in the slightest begrudge his omnipresence behind the scenes at Upton Park, popping up on the Sky Sports cameras to shower the gaffer with kisses; if I ever attain celebrity status then I'll use it shamelessly to penetrate the corridors of power. Brand's regular attendance demonstrates the zeal you'd expect of someone with an addictive personality, and having run to the stadium to be present for the final match against Manchester United and the subsequent closing ceremony, one wonders why he wasn't on hand to take over MC-ing duties from the insipid Ben Shephard? Hopefully because he's being held back for the opening ceremony at the Olympic Stadium, a harbinger of bigger, brighter things. If the delectable Katy Perry were still Mrs Brand then I'd certainly make space for her too but I imagine her enthusiasm for all things Irons has waned somewhat since the couple's estrangement.

What with Brand's nihilistic excursions into politics, it's almost a shame that Mr Cameron isn't a true claret and blue. Prime Minister's Questions has never been scintillating viewing but I'd pay good money to witness a verbal joust between the Etonian toff and the revolutionary dilettante. Staying in the political sphere, we're privileged to be able to bar the (alleged) swine-fancier but to instead admit a more celebrated leader of the free world: President Obama. Barack (I'm sure he wouldn't mind me calling him by his first name) qualifies thanks to his sister, who lives in East London. The story goes that all her side of the family are Hammers devotees and they got Uncle Obama hooked on a visit to London back in 2003. While readily accepting that he's more of a Chicago Bulls fan, we could have fun testing his knowledge of our club with quick-fire questions such as Slaven or Sam? New crest or old? AVCO or BAC? Watching the incumbent of the world's highest public office growing ever more discombobulated counts as a satisfying pastime to someone possessing literally no authority.

And we could have another leading world dignitary join in the game if rumours that Queen Elizabeth II is also a West Ham fan are to be believed. For a long time she was thought to be a Gooner, until she was reported to have baited Millwall-supporting handservants with the news that she was West Ham through and through! Kudos for that Your Majesty, regardless of your true allegiance. My prime reservation for setting a place for you is the need for everyone else to mind their Ps and Qs. Having a spirited football chat without recourse to expletives is nigh on impossible. Now it might well be that Her Majesty swears like a trooper on the subject of Michail Antonio being deployed at right-back, but I still wouldn't care to run the risk of conversation being inhibited by archaic notions of decorum.

Decorum is certainly not a sticking point in Hollywood, and we can also lay claim to a few stars of the silver screen. Elijah Wood's affinity with us grew thanks to *Green Street*, where conversely that film is a black mark against his name for me. Matt Damon has professed a fondness that's basically explained by a preference for plucky losers over perpetual winners, so let's hope he's not a fan for much longer. Overuse of the Americanisation 'soccer' would undoubtedly grate, so turning our attention to thespians closer to home, we have the daddy of the British gangster genre to keep everyone in line: Raymond Winstone. Some of his output is so low grade as to rival professional twonk Danny Dyer but there are enough stone-cold classics in Winstone's oeuvre to command respect. Whether the actual films are good or bad, the thing with Ray is you know what you're getting; like Caine before him and Dyer after, he's perfected the art of being himself no matter what the role. My erstwhile university tutor, Richard Dyer (no relation to Danny as far as I'm aware), famously theorised that Hollywood stars shouldn't be seen as real people but as constructed images. I'd be keen to find out if Winstone in the flesh really is the walking, talking stereotype that he appears. Even if he is, the persona he projects is basically the archetypal West Ham fan, so far from the worst person to have a beer with, as long as you stay on his right side.

A very different Hollywood star is next on the guest list. Keira Knightley, the waif-like English rose with the plummy accent is the most atypical of Irons yet was apparently once in possession of a season ticket in the East Stand. She espoused her love of West Ham on *Late*

Night with Seth Meyers (the US host also staking a claim to fandom, having once chosen to take in a match at Upton Park over a visit to the Valley) back in 2014, getting excited at how high in the table we were riding while accurately predicting the impending fall. It's a pleasure enough to gaze on Keira's face when she's duelling pirates on the big screen; to do so while she talks breathlessly about Europa League adventures would be heavenly.

You'd think by now we'd be running out of A-listers but there's still James Corden and Lennox Lewis, plus plenty of B/C/Z-listers, including Pixie Lott, Bruce Dickinson, David Essex, Frank Bruno, Kriss Akabusi, Len Goodman and Noel Edmonds. I've been restricting myself to those still with us but if resurrection were possible then Alfred Hitchcock would be a dead cert. It's tempting to veto anyone who's not recently been seen at Upton Park but my last place is reserved for someone about whom there's a fair degree of online debate regarding their footballing kinship. Bristol City are the competition based on his childhood habitat but general consensus seems to be that John Cleese is in fact a steadfast West Ham fan. Maybe, as with many icons who've adopted pseudonyms, he's a little bipolar – plain old John Cheese supports Bristol City but the legendary Python known as John Cleese follows West Ham. He needs inviting a) so that we can sort out once and for all who he actually supports, and b) so that Brand, Obama, Winstone and Knightley can join him in doing the Ministry of Silly Walks after they've had a few bevvies.

That's quite an assortment of celebrity supporters we boast. The entertainment roster for the evening must also include a spot of five-a-side. Myself managing, we'd have

Obama in goal (American sportsmen are better with their hands than their feet), Winstone as defensive enforcer, Brand and Cleese using their lankiness to get up and down and Knightley up front bending it like Beckham into the net. If the aforementioned trio of Villans want to take us on then we'd let them supplement their numbers with last season's two best first-teamers, say Micah Richards and Jack Grealish, to make it a fair game. I'd even consider a last-minute substitution of Winstone for Her Majesty and still fancy our chances.

Mike Bassett: The Second Coming

22 July 2016

Well, knock me down with a feather. Press reports told us it was on the cards but the FA have actually gone and done it, despite being called 'Clueless, Classless, C***s' in *Big Sam: My Autobiography* (the ghostwriter's emphatic capitalisation, not mine). I really don't know what to make of Allardyce being given the England job so I'll keep this mercifully short.

The appointment seems to have met with muted approval, not dissimilar to when he strode into Upton Park and we were all too numb from a bruising relegation to muster either enthusiasm or opposition. Nearly every fan respects Sam, even if grudgingly, as a specialist in making the most of the resources at his disposal. In this sense at least, he's a perfect match for national team manager. Speaking from personal experience, he did a very good job for us in the first two years but his last two years at Upton Park exposed limitations in public relations and playing style, both of which could prove major stumbling blocks in his new role.

He's always thought that he belonged at the top table so I guess now we'll find out who was right: the man himself or 30,000-odd Cockney naysayers.

Vintage Carr Requires Some Repair

28 July 2016

> Academy veteran departs with a pang of sadness this summer having overseen the development of some of the club's brightest stars of the past generation. (*The Guardian*)

The word lynchpin rather underestimates a man who's dedicated 43 years of service to our football club, so it would be fitting if the HR slight to Tony Carr were rectified by him being honoured in some way along with legendary players and managers at the swanky new stadium.

Carr obviously did some sterling work down the years but, before anyone gets on their high horse about the spirit of West Ham being sold off (the breaking stories of the Tesco Stadium were particularly untimely, coinciding with news of Carr's departure from his ambassadorial role), it's worth pointing out that his crown jewels – Ferdinand, Lampard, Carrick, Cole, Defoe and Johnson – were less likely to have left under a regime bringing in 60,000 punters every week.

It's the way of life that as one door closes another one opens, and since inheriting control of the academy from Carr in 2014, Terry Westley has already delivered one trophy and, more importantly, supervised some mouth-watering young talent, so life goes on even if we'd like some people and some things to hang around forever.

Thank you to Tony for helping to write the DNA of the West Ham United that I know and love, and I hope that you continue to feel part of the family wherever the future takes us.

Classic Carr:

- Signed apprentice terms the year that West Ham won the World Cup. However, Hurst, Roger Byrne and Clyde Best barred the young striker's path to the first team.
- Recruited by John Lyall in 1973 to train junior players on a part-time basis, Tuesday and Thursday nights, outside on the forecourts, on concrete, around a parked car if necessary. 'Street football,' Carr said.
- Became head of academy in 1980 and Paul Allen was his first claim to fame. 'The anomaly with Paul is that he won an FA Cup medal in 1980 and an FA Youth Cup medal in 1981.'
- Highlight of his career? The 6-0 thrashing of Coventry at Upton Park to make it 9-0 on aggregate in the 1999 FA Youth Cup Final. 'We won the game in real style, a full house. It was rocking. We won the game quite early and you could sit there and just admire the football.'

Always Look on the Bright Side of Life

29 July 2016

[Europa League qualifier, first leg: NK Domžale 2-1 West Ham]

After another chastening Europa League qualifying tie, I've been searching for positives and here's what I've managed to scrape together:

1. It could have been worse were it not for Adrián's right boot. A one-goal deficit is very much surmountable.
2. Should further ridicule follow next week, we should recall that a premature European exit didn't do us too much harm last season.
3. There may be new-found urgency in the summer recruitment drive. The bosses are right to advocate not spending money for the sake of it but the need for reinforcements at full-back and up front was again exposed.
4. One of our new acquisitions, Feghouli, showed glimpses of class.
5. The Antonio at right-back experiment must surely now be terminated. It nullifies one of our most potent attacking threats and makes him culpable for goals conceded rather than goals scored, which is unfair on a lad who's hauled himself from non-league to the verge of England recognition. Last night it was also unfair on Byram, shunted over to left-back in a very unsteady and makeshift back four. Is it a plus that Burke and Oxford were spared the ignominy of playing an active part in it all?
6. The curtain-raiser at the Olympic Stadium is now a must-win if we're to christen the maiden campaign there with Europa League glitz, and that makes Domžale's visit more tantalising. I booked my ticket only yesterday afternoon and was surprised at how much available seating remained for a landmark fixture. No matter how much cause they give us to grumble, fans must

unite behind the team and show the players and the watching world that our new home will be a cauldron of claret-and-blue ardour.

Stadium Verdict: SUCCESS (Pending Approval of Noisy Fans)

4 August 2016

[Europa League qualifier, second leg: West Ham 3-0 NK Domžale (4-2 agg.)]

The last time I attended the inaugural match at a new stadium was England U21s versus Italy U21s at the rebuilt Wembley in 2007. I recall feeling distinctly underwhelmed; it was comfortable, good leg room in particular, but soulless. I kept thinking back to the last time I was at the old Wembley, stood in the centre of the pitch for an Oasis gig shortly before it was bulldozed, and marvelling at the architectural pomposity of the Twin Towers, the grandeur of which Upton Park's own dubious faux turrets came closer to emulating than a wonky arch ever will.

First impressions of the London Stadium are, I'm pleased to report, far stronger. Or perhaps I should say second impressions, because I've already visited the place in its previous guise as the Olympic Stadium.

There probably aren't many Hammers for whom this construction already holds such a special place in their heart. I watched it slowly rise on the horizon when I went running on the Newham Greenway and, four years ago today, I set foot in it for the first time to watch Jess Ennis get one hand on her gold medal on the morning of Super Saturday. To top it off, I spent my last night as a Londoner there, enjoying more Olympic action, before moving north in that glorious summer of 2012.

At the crux of many objections to our relocation has been the difficulty of being yanked from our roots. I left my roots behind four years ago and, although I'm constantly looking back, I don't have any regret, and I'm confident that the West Ham United of the future will be equally unwavering. Looking much further into the past, fans need also be aware that the club's roots spread wider than Green Street to Priory Road. Derided as a money-making exercise, the commemorative dark blue kit that we're wearing for Sunday's official opening against Juventus harks back to our origins as Thames Ironworks, who themselves moved to a multi-sports arena with a banked cycle track around the pitch, the Memorial Grounds, in 1897. The ambitious founder of the Thames Ironworks, Arnold Hills, would approve of the social mobility shown by our fresh relocation to a bigger, better arena.

And nostalgia aside, it is better than the Boleyn. I've previously criticised our old home and Newham in general as being, well ... grim. Our new surroundings are far more spacious and inviting, the equivalent of moving from an East Ham tower block to a waterside complex with a private park. There's ample room for families to mill around outside in the evening sunshine. Favourite pre-match sights included people searching for and photographing their personalised paving stones on Champions Place, an old dear with claret-and-blue-rinsed hair looking properly chuffed with life, and mounted police chatting to a partially blind man (whose canine companion was covered in claret and blue ribbons) about whether his guide had sussed the place out yet. All in all, a more genial picture than many of us will have of Upton Park's lively farewell.

Some might stop me here to say that football stadiums aren't supposed to be *nice* and I'm inclined to agree, within reason. They're gladiatorial arenas, flanked by thousands baying for blood. As long as everyone remembers before the whistle blows to get the conflict underway and at the end of the 90-plus minutes that it's *just a game*, albeit one with the power to consume us. And just because football gives us licence to vent our wild sides for an hour and a half doesn't mean that the environment in which we do so has to be unpleasant.

My dominant reservation concerns the stands' distance from the pitch. While enjoying the external capaciousness, a large gap between the fans and the action isn't conducive to generating the febrile atmosphere that football thrives on. The players' emergence from the tunnel, greeted by the first rousing rendition of 'Bubbles', was enough to give me goosebumps and showcased the impressive acoustics of the new roof. The bubble machine, on the other hand, looked wholly inadequate, the bubbles lost in the wide-open space between tunnel and pitch. My humble recommendation, therefore, to partially fill the pitchside gulleys, is to install giant machines to crank out millions of bubbles at opportune moments.

Despite the distance, views were impeccable, save for the eye-line from my cheap seat in the Bobby Moore Upper Tier being disturbed by an ugly yawning chasm between tiers. I know that it's been hurriedly reconfigured from athletics to football mode so I'll reserve judgement in the hope that this will be prettified one way or another.

With all mod cons, the only other grumble I heard all night (leaving off some of the football!) was from an agitated member of the catering staff at the pie, mash and liquor stand, which had run out of liquor. It wasn't the only liquor missing, this being a UEFA fixture, but new watering holes seemed to have been located across E15 as Stratford was turned into a sea of claret and blue and even pubs that are more gastro than boozy, such as King Eddie's, had hung out flags to welcome new customers who were making themselves very much at home.

And it's already beginning to feel like home. The favourable terms of tenancy struck with the London Legacy Development Corporation (LLDC) have attracted streams of negative comment from third parties, mostly fuelled by tribal jealousies, but I'm still amazed at how much we've been able to stamp our identity on to a multi-purpose venue that we don't actually own; leaseholders in London's cut-throat property market aren't allowed a fraction of the creative freedom that we've had with the décor. Even the ArcelorMittal Orbit seems to have faded a deeper shade of red to blend in.

Of course, the edifice is only part of the equation. Bilić, speaking sense as always, has acknowledged that on-pitch success ultimately rests with the players: '50,000 season tickets won't get you even a throw-in.' However, he also alluded to the importance of the support in helping the players to settle quickly, adding that 'fans who are well known to be very loud and a little bit intimidating [can improve] our performance'.

St James' Park, perched atop Gallowgate, remains one of the most aesthetically majestic arenas that I've visited, but it failed to live up to its cacophonous reputation on the day that I was there, for a nil-nil bore draw with Aston Villa in the early days of the ill-fated Allardyce era, during which the fans may as well have been sat on their hands for 90 minutes. At the other end of the spectrum, at least prior to Barry Hearn turning one end of the ground into apartments, I've known little Brisbane Road to rock even when under capacity.

The board, courtesy of the LLDC, have gifted us a magnificent shell, undeniably befitting a club with ambitions to be among the elite. However, in the spirit of home being where the heart is, the success of the new stadium will only truly be measured against what we – the fans – inject into it. The players and supporters have to make sure that they lift each other, so those who deemed it a good idea to leave ridiculously early on this special night with the score at 2-0 and the tie still in the balance needn't bother returning if we want to turn the new digs into a formidable fortress.

If You've Not Got Anything Nice to Say, Then Don't Say Anything at All

26 August 2016

[Europa League qualifier, second leg: West Ham 0-1 Astra Giurgiu (1-2 agg.)]

So goes the maxim, but that would lead to an entry reading no longer than 'Ashley Fletcher showed promise'. In truth, even having slept (uncomfortably) on it, I'm having trouble writing today, having been numbed by the ineptitude of last night's display.

It's hard to believe that at the age of 35, after dreams have faded and died on countless occasions, West Ham still have it in them to make me feel physically sick. This journal began with a rumination on whether I should coerce my Cestrian son – now approaching two – into following in my footsteps, in which supporting the

Hammers was described as a life sentence; as I packed him off to nursery with a newly purchased West Ham rucksack this morning, I felt ashamed at the cruelty I'm trying to inflict upon him. If I can't find the receipt and the next 12 hours do nothing to assuage my distemper then I'll be sorely tempted to toss the thing on this evening's barbecue. Better a piece of fabric going up in flames now than my little boy's hopes and desires in years to come.

The subject of European football has been classic West Ham. As it looked like Champions League football could be a possibility we imploded against Swansea [West Ham 1-4 Swansea]. Automatic Europa League qualification seemed nailed on until we contrived to throw it away in the second half at Stoke [2-1]. And after a scare from Slovenian minnows NK Domžale, who would have thought we'd make nemeses of Astra Giurgiu, whose manager is currently serving a six-month suspension from domestic football and whose owner is in jail?! What makes the failure so seismic this time around is that it feels as if the foundations of our brave new world are already crumbling. The stadium's not even at full capacity yet, and yesterday there did seem to be more atmosphere than there was against Bournemouth, but when the ground reverberates to the sound of booing after just 225 minutes of competitive football in our new home then that's not a good sign.

Fans were quick to vent their fury on Facebook and Twitter too, and I could only grunt in agreement at much of what I read. David Gold's half-hearted excuse of nine first-team players missing met with much derision, which was fair enough given that Enner Valencia, sat on the bench, cost more than the opposition's entire squad.

Gökhan Töre replaced Valencia as the fans' favourite scapegoat last night and his defensive awareness, or lack of it, was what ultimately cost us. Fellow new recruits Håvard Nordtveit and Jonathan Calleri were equally woeful but let's not be too premature in casting aspersions and writing off their West Ham careers; it took Antonio a little while to come good last season and, although the Hammer of the Year runner-up's effort couldn't be faulted last night, his touch and his decision-making certainly could.

Cries of 'Bilić, Gold and Sullivan out' are preposterously impetuous – let's not throw the baby out with the bath water! We've had cause to question a few of his decisions lately but I certainly don't buy into the belief that Bilić showed contempt for the competition; balanced against the injury list, he fielded a strong line-up and looked as shocked and disgusted with their performance as we were. As for the accusations that Gold and Sullivan have been ineffectual in the transfer market, just as Bilić decreed that he won't resort to begging players to sign, the chairmen can't tie them up and hand-deliver superstars. They reportedly put up good money for Alexandre Lacazette and Carlos Bacca but neither player could be tempted by a move to East London. We have to accept that it's evolution, not revolution, which makes our Europa League humiliation all the more disappointing, because it represented an opportunity to put our name in bold on the European football map. There will be repercussions in the make-up of the squad; Bilić had no doubt planned to use the additional game time to blood the likes of Oxford, Burke and Calleri. And will the mooted transfer of Simone Zaza still take place? I know he wasn't first choice but signing an Italian international centre-forward was the stuff dreams were made of in my youth, so we're still moving in the right direction, if not at the pace some of us demand.

A true fan will stick around (yes, that's a dig at those again leaving before 90 minutes were up) through thick and thin. So let's rally and start believing that Europa League disaster can lead to another positive Premier League season. Clutching at straws, we were never going to win the Europa League but we could win the League Cup and European participation got us a bye into round three. Surely we can beat Accrington Stanley at home …

And That's a Wrap

12 September 2016

There's a misapprehension that film sets are as glamorous as a Champions League Final against Real Madrid on a warm summer evening in Paris. They're not. They're as glamorous as an EFL Cup tie away to Accrington on a damp Tuesday night. But when said film set is Upton Park several months after you thought you'd waved goodbye to the place, then it carries a certain romance, as if recently-closed superclub Fabric were to reopen its doors for one night only for a good old-fashioned clandestine rave.

It was probably in Fabric's halcyon days that I last attempted to stay awake for 24 hours but, having signed up for a night shoot care of Jack Sullivan tweeting the call-out for extras, I was about to visit the witching hour stone-cold sober. West Ham have been known to make 90 minutes feel like a lifetime but this promised to be a real test of stamina, ten hours of shooting (from 7pm till 5am) being distilled into what will probably amount to about a hundred seconds of screen time.

It turns out that our last match at the Boleyn wasn't that fateful night against Manchester United. It's a League Semi-Final(!) against fictional Russian team Dynamo FC. And something far worse than the smashing of coach windows is afoot … Russians have taken over, and we're not referring to oligarchs in the boardroom. Eastern bloc terrorists have planted explosives in the stands and Pierce Brosnan, presumably playing David Gold, is out to foil them. Essentially it's *Die Hard* in a football stadium.

This high-concept masterpiece is titled *Final Score*, the Saturday afternoon version of which hasn't been so engrossing since the vidiprinter was retired. On the subject of which, I still eerily recall Mitchell Thomas prophesying in an early '90s matchday programme that in the future we'd all be watching events unfold via Ceefax; update Ceefax for smartphones and it looks as if he was better with a crystal ball than a football.

Sharing a mock-up poster of the make-believe match via Facebook probably contravened the terms and conditions of the release form signed by all but read in depth by no one upon entry. Led through back rooms where production equipment mingled among Barratt Homes gear – pointing to a fate for the stadium marginally better than being blown to smithereens – the dishevelled look of the place after all the fixtures and fittings had been auctioned off had me humming 'Ghost Town' to myself, so it didn't click that I was emerging from the tunnel until the hallowed turf was right there in front of me. Cue gratuitous selfies from the vast majority of extras around me, while I fought against the in-built instinct that it would be improper to encroach on to the pitch! Seeing Upton Park empty save for 60-odd people, an ambulance and a lighting rig was strange to say the least; David Lynch is supposed to be the master of surrealism but this had me more freaked than anything Agent Cooper encountered in *Twin Peaks*.

Under instruction to bring two sets of clothing – one to represent Dynamo fans and one to represent the West Ham faithful – it was notable that all but a couple were wearing claret and blue as option number one. I dreaded being picked out to play the other side. However, it turns out that extras are masters of disguise, because across the night we all had to be both, while some got kitted out as stewards and rozzers too. Given the attention to detail in other areas – those wearing the newest kit were asked to cover the changed crest so as to avoid some *Back to the Future* time paradox – one assumes either that movie viewers aren't eagle-eyed enough to spot the same faces adorned in different colours at opposite ends of the ground, or else half of us will end up on the cutting room floor.

Background continuity ought to have been less of a concern than the on-pitch action. The most entertaining moment for a long time came when the extras plucked from Wanstead Flats kicked off their own game of fantasy football, and the standard was no worse than much of what we've seen at the London Stadium so far this season, but several were so 'experienced' as to make Kevin Nolan look like a spring chicken. Spoiler alert: apparently West Ham win, as they should do given the sub-Sunday league physique of Dynamo's No. 9. In the stands, those of us in the guise of Dynamo fans were given the direction to act angry and frustrated; not exactly a stretch for anyone that's suffered the slings and arrows of following the home team's fortunes – we've been method training for years!

A popular theory posits that the director is the auteur of a film, the driving force behind all the action. Watching Scott Mann – one-time director of *Hollyoaks* and *Stars in Their Eyes* – try to marshal a mass of units made me pity football managers who helplessly conduct from the touchline, with negligible impact on what their troops are actually doing. Then the West Ham injury curse of 2016 struck again as amiable man-mountain Dave Bautista, recognisable from his forbidding cameo in *Spectre* and here streaking on to the pitch to prevent a bomb detonation, went down with a hamstring injury, prompting an unsympathetic outbreak of terrace humour from us extras with taunts of 'Diver!' and calls for the magic sponge.

Dealing with a crowd of extras is much like dealing with a crowd of small children: it's impossible to get their collective attention and there's always one in need of the toilet. The handful of professional extras among the volunteers didn't help matters, with one complaining about the poor quality of soup and instigating a chant of 'we want tea'! Another vowed to contact her union about the lack of a break from sitting and cheering, sitting and cheering. It might have been sleep deprivation sending my imagination into overdrive but by 4.30am I swear I heard Ricky Gervais's reedy voice whining about the need for rest! Despite the monotony, I'm still seriously considering registering with a screen extras agency; after all, some people were paid 75 quid to be there while I'd paid that much in train fares for the privilege. Having dismissed myself as far too self-conscious to be a natural actor, even as a distant blur in the camera lens I became strangely aware of my own performance after multiple takes, asking whether I got the miming of 'Irons! Irons!' right that time.

I suspect that after the release of *Final Score* next year we'll still be awaiting a truly great football-set film but this film's setting will always be special to scores of Hammers, and I for one eagerly await my big screen debut. I'm the guy in the claret-and-blue bobble hat; you can't miss me.

Keep Calm, This Can't Carry On

18 September 2016

Some so-called supporters reap what they sow. You won't find anyone who's not frustrated by the season so far but some reactions border on the hysterical, which only deepen the gloom and the sense of panic rather than lending the support that might help lift the team out of its current malaise.

For example (all direct quotes from the official West Ham United Facebook thread following the West Brom defeat):

> Upton Park was a great stadium and we should still be there as our new stadium is not doing us any favours.

Teething issues were to be expected and some are revelling in 'I told you so' forecasts of doom but most are taken aback by the extremity of our grievances. Hostile stands (more on the sitting/standing issue to come later) understandably unsettle the players but a 4-2 defensive horror show at The Hawthorns can't be attributed to a change of climate in the way that the Watford debacle [2-4] could. London Stadium detractors with short memories are also conveniently ignoring the fact that

Upton Park wasn't exactly a safe zone in which we were immune from feckless displays that often had grown men wailing.

> Mark my words Brady and co better have foreign bolt holes if they fk up this club chasing money yet selling us down the swanny!!

Is the club run using a 21st-century business model? Yes. Do mistakes get made? Yes. Would I swap our current owners, lifelong fans with a wealth of football experience, for a Chinese, American or Saudi investment group? Hell no.

> Tore isn't good enough. Nordviet isn't good enough. Masauku isn't good enough … Why the hell sell Tompkins.

Misspelling the names of foreign newcomers, fair enough, but a homegrown lad who you profess to merit a starting spot, at least have the decency to spell or pronounce his name right. Any discussion of the line-up when the team are on a bad run reveals the fickleness of many fans … COLLINS OUT, REID OUT, NOBLE OUT … we'd struggle to scrape a team together based on form alone. But the old adage goes that class is permanent, and if any of Töre, Nordtveit or Masuaku, as shit as they might currently look, prove in time that the cream rises to the top, then the same fans cursing them now will be singing their praises.

West Ham till I die, only some of us seem to require resuscitating on way too regular a basis.

The Great Popcorn Debate

Is this really a debate? On the one hand, I don't personally know anyone who would choose salted or sweet to go with the football. On the other, what would it matter if they did? I like a pie or a burger. My dad prefers a packet of Werther's or Fruit Pastilles. It takes all sorts, although I've yet to see Bertie Bassett selling his sugary wares alongside Herbie Hammer flogging kits.

I want to make light of this, except there are those frothing at the mouth over popcorn and I surmise their anger derives from its association with 'light' entertainment, whereas 90 minutes of football action sits a lot heavier with the majority of us. I don't know what the going rate is for a tub of popcorn at the London Stadium but I hope it's at least as extortionate as it is at my local Vue. I say keep popcorn prices high and ticket prices low; let the new breed of popcorn munchers subsidise the traditionalists and let's just laugh at them rather than choking on our own choice of snack.

Sit Down for Your Rights

20 September 2016

What's your definition of a football club? Is it the players that take to the pitch? Is it the arena in which they play and in which you support them? Is it all the supporters around you and the camaraderie that you generate? Or is it something more, something even less tangible?

If we were to accept that a football club is made up of multiple components, then would we at least be able to ascertain which is the most important? I ask these questions because at the moment West Ham seems to be a club that's disunited, the fans at war, tearing it apart from the inside out and creating a sour, poisonous atmosphere.

It's difficult to tell which was worse against Watford: the team disgracing themselves or the fans doing likewise. I wouldn't suggest that when the team delivers a miserable, unedifying performance the fans should just sit in silence, but there's a middle ground between that, throwing missiles at the away support and having punch-ups among themselves. The behaviour exhibited on that afternoon represents a very strange kind of 'support'.

Of course supporters needn't be in agreement with each other all the time and support of the club needn't be absolute, we're not in *1984*, although some supporters evidently wish we were. The Against Modern Football movement has my sympathy in many respects – gross pay packets fuelled by extortionate ticket prices, the self-serving elite growing rich off the Champions League and Sky Sports cash cows – but the horse has long since bolted; if you find the corporatisation of the Premier League that distasteful then get down Victoria Road to support Dagenham & Redbridge, but don't then complain that there are no entertainers in the class of Dimitri Payet or that your new team stands no chance of going all the way to Wembley.

Crucially, there'll be no trouble with standing if you go to watch the Daggers. One reason for this is that the 6,000-capacity Victoria Road (currently known as the Chigwell Construction Stadium for sponsorship purposes, natch) is rarely more than a quarter full, so it's easy enough to accommodate all types of fan. Another reason is that they don't even have seats at the Bury Road end. And the reason for this is that they've never been higher up the football pyramid than League Two (the Fourth Division in old money), so haven't been subject to the same legal requirements as Premier League and Championship clubs.

The last Premier League club to lawfully accommodate standing fans was Fulham in 2001. I have family and friends who are Fulham season ticket holders but I don't recall a single grumble as the terraces were pulled down and replaced by seated stanchions, necessitated by the meteoric rise up the divisions funded by Mohamed Al-Fayed. I have relatively fond memories of accompanying my dad to Craven Cottage and sitting on the crush barriers back when they languished in the bottom division of the Football League and played to crestfallen crowds of a few thousand; I also recall having to be lifted on to the barrier to see anything but the backs of grown men and feeling a bit scared on the rare occasions that the crowd surged forward.

I never actually stood on the terraces at Upton Park, my first visit coming in 1989 at the age of eight, shortly after the initial publication of the Taylor Report instigated the phasing out of standing areas. You'd be hard pushed to find anyone under the age of 35 with a vivid recollection of standing at top-flight football. An older generation for whom the experience of standing was entrenched but who are now reaching pension age would probably rather not be on their feet for 90-plus minutes, which leaves a relatively small window of supporters who would strongly advocate standing under existing conditions.

When I say 'standing', I'm referring to being in an upright position for the entirety of the match. If you enjoy the comfort of a seat for even a few minutes but assert your right not to use it then you're a hypocrite. Naturally we all rise to our feet at certain moments, such as the teams' emergence from the tunnel and the scoring of a goal, which are deemed socially acceptable. It isn't socially acceptable to obscure the views of others, especially the frail and infirm who hero-worshipped Charlie Paynter, or the kids who form the club's future, just because you want to 'give it some'. I'm fed up with hearing and reading the loutish attitude of 'I'll stand if I wanna stand'. You know what, I'd like to play up front but it doesn't give me the right to go and elbow Zaza out of the way, even if he's not currently looking any more like a £20m striker than I would. When you bought your season ticket for the new stadium you were assigned a seat, not a personalised X that marked where you could stand each week; the rules and regulations have been clear for a long time.

Now, rules are made to be broken and many will claim that they were persistently flouted at the Boleyn, where there were sections that turned a blind eye to standing. Give it time and pockets of the London Stadium will emerge as standing-friendly, where those of a like mind can congregate. The ticket office is already working behind the scenes to reorganise season ticket holders according to their penchant for being fully vertical or otherwise, but they have to do so quietly and tactfully while Newham Council and stadium operators LS185 withhold the safety certificate for an additional 3,000 seats and with the board wishing to expand capacity to 66,000 next year.

There's no doubt a handful of supporters who can reasonably complain of mistreatment – the world, sadly, isn't always a fair place, hence Baroness Brady being allowed to stand in the executive box – but to my mind the club is being as fair as can be. The letter signed by

Brady but sent in the club's interests prior to the Watford match was clearly not intended to rile fans; it was a polite reminder of the need to abide by the laws laid down for all top-tier clubs, stating what the consequences would be for individuals who chose to ignore its message. If you proceed to get yourself ejected from the ground then good riddance, there's a waiting list of thousands who would still happily take your vacated seat. Worried about the sterile atmosphere that the absence of a few ultras might breed? Well, 60,000 harmonious supporters ought to be capable of generating a pulsating noise more conducive to on-pitch success than that created by a vociferous but mutinous minority.

Nor are claims of even-handedness on behalf of the club derailed by it allowing away supporters to stand. As David Gold pointed out when wading into a heated Twitter debate, the game has evolved in such a way that travelling spectators, mostly well known to one another and to the club, largely police themselves. Stewards were rightly instructed to concentrate on areas where standing was causing problems as views were obstructed, meaning that the rules haven't been strictly enforced in swathes of the Bobby Moore Lower blocks either, buttressing the request for patience and consideration as these things sort themselves out.

Segregation and security look to be more pertinent issues, although just as rugby fans and civilised people in general are able to mix with one another, it's a sad state of affairs if anyone is so enraged by the sight of a Watford, Manchester United or even Spurs shirt that they feel compelled to start a fight. The biggest concern revolves around the club not being responsible for security and the Met refusing to police the stadium because it doesn't have a satisfactory radio system, which is quite alarming given the terror alerts around the Olympics! The club, however, seems to be doing its best to work with all parties, including inviting those who have contributed Founders' Feedback – as I did, both positive and negative – to partake in a fans' forum, in order to resolve matters as soon as possible.

If I were to design the perfect stadium then there would definitely be safe standing areas and Gold has stated that he too would introduce it in a heartbeat, if it were permitted by the authorities. The Taylor Report, while recommending that all major stadiums convert to an all-seater model, recognised that standing isn't intrinsically unsafe. Fans of various creeds and colours have campaigned for the return of standing on the terraces via the Football Supporters' Federation, and Celtic are currently trialling what's known as rail seating, a German system that allows easily for both standing and sitting.

But those that continue to pine for Upton Park need to move with the times. I used to relish picking up my copy of *Over Land and Sea* on matchdays but you won't find me smashing up my laptop just because it's migrated online and ceased being printed. If further analogy were needed, our defence might be a chaotic mess but it won't be fixed by Dicksy telling the back four to get stuck in like he used to; we might applaud the passion but it won't help much if we end every match with seven men! The football world has changed, for better or worse, but, rather than try to force back the hands of time, fans would be better advised to look to the future and join the nationwide campaign for the reintroduction of safe standing rather than undermining the position of the club they claim to support.

The wish for our next match, at home to Accrington tomorrow night [1-0], is a trouble-free evening both on and off the pitch, the fans making the London Stadium feel more like home and the players responding accordingly with an uplifting victory. Lifting the League Cup for the first time, combined with mid-table safety, would represent a very successful 2016/17, a year in which, despite its calamitous beginnings, there's still cause for hope. Indeed, let's count our blessings that we have a realistic chance of winning any major trophy, as opposed to about 80 per cent of the teams that just make up the numbers. If life as a Hammer still isn't to your satisfaction then Dagenham & Redbridge – ineligible for the EFL Cup this year but striving to be back with the big boys next season – isn't yet a sell-out for the visit of Tranmere, although funnily enough the cheapest tickets cost more than their equivalent at the London Stadium, and you don't even get a guaranteed seat for that!

FINALLY, We Have LIFT-OFF!

17 October 2016

[West Ham 0-3 Southampton]

[West Ham 1-1 Middlesbrough]

[Crystal Palace 0-1 West Ham]

In the time-honoured tradition of the Monday sports supplements, here's a list of five things we learned from the weekend's action ...

1. The players do care

It's an easy accusation to throw at somebody who earns more in a week than most of us do in a year: that they've grown complacent and fat, that their heart's just not in it anymore. It's also an insult to any sportsperson's competitive streak. With all the stick thrown their way so far this season, when the final whistle blew, the West Ham players looked as if they'd just got a ten-ton monkey off their backs. How much of that weight could be apportioned to their own shortcomings and how much they were carrying the burden of unrealistic and unforgiving fan expectations is open to debate, but if they really didn't care then they could be equally well remunerated as actors because they gave a bloody good impression of players whose sheer will to win had just brought them a much-needed three points. Winston Reid, Cheikhou Kouyaté, Mark Noble … all victims of the boo boys at times this season, all stood up to be counted on Saturday.

2. Goals change matches

They also have the potential to transform whole seasons. It's to be hoped that a narrow one-goal victory will provide the lift-off for a more routine win against beleaguered Sunderland [West Ham 1-0 Sunderland], who themselves need a stroke of luck to raise spirits, followed by a potentially season-defining EFL Cup match against Chelsea. The atmosphere at the London Stadium should be altered dramatically by Lanzini's classy strike at Selhurst Park.

We might not have been in such desperate need of this tonic had we scored first against Southampton, in what was quite an evenly contested first half prior to our sorry second half, or had Nobes' effort that hit the crossbar against Middlesbrough been a fraction lower. And not conceding goals can have as big an effect as scoring them. Had Christian Benteke not fluffed his lines from the penalty spot shortly before half-time or brushed the post with his header moments later, who knows what the outcome might have been? At the risk of sounding deliberately obstinate, especially given Benteke's six goals in all competitions this season to Zaza's none (the winner against us in a glorified friendly aside), I'd still rather splash £20m on the Juventus loanee than in excess of £30m on the Belgian target man. That's not to malign Benteke, who I think will score goals in a system that plays to his strengths, as Palace's use of two traditional wingers does. I don't think he'd have clicked with Payet and Lanzini, and he definitely wouldn't have offered the mobility and work rate that Zaza did, further proving point one.

3. As can refereeing decisions

Had a penalty been given for Yohan Cabaye banging knees with Aaron Cresswell, then I'd have considered it fortuitous. Equally, if Wilfried Zaha had been booked for simulation when he tumbled under minimal contact from Cresswell a minute later, then I'd have called it a harsh yellow card. But it's impossible to be magnanimous about what actually happened; for these two incidents to have resulted in a red card for our man was nothing short of ludicrous. There isn't a single commentator who's even tried to defend referee Martin Atkinson's call; if Arsène Wenger termed Granit Xhaka's dismissal for a forceful professional foul a 'dark yellow' then Cresswell's was positively anaemic. In the end, the backs-against-the-wall mentality created by this injustice could work in our favour in forging a steely team spirit, but had we not seen out the last 15 minutes with ten men, then the sinking feeling of the fates conspiring against us would have increased tenfold.

Crowds gather for the final match at the Boleyn.

The Champions (aka The World Cup Sculpture) on the junction of Barking Road and Green Street. ©WHUFC

Seats to be taken for the last time.

Winston Reid's header provides the perfect finale against Manchester United. ©WHUFC

Fireworks on and off the pitch. ©WHUFC

Resisting the gentrification of 'Upton Gardens'.

Laying the foundations. ©WHUFC

Rolling back the years. @WHUFC

LEAGUE
SEMI-FINAL

VS

DYNAMO FC

THE FINAL GAME AT THE BOLEYN

FOREVER BLOWING BUBBLES

After the official farewell came Final Score

Welsh, ginger and proud. ©*WHUFC*

'Ready' for Juventus.

One way of getting closer to the action.

Snake or GOAT?
©WHUFC

Massive everywhere. ©WHUFC

Against modern football.

4. A rule change is overdue

Several rule changes came into effect at Euro 2016, from the relatively benign possibility of being able to kick the ball backwards from kick-off to the much-needed eradication of the triple punishment (penalty–red card–suspension) when denying a clear goalscoring opportunity. Cresswell's misfortune provides further evidence that the FA needs to dispense with the ruling that yellow cards leading to red cards, and therefore suspensions, can't be appealed or rescinded. It's not coincidental that the presence of our regular left-back resulted in the rediscovery of defensive stability and to lose all that he brings for yet another match following his lengthy injury lay-off adds another layer of farce to Atkinson's poor judgement.

5. Panicking never solved anything

I've refrained from titling point five 'the only way is up' so as not to tempt fate, but when we've played as badly as we have and still sit in 15th place, then the doom-laden talk of a relegation fight should be banished. Football is a high-octane sport, whether playing or watching, but the passion needn't be accompanied by panic every time things go a bit wrong. Gone wrong they have, for reasons that remain something of a mystery, but the players regained their composure at the weekend and Hammers fans would do well to heed the words of Rudyard Kipling (or the Hovis ad for the uninitiated): *If you can keep your head ...*

Class Warriors

26 October 2017

Coopers' Company and Coborn. Sounds posh. Could be a Masonic lodge or a royal warrant holder. It is in fact the name of my old secondary school in Upminster, Essex. Its history is a long and winding one, beginning life back in 1536 as the Nicholas Gibson Free School in Stepney, which sounds more like a precursor to obnoxious media personality Toby Young's government-backed vanity project, the West London Free School. In the 18th and 19th centuries it moved around a few sites within earshot of the Bow Bells before settling in Upminster, at the end of the District Line, in 1971.

Despite the upper-crust name, Coopers' is a comprehensive, but not a bog-standard one. In my day it enjoyed grant-maintained status, which in our confusing educational system seems to be an antecedent to academisation, allowing it to be semi-selective. Accordingly, football was frowned upon, rugby and cricket being the upper-class sports that curried favour with the disciplinarian PE department as they strove to keep up with the Joneses in the private sector. When, in the mid-90s, we visited the old school site in Bow for a special anniversary church service, our bus was attacked by a mob of the present-day local kids who presumably took umbrage at their turf being invaded by the very people who stole their school and transplanted it into a middle-class suburb. The image of our prim and proper deputy headmaster swinging punches as if he were at the siege of the Alamo traumatised a batch of bright Essex teenagers with very little exposure to ethnically diverse East London and with the Stephen Lawrence tragedy fresh in their thoughts.

I recount the story of my own schooldays partly out of nostalgia prompted by being back in the bosom of family after my dad was taken ill last week, and partly for its parallels with the modern history of West Ham United. The move out of E13, even when only going so far as the newly established E20, seems to have given rise to class warfare over the soul of the Irons.

That very nickname and our hallmark 'Come On You Irons' chant is a romanticisation of the club's working-class roots. The rivalry with Millwall has survived the death of the dockside industries that gave birth to it, as well as Millwall's move south of the river in 1910. Indeed, in the pessimistic talk of betraying our roots by leaving Upton Park, it's conveniently forgotten that Thames Ironworks changed ground twice in their brief five-year existence.

The real issue, I think, is that the displacement of my school from the East End to Essex mirrors that of our fanbase. The affluent Havering suburbs are a greater source of Hammers support than the Newham council estates. The predominantly white British pupils of Coopers', despite its rugby prejudice, are far more likely to be seen sporting Hammers strips than the ethnic minority boys of Rokeby and Brampton Manor, who are as likely to don Manchester United kits or Chicago Bulls vests. Getting on the c2c to West Ham and marching down Barking Road every other week was a means for those living in gauche mock-Tudor mansions to reconnect with their ancestral heritage, an opportunity cruelly denied them by the commercial Westfield thoroughfare to the Queen Elizabeth Olympic Park.

As with the schoolkids who assailed the bus in Bow, it's those left behind in the East End who have the greatest right to vent their anger. Besides a handful of local businesses that will suffer from the decrease in footfall, the dominant feeling among my former neighbours in

Newham is pride that their local team has bettered itself by relocating to a state-of-the-art stadium, plus some relief that residential streets are no longer being overrun by a swarm of overbearing oiks on matchdays. The ripple effect on property prices might be an added bonus for any of the populace looking at relocating themselves.

That complaints about public transport and even a lack of convenient parking facilities is one of the sticks being used to beat the new stadium with is testament to my belief that the naysayers are no longer locals, they're East End tourists angry that the proletarian authenticity of days away from their bourgeois comfort zone is threatened by niceties such as popcorn! Truth is, even at the more affordable prices made possible by the move to a larger stadium, if you can afford a Premier League season ticket then you lose your claim to be one of the common people.

Chelsea is a club that shed its working-class roots in the 1990s, when the metropolitan sophistication of Glenn Hoddle, Ruud Gullit and Gianluca Vialli coincided with the rapid modernisation of the game, which helped usher in the nouveau riche era of Roman Abramovich. That the trend towards staid opulence brought with it some success no doubt helped to ease the pain of any working-class heroes who fought in vain against the forward march of time and money. Chelski has become shorthand for the ostentatious wealth that's flooded football and taken the people's sport out of the hands of the hoi polloi, so I do get fans' unease that our new home is more stylish and modern than Stamford Bridge, even if the restlessness propagated by this alien luxury is mitigated by discounted ticket prices.

Snapping up a last-minute ticket for tonight's visit of Chelsea for a relatively measly 20 quid, as I was able to do due to the unscheduled trip south to see my stricken father, would have been unthinkable in an Upton Park constantly straining at the seams of its limited capacity. Paradoxically, the gentrification of West Ham United reopens doors to lower-paid supporters who found themselves inadvertently barred from the Boleyn. Here's hoping that the Irons put on a rabble-rousing display tonight and that any supporters continuing the fight against the club's progressive identity don't equate its blue-collar origins with picking fights against the Blues.

Won't Somebody Please Think of the Children!!!

28 October 2016

[West Ham 2-1 Chelsea (League Cup fourth round)]

To carry on directly from my last entry, we got the rabble-rousing performance desired but the second part of my wish sadly failed to come true, with an imposing display by the team and 99 per cent of the crowd overshadowed by the thuggish behaviour of a small minority.

Stadiums don't cause trouble. Stadiums don't throw coins and bottles. People do, although the uncivilised individuals that this applies to only just classify as making the evolutionary leap to *Homo sapiens*. So let's stop the charade that the London Stadium is seriously defunct; the problems are psychological and emotional, not constructional.

It was third time unlucky for me. I've read with dismay about unsavoury scenes at the matches against Watford, Middlesbrough and Sunderland but hadn't witnessed anything untoward in the matches I'd attended against

NK Domžale and Juventus. Granted, the first of these was a relatively humdrum victory and the second a glorified friendly, both against foreign opposition who brought only a couple of hundred fans with them, but I've struggled to square my experience of stewards being inconspicuous and unneeded with the relentless press portrayals of Armageddon in E20.

Having seen at first hand the disturbances on Wednesday night (although not at close quarters, sat as I was in the upper tier of the East Stand adjacent to the Bobby Moore Stand, about as far as could be from the 'action', although it does seem to be true that every seat in the house offers a superb panoramic view) I still struggle to square my reality with some of the media hysteria. Until about the 85th minute I observed nothing more unseemly than some indecorous hand gestures between the home and away fans. The segregation of away supporters was very clearly delineated, with two walls of stewards and a column of empty seats separating rivals, and the spectre of Chelsea fans buying tickets throughout the stadium failed to materialise since the general sale was sensibly restricted to one ticket only to fans with a purchase history.

The relative calm was shattered by a Chelsea fan breaking through the cordons into no-man's land and baiting the jubilant home crowd, who had been goading their adversaries all evening, as is pretty much par for the course in any football stadium. This led to much jostling on either side, and this is where I have the utmost sympathy for the stewards, who have been roundly disparaged all season. Nobody else, at least that I noticed (a 2-0 lead making the match virtually over as a contest, it was the troubles that held my attention for these few minutes), broke through into the safe space, with stewards who are presumably not handsomely paid, including a number of women, standing strong against mostly virulent young men. The idiots' recourse was to congregate on the walkway running atop the lower tier of the Trevor Brooking Stand. The fluid curvature and openness is a welcome aspect of modernity, but here the stadium's design does necessitate extra precaution on a night like this, and the area was well-manned by security so even though it became horribly congested as foes surged towards one another, reports suggest that no hand-to-hand combat was able to take place, leaving indiscriminatory projectile objects to do the damage.

The vast majority of spectators gave this fracas the muted response it deserved, mostly condemnatory sighs rather than incendiary roars, which is at odds with the inflammatory headlines. As I've seen remarked elsewhere, Black Friday brings worse scenes of crowd violence, yet I don't hear any self-aggrandising MPs calling for Tesco to stay closed on 25 November. This is not to play down events or to absolve ourselves of responsibility, merely an attempt to put things into perspective.

Some of our own have been equally guilty of overreaction, although far better to be guilty of this than ABH. On one Twitter debate, fans condemned anyone foolhardy enough to take children to the match. It should go without saying that I'd prefer children not to witness the scenes described above but I'd have had no qualms about the welfare of a child sat next to me, a safe distance from opposing fans. There's always the potential for unrest outside the ground but, in trying to navigate my way towards Stratford High Street and the Greenway (note to those complaining about public transport: I was home – a 15-minute walk from Upminster station – within an hour of the final whistle, and I didn't leave my seat a second beforehand), I inadvertently found myself walking among the Chelsea supporters, who had been directed towards Pudding Mill Lane station, and yet I felt perfectly at ease. Riot police were present but surplus to requirement; I've seen more stringent police measures in place for the cross-border derby between Chester and Wrexham. It's a fairly stable law of life that trouble is only easily found by those who go looking for it.

Also making undesirable news headlines were homophobic lyric sheets circulated before kick-off making imaginary reference to John Terry and Diego Costa sexually arousing one another.

Should my son, or any young man, grow up sexually confused then heaven forbid their lifestyle choices be swayed by a depressingly unfunny football chant about John Terry's predilections. Making a case in defence of the composer, judging by the spelling, punctuation and grammar, I think the lyrics were less anti-gay than they were anti-intelligence. Furthermore, no football stadium is a haven of politically correct sensitivity and I do applaud the concerted effort to ensure the fans were vocal, even if I didn't hear a single rendition of this magnum opus. The last few moments aside, the atmosphere was easily the best I've experienced at the London Stadium but let's not rest on our laurels; rather than signing a FIFA pro gamer to represent us at international nerd conventions, the club would be better advised to appoint a poet laureate, a skilled songsmith to get us all singing in harmony week after week.

Like it or not, we have to accept that the former Olympic Stadium is a matter of national interest, meaning that the media will continue to magnify proceedings. Galtung and Ruge famously listed negativity as a news value: bad news trumps good news, which explains why small-scale hooliganism will always stand out more than an enthralling match. It doesn't help that a section of fans want to see the move to Stratford fail, resulting in a form of self-sabotage not evident in the rehousing of any other club in recent years.

Despite the incessant griping against them, I'm thankful that we have an unwavering board that continues to work diligently with all parties to resolve painful teething issues. However, I'd dispute the wording of a statement thanking 'genuine supporters' for their good behaviour. Much as I support the policy of banning anyone found guilty of gross misconduct, it's dangerous to disown all who have been causing discordance this season. A propensity for violence is, unfortunately, far from mutually exclusive with a passionate fanbase, but those who continue to seek trouble need educating that there are alternative channels for this passion rather than being given more protocols to kick against.

My earlier musings attempted to tap into the mentality of those who genuinely believe that they're somehow defending the honour of the club when in fact they're having the opposite effect of wrecking it. Life bans send out the right message but there's no quick fix to all the underlying tribulations. But just as the team are now very much on the ascendance, being in attendance again did reassure me that those in dissent are in descent, even if some of them are going down fighting.

Who's Next?

25 November 2016

The #BilicOut brigade have got up a head of steam thanks to our pitiful start to the season but I still believe them to be woefully premature with their brash proclamations of doom. I for one most definitely do not advocate sacking our most adventurous and erudite leader for some time. However, the question marks hanging over the manager have got me thinking (unlike many who are quick to call for change without a second thought for the repercussions): should the worst happen, where next? Bilić out! Who in?

Saturday's late collapse [Tottenham 3-2 West Ham] was precipitated by some questionable substitutions that have given the haters more oxygen. But isn't hindsight a wonderful thing?! Simone Zaza, for all his travails, was more of a presence than the man he replaced, Diafra Sakho – understandably raw after his protracted absence – had been for the previous ten minutes. And had he released the ball to Payet a few seconds earlier then he could have registered a quite sublime assist; the line between success and failure isn't just thin sometimes, it's skeletal!

To my mind it's a source of pride that we've had as many managers in our history (15) as some clubs have gone through in the past decade. We live in an age of instant gratification, with social media propagating impatience, yet evolution has obviously skipped a beat because scientific studies have consistently shown that deferred gratification is a sign of higher intelligence. Bottom of the brain cells league are Leeds United, where some fans still cling to the fallacy that their size and history mean that they somehow deserve to be among the present-day elite, and yet their managerial merry-go-round has done little to change their fortunes, to the point that level-headed fans are now craving a period of stability under Garry Monk, who's steadily growing into the role, having farcically faced the chop after an unconvincing first month.

Question for Massimo Cellino and co.: do you think a playing staff who have little to no affiliation to your club will really be responsive to their fifth manager in two years? All are portrayed as numpties on their way out but you don't land the Leeds United job in the first place without something to recommend you. 'Quick-fire Cellino' tried to buy West Ham in 2010 so fans should maybe think twice before disparaging our club's current statesmen. True to the fabled West Ham Way of not dispensing with managers at the first sign of trouble, they've shown an unusual level of loyalty in standing by their employees through sticky patches, even when their faith has ultimately proven misplaced, as with Avram Grant (a highly suspect appointment in the first place).

Fans should be passionate creatures so it's perhaps understandable that they get carried away when times are bad, quickly forgetting how they also very recently got carried away when times were good with all that foolhardy Champions League chatter. Owners, on the other hand, should be ice-cold businessmen with one hand on the tiller at all times. There are many who accuse the board of having their hands in the tills rather than on the tiller but this should be taken as a back-handed compliment in some ways: if we want to be a successful football club then it's almost essential, like it or not, that we're first run as a successful business with a close eye kept on cash flow. It beggars belief how many football clubs, despite being multi-million-pound organisations, adopt short-sighted, indiscriminate strategies. There's no such thing as a quick-fix solution and surely this is more apparent than ever when Mr 'Wham Bam Thank You Ma'am' Mourinho is looking fallible at Man Utd and 'Mr Perfect' Pep Guardiola is on a personal record winless streak. Furthermore, despite evidence of a 'bounce' provided by having a new man at the helm, overall statistics show that multi-million-pound severance payments are very rarely a step in the right direction and the lower reaches of the Football League are littered with solemn case studies that bear this out.

Part of the problem these days – in terms of both cost and continuity – is that owners rarely sack just the manager, or head coach as they might also be known (with the remote, shadowy figure of the director of football supposedly providing unity and cohesion). With them go their assistant manager, goalkeeping coach, fitness coach, etc. I get the sense that only the tea ladies are still employed directly by the club, the rest are sub-contracted through the manager. This has its perks: the coaching staff come as a team who should be bound by a sense of unity, loyalty and security. On the downside, these qualities only exist for as long as their boss remains the boss. When the manager is shown the door and they all follow, presumably the tea ladies step in to take training until the next manager and his entourage arrive. The current practice takes a sledgehammer to stability!

In hardly any other business do you get to give jobs to your mates and there are several reasons for this. Uppermost among them is that cushiness is generally not good for business. And I'm now going to contradict that statement by suggesting that West Ham ought to develop a more family-oriented approach, by which I mean employing ex-players who are entrenched in West Ham's genealogy.

Despite deserting us for Everton after little more than a year at Upton Park, Bilić connected with the club and that rapport was quickly re-established upon his return. Despite experiencing a downturn in his sophomore season, he shouldn't fear being handed his P45 just yet; however, it would be remiss of the owners not to have a contingency plan in place.

What exactly should that plan be? Well, options are severely limited when the prestigious national job goes first to a West Ham reject and now Gareth Southgate, not exactly batting away suitors, looks set to get it almost by default. Flavour of the month with fans and press seems to be Rafa Benítez. I've previously shared my reservations about his candidacy and they'd only be added to if he were to up and leave Newcastle at such a pivotal moment for them; loyalty has to work both ways. Remember also that Rafa was rumoured to have a gentlemen's agreement to take over at Upton Park before hopping aboard a first-class flight to Madrid. Fair enough that the Bernabéu trumped the Boleyn as an office space but if the London Stadium manages to usurp St James' Park then protecting prize assets from headhunters becomes a perilous task with a leader proven to be fickle himself.

Benítez's heart belongs to Liverpool, just as Bilić's – despite his dalliance with Everton – belongs to West Ham. And it's to the red half of Merseyside that I'd turn for inspiration. This isn't an expression of a whimsical belief that Jürgen Klopp, who resisted overtures from the mighty Bayern Munich while defying the odds with Borussia Dortmund, could be lured down south. Rather,

I'm looking to Anfield's glorious past and the boot-room dynasty that saw six consecutive managers – Bob Paisley, Joe Fagan, Kenny Dalglish, Ronnie Moran (in a caretaker capacity), Graeme Souness (a former Liverpool captain poached from Rangers) and Roy Evans – appointed from within to build upon the foundations laid by Bill Shankly. The popular view is that the house that Shankly built crumbled under Souness and then Evans but the bad seasons that saw them derided as pariahs weren't an awful lot worse than those that later saw Benítez hailed a legend.

There's probably more chance of Klopp being appointed Bilić's successor than there is of Bilić's faithful assistant, Nikola Jurčević, getting the job, which is just plain wrong. We don't want a number two actively coveting the top job, as was rumoured to be the case when Harry Redknapp's succession of Billy Bonds soured their friendship, but it would be expedient to always have one or two potential managers-in-waiting.

Ghosts of West Ham past do still haunt the training pitches; loyal servant Steve Potts is a supremely sensible selection as educator of the U18s and I was pleased at Dicksy, my all-time favourite Hammer, being plucked from the relative obscurity of managing the ladies' team to exert his forceful influence on the first team.

Like Lyall, Greenwood and Fenton before him, long may Bilić reign, but where will our next manager eventually come from? As with the current incumbent, I'd like it to be somebody with claret and blue pumping through their veins. How motivated will ex-professionals with multi-million-pound fortunes be though? That's why it's imperative that they have a burning passion for the club and are in it for the love rather than the money. One wonders whether Mark Noble will soon start his coaching badges as the years catch up with him. One also fears that some supporters would never give him a fair go as manager because internal appointments buck the present trend for stellar 'marquee' managers.

If forced to look for richer pedigree, we should move quickly to secure the services of Rio Ferdinand on the coaching staff before he's soiled by Leeds. As with Slaven, who was something of a mentor to young Rio in the previous brief overlap in their careers, he might not have spent too long at West Ham but in this case that's to his advantage. Even had we kept the homegrown crop of Ferdinand, Lampard, Carrick, Cole, Defoe and Johnson together, it's unlikely that Ferdinand would have enjoyed the success that he went on to achieve at first Leeds and then Manchester United, and bringing this wealth of experience back to East London he'd undoubtedly command the respect of all. Moreover, he's occasionally been caricatured as a bit dim but he's probably matured into one of the more cultivated members of the Golden Generation, the drug test mishaps and the incredibly sad death of his wife creating an empathy that should only enhance his man-management skills. If introduced as a defensive coach, surely a line-up of Bilić, Dicks and Ferdinand between them possesses the nous to shore up our leaky defence!

Looking back to look forwards: surely it makes more sense than clutching at straws.

Rainbow Connection

30 November 2016

Back in the day, it was a bit 'gay' to wear coloured boots, never mind rainbow laces. Flamboyant wingers in garish footwear were considered fair game for some rough treatment. But surely we've moved on from such primitive reasoning, right? Colour and diversity are to be welcomed. By the time I finished playing, it was only the old guard still in black boots, although none of those in red, blue or luminous yellow were actually homosexual, to the best of my knowledge, although I certainly wasn't privy to all my team-mates' private lives. Why would I be? It has no bearing on their ability to pass the ball accurately, as long as their headspace is right. Maybe that's one of the barriers to being a gay professional footballer: it's hard enough to stand out from the crowd of wannabes without worries of acceptance swimming around your mind.

Why does coming out as gay seem to be football's final frontier? The tragic death of Justin Fashanu undoubtedly cast a long shadow but the generation emerging today are more au fait with the songs of Justin Bieber and the silliness of Justin Fletcher than they are with the suicide of a man who shouldered the double burden of racism and homophobia. His brother John might have been revered as one of the game's hard men but it took balls of steel for a high-profile black British footballer to come out as gay in 1990.

The number of footballers to have come out since could be counted on one hand, which is ludicrous when you consider that, according to population percentage estimates, there should be one in each team. Of course it doesn't work this neatly; people aren't apportioned according to sexual orientation, skin colour, religious belief or any other demographic, and any conjecture about who West Ham's resident gay player must be is about as helpful as the immature boys I went to school with forlornly trying to guess which of their classmates played for the other side. Who would have guessed that 'Der Hammer' Thomas Hitzlsperger was hiding in the closet throughout his career in England, Germany and Italy? Always popular, it's a shame that he felt unable to test the acceptance from the terraces and waited until retirement to reveal his sexual inclinations. Not that these should matter to anybody, but then that's entirely the point. If anything, the only people it should mean anything to are the gay boys among the crowd who could seize upon a positive role model. The girls are a lot better catered for; colourful US superstar Megan Rapinoe is a vocal activist who even has a day and a parade named in her honour, while Lily Parr established the acceptance of lesbians in the British women's game by being openly gay at a time when male homosexuality was still illegal.

It discredits football that rugby union, a sport for much more rugged men (and one that requires forwards in the scrum to place their heads between others' backsides, the intimacy of which should surely further inhibit revelations of homosexuality), can boast trailblazers such as Wales legend Gareth Thomas and referee Nigel Owens. It certainly wasn't easy for them. The struggles with their inner demons have been well-documented but so has their relief at taking one small step for man, one giant leap for LGBT relations. Perhaps rugby's reputation as an all-boys public-school sport and the commonly held image of such institutions as a breeding ground for homosexuality eased the passage from antipathy to acceptance. An interpretation that's more damning on the football world makes use of the old adage that rugby is a game for thugs played by gentlemen and football is a game for gentlemen played by thugs – perhaps those in the oval ball game are genuinely better educated and more tolerant than their counterparts with the round ball. The following uninformed responses to an article on the league table of football-related arrests during the 2015/16 season (West Ham placed a semi-respectable seventh) prove that the liberal social conscience is about as well acquainted with the so-called 'beautiful game' as our back four is with clean sheets:

> Notherners think they can fight all they know
> is how to batter there women mugs [sic]
> Arsenal in 2nd place... must have been
> for noncing
> Bloody hell we can't even win this

What's required is someone in the mould of Gareth Thomas. Someone who's not only brave but who's at the top of his game, indispensable to his team, thereby making acceptance a formality. Had one of Arsenal's Invincibles – several of whom managed to combine toughness with effeminacy – come out at the time of their success, it's hard to imagine them being ostracised. The expectation is that they'd have taken stick at away matches, with fans outside the liberal metropolitan elite perhaps proving less accepting, but the condemnatory press coverage that this would invite would soon put a stop to targeted abuse. The prominence of black players (if not managers and coaches) in today's game shows that hatred and rejection should eventually perish along with banana peels.

Until a breakthrough moment such as Lionel Messi disclosing a secret tryst with Sergio Busquets, the boundary-pushing of the cutely named *The Pass* – in which out-and-proud actor Russell Tovey plays a Champions League footballer wrestling with his sexuality – will remain in the realms of fiction. Meanwhile, Stonewall's rainbow laces campaign shines a beacon of acceptance, supported by club captains wearing a rainbow armband this weekend. It's a small gesture but it stirs the soul and could herald the time when an active footballer holds aloft a rainbow banner at a Pride rally. In the words of another Stonewall campaign: 'Some people are gay, get over it.' It's about time football did.

So Long 2016

31 December 2016

National and global reviews of 2016 will tell of societies torn asunder and a Hammers review of the year, including a highly divisive switch in our geopolitical identity, unwelcome overseas arrivals and dissent over expenditure, is basically a chaotic world in microcosm. So to lighten the mood I'm gonna put a Cockney spin on some of the major events and figures of 2016, both in E20 and the wider world, by using them as inspiration for new entries into a rhyming slang dictionary …

Donald *n.*
Etymology: Donald Trump > dump
Usage: 'If there's at least one thing that can be said for the new stadium, it's got better facilities for squeezing out a nice big Donald.'
Theresa *n.*
Etymology: Theresa May > payday
Usage: 'Gold, Sullivan and Brady are gearing up for the Arabs or the Chinese to gift them one final Theresa.'

Zsa Zsa *adj.*
Etymology: the late Zsa Zsa Gabor > poor (any similarity to the much-maligned loanee Simone Zaza is purely coincidental)
Usage: 'That finish was seriously Zsa Zsa!'
Princess *n.*
Etymology: Princess Leia (pronunciation LAY-uh rather than LEE-ah, as verified by a survey of geeks) > player
Usage: 'When he sets his mind to it, Payet is one helluva Princess.'
Aladdin *n.*
Etymology: Aladdin Sane > pain
Usage: 'It's a right old Aladdin listening to people whinge on and on about things that can't be changed.'

The Mad Hammers

7 January 2017

I've been seeing a psychologist since October but can confirm that no, despite all that they put us through, my visits aren't the result of any West Ham-induced trauma. I was referred by a neuropsychologist, who I was referred to by a neuroradiologist, who diagnosed me as having a severe head injury as a result of being hit by a Land Rover. Yet I can still claim with some confidence that I'm far more sane and rational than many West Ham fans.

Yes, being thumped 0-5 at home by Man City [FA Cup third round] is embarrassing, but not as embarrassing as the petulance of fickle fans throwing their toys out of the pram and demanding that heads roll. My two-year-old toddler throws fewer tantrums than our Facebook followers and probably has more realistic expectations, having learned some of the words to our signature song:

'fortune's always hiding' ... there's a big clue to the masochism that being a Hammer entails right there!

Let's get some perspective. We lost to what may well be the most expensively assembled squad in the history of world football, led by a manager seeking to emulate his own Barcelona blueprint that's widely considered to have given us one of the finest teams ever to grace the planet. There's certainly no shame in losing to them, and for 40 minutes it was quite a finely balanced contest in which the two teams were only separated by a diabolical refereeing decision.

The players must have felt a sting of injustice coupled with a sense of fatalism when Michael Oliver put the whistle to his lips to penalise Angelo Ogbonna's tackle-that-never-was. On top of playing 75 minutes a man short, plus Mike Dean and his assistant also seeming to don Manchester United kits on Monday night [West Ham 0-2 Man Utd], once the luckless Sofiane Feghouli spurned a gilt-edged opportunity to equalise, quickly followed by the equally hapless Håvard Nordtveit's own goal, it's only human nature that their heads dropped in resignation and they were subsequently a yard off the swift pace set by City. 0-3 ... 0-4 ... 0-5 ... doesn't make much difference, especially in cup football. The fight was gone and the team display so tame in the second half that it wasn't just regular fall guys Feghouli and Nordtveit shouldering the blame on social media. They say that the first yard is in the head so what concerns me is that they get their heads straight and bounce back in a week's time, just as they did after the 5-1 Arsenal drubbing.

The trend is for specialist sports psychologists to work with athletes to overcome setbacks and visualise success. I don't honestly know whether we hire such a person to work with the players but we need a whole team of season ticket psychologists to help some get over the mental barrier of moving to pastures new and to realise that things could be an awful lot worse than they are.

I was at the third-round tie against third-tier Wrexham in January 1997 and that was definitely worse, although the team's abysmal performance was again surpassed by that of the fans, with those who are possibly now proclaiming their eternal love for Upton Park commemorating a humbling defeat by defacing the stadium, with seats ripped from their stanchions and hurled over my shaking teenage head. Those who misguidedly think we're at a particularly low ebb right now should perhaps draw some comparisons between today's match reports – largely focusing on City's exquisite movement – and a report from that day:

> Harry Redknapp is expected to battle on through West Ham's escalating crisis … But there is a new fear for the Hammers after furious fans invaded the pitch upon the final whistle and screamed abuse at the chairman, Terence Brown, and his directors … Peter Storrie, the managing director, is worried the Football Association could take disciplinary action … Slaven Bilić, the big Croatian defender who has been one of Redknapp's few successes among a flurry of foreign signings over the past year, stepped out into the Upton Park forecourt, ignoring police advice, to appeal

> for calm and unity among the protesting fans. (*The Independent*, 27/01/97)

My own treatment involves acceptance and commitment therapy (ACT), the tenets of which are relevant to our knotty scenario. To quote:

> The objective of ACT is not elimination of difficult feelings; rather, it is to be present with what life brings us and to 'move toward valued behaviour'. ACT invites people to open up to unpleasant feelings, and learn not to overreact to them, and not avoiding situations where they are invoked. Its therapeutic effect is a positive spiral where feeling better leads to a better understanding of the truth.

I can't vouch for its effectiveness at this moment in time but it certainly beats criticism and caterwauling if we genuinely want a brighter future.

In a league full of crackpot owners, I'm again thankful that our owners' most outward sign of madness is Mr Sullivan's eccentric fashion sense. Even if it's not on the grand scale desired by some, the owners will doubtless embark on a bit of retail therapy to put everyone in a more positive mindset. And splashing out £20m or more on a highly regarded international striker will *definitely* solve all our ills.

Now what's that phrase about the definition of madness? Something along the lines of repeating the same action and expecting a different outcome …

And in Other News ...

20 January 2017

Tomorrow's match on Teesside seems no more than a sideshow to Payet-gate. And I'm possibly alone in having a degree of sympathy for the bloke. If he were agitating for a move to Arsenal, Chelsea or China, rather than the proposed pay cut that a move back to Olympique de Marseille will entail, then that would be another matter entirely, and making comments such as 'when you see [Arsenal] playing, as a technical player, you could only have fun in that team' in between a 5-1 hiding from the Gunners and the transfer window opening was neither smart nor endearing. However, his actions at present seem to be those of a man who desperately wants to go home to a settled family and not a money-grabbing mercenary. Signing a five-year deal and taking a million-pound loyalty bonus upon the closure of the last transfer window, when he knew his family were unsettled, were perhaps not the smartest moves either. And his refusal to play is what differentiates this case from many before him, including that of his manager wanting to swap the claret and blue for the plain old blue of Everton in his own playing days. I can't begrudge a player wanting to better himself, or one looking out for his family's interests, but there are better ways of going about it than appearing to be an avaricious idiot and alienating both your team-mates and the entirety of the club's fanbase.

Payet is both a beneficiary and a victim of modern football. So too are our owners, caught between a rock and a hard place: they're damned if they sell him and damned if they don't, even at a double-your-money deal on what they paid. Similarly, they're damned for being old-school local lads made good via the adult entertainment industry, and damned for being corporate whores. In the great sitting versus standing debate of late 2016 I expressed sympathy with the Against Modern Football movement, while siding with the sitters. I suffer frequent pangs of nostalgia myself and found an article on the prospect of an FC West Ham Utd of East London breakaway club highly thought-provoking, yet couldn't help concluding that its author was guilty of navel-gazing. They really lost me with the use of Cass Pennant as a figurehead, a character who revels in the infamy earned as leader of the Inter City Firm. He may well be a reformed character but that gives hope that Payet could yet see the error of his ways, and I'd rather welcome a repentant Frenchman back to the London Stadium than the thugs who reportedly saw fit to vandalise his car this morning.

The other aspect of the breakaway idea that perturbs me is the suggestion that disgruntled Hammers fans commandeer the Old Spotted Dog ground, home to Clapton FC. That's Clapton FC who were established in 1878. Guess what? They've had a change of name and a change of address in that time but, having played at the Old Spotted Dog since 1888, invading their turf feels akin to how we might have felt had Spurs succeeded in misappropriating the Olympic legacy. Here's a radical idea for those who are truly disenchanted with top-flight modern football: get down to Forest Gate and cheer on your other local team.

Back to the here and now, or at least the London Stadium last week, it was gratifying to read from several sources that the atmosphere against Crystal Palace [3-0] was electric. Cheers to Payet for uniting the supporters, which is perhaps an even greater feat than any of his sublime achievements on the field. And kudos to Andy

Carroll for proving that moments of individual brilliance won't disappear along with Dimitri. Palace must be sick of being on the end of our goal-of-the-season contenders; the 'can we play you every week' chant is clichéd and a bit disrespectful but it's probably a fair summation of what most supporters feel having produced arguably our two most spirited performances of the season against the Eagles.

And taking us back in time, delving into their well-worn '60s costume vault, ITV issued a timely reminder that the bygone days weren't quite as rose-tinted as we Hammers might care to remember, with gaudy biopic *Tina and Bobby* depicting the legendary Bobby Moore as a turncoat who wanted a transfer to Tottenham to help pay for a fancy new car! The standard disclaimer that some aspects of the true story had been fictionalised for dramatic purposes shouldn't gloss over the fairly well-documented fact that our captain wanted out, but nor does it diminish the many momentous moments that he did bestow upon us, both before and after this episode.

So let's not consign our extant virtuoso to the history books until a deal reaches its denouement and let's please cease our own rewriting of history with the unremitting romanticisation of the past.

All the World's a Stage, for the Critics

17 March 2017

Earlier this week the club announced season ticket arrangements for 2017/18, including price freezes. And a social media shitstorm ensued. Now, being far removed from the capital and a relative pauper who probably couldn't stretch to even the cheapest season ticket anyway, this news was of limited interest to me. But after reading

30 or more universally negative comments on the club's Facebook feed I felt moved to add my own tuppence worth.

Gratifyingly I'm not alone in thinking that Gold and Sullivan, if not messiahs, aren't exactly the spawn of Satan either, as indicated by the number of likes pushing my comment above all the ones aggressively telling them to put up or shut up. To summarise, I declared myself thankful to have fans as owners, even if they're less than perfect. Similarly, I respect that our manager and captain genuinely care about the football club, even if neither is enjoying the most impressive of seasons.

In firing out my riposte to the trolls, I was reminded of a recent editorial ('A Sense of Responsibility') in *The Blizzard*, a bastion of balanced and intelligent football journalism, which opined that 'in early 2017, we seem to have entered a world in which there are so many voices all demanding to be heard that any notion of authority is problematic, that the very concept of truth is being eroded'. As an amateur blogger it would be highly hypocritical of me to criticise the rise of citizen journalism but it's well documented that social media, and Twitter in particular, is an echo chamber that promotes hate rather than debate, where the trolls reign supreme. Yet judging by the conviction with which they type there must be an awful lot of trolls with a PhD in their chosen subject. If I could encapsulate in a single sentence the problem of which editor Jonathan Wilson so scrupulously writes it would be this: 'Too many experts, not enough expertise.'

Football-wise, there's the particular quandary of armchair pundits and fantasy football managers poring over the minutiae at the risk of losing sight of the bigger picture. I blame Alan Hansen. His articulate and composed analysis set the trend for finding fault, and the hysterical have followed in his wake. Hansen, stereotypical of both a Scot and a defender, developed the parsimonious habit of never crediting the cunning of the attackers but instead highlighting every possible error in the build-up to a goal, seemingly forgetting in his dotage that not all are blessed with his clairvoyance and to err is human. Were it not for these factors, teams would continuously cancel each other out, resulting in an unwatchable stalemate.

There's a place for scrutinising performance and dissecting tactics, and that place is the changing room and/or the training ground (where the true expertise and inside knowledge resides), not the TV studio and definitely not the Twittersphere, for you can't possibly do justice to 90 minutes of football in a few edited clips and certainly not in 140 measly characters! It's probably fair to say that standards have risen under the glare of this harsh spotlight but any advancement is exceeded by the surge in unrealistic expectations; mistakes are analysed ad nauseam, as if on a quest for perfection that's unattainable in any sphere, never mind the cut and thrust of the heated sporting arena.

Does being so censorious make us supporters any happier? It's one thing to aim high, but at what cost to our sanity? Having fallen victim in the past to my own perfectionist streak, I'll direct you next to Dr David Burn's psychological treatise *Dare to be Average*, the point in the title being that 'perfection' is a Holy Grail and that lowering expectations accordingly can lead to a happier existence.

How exactly does this apply to football? This goes against the grain that's sown by modern media but perhaps being a yo-yo club that enjoys the occasional cup run is actually more rewarding than being a member of the 'big six'? Too many supporters are led to believe that their team should be winning the league/winning a cup/qualifying for Europe, oblivious to the simple mathematical logic that across a season there are always destined to be far more 'losers' than winners. As a beleaguered Arsène Wenger notoriously claimed this week, 'Nothing is good enough anymore.' While I have a degree of sympathy with the groundhog-day frustrations of Gunners, 95 per cent of Football League clubs can only dream of matching Arsenal's achievements over their supposedly fallow last decade. I wonder who's derived more pleasure from this season: the fans of Arsenal, watching Champions League football, or the fans of Newcastle, watching Championship football? Highs can't be appreciated without lows, so although I warn all spoiled and ungrateful fans to be wary of what they wish for, especially at Arsenal where Arsène is such a big part of the club's fabric that under different management it would be in danger of quickly unravelling, a fall from grace could in fact be the making of them, making cup finals something to be cherished again rather than a mere consolation prize.

The bigger picture in East London is that, even with the raised expectations that the club has actively encouraged with the move to a plush new stadium, we remain rooted to our core values and identity to an unusual extent in the 21st century. Traditionally clubs have been owned by local businessmen who have some affinity with the community. Traditionally clubs have been managed by former players who recognise their culture and requirements. Traditionally clubs have been captained by loyal servants (ideally youth team products) who understand what it means to wear the shirt and to proudly lead out their team-mates. It's debatable to what extent the current occupants fulfil these roles. It's also debatable to what extent these traditions remain desirable. However, in the rarefied environment of the Premier League, I'd contest that such values are more important than ever, so will leave you with an alternative league table that shows our club to be in considerably better shape than the naysayers would credit:

League Table of Affordable Season Tickets 2016/17
Source: mirror.co.uk, 02/07/16 Additional information correct as of 14/03/17 (those meeting traditional values in **bold capitals**)

	Owners	**Manager**	**Captain**
West Ham	**BRITISH**	**SLAVEN BILIĆ**	**MARK NOBLE**
Stoke City	**BRITISH**	Mark Hughes	Ryan Shawcross
Manchester City	UAE	Pep Guardiola	Vincent Kompany
Hull City	Egyptian	Marco Silva	Michael Dawson
Sunderland	American	David Moyes	John O'Shea
Burnley	**BRITISH**	Sean Dyche	Tom Heaton
Leicester City	Thai	Craig Shakespeare	Wes Morgan
West Brom	Chinese	Tony Pulis	Darren Fletcher
Swansea City	American	Paul Clement	Leon Britton
Watford	Italian	Walter Mazzarri	Troy Deeney
Manchester United	American	José Mourinho	Wayne Rooney
Crystal Palace	American	Sam Allardyce	Scott Dann
Bournemouth	Russian	**EDDIE HOWE**	Simon Francis
Middlesbrough	**BRITISH**	Aitor Karanka	Grant Leadbitter
Everton	Iranian	Ronald Koeman	Phil Jagielka
Southampton	German	Claude Puel	Steven Davis
Liverpool	American	Jürgen Klopp	Jordan Henderson
Chelsea	Russian	Antonio Conte	**JOHN TERRY**
Tottenham	**BRITISH**	Mauricio Pochettino	Hugo Lloris
Arsenal	American	Arsène Wenger	Per Mertesacker

Can I Have a Minute?

5 May 2017

It's been mooted that tonight's home match against Tottenham be marked by a minute's applause in the seventh minute in honour of Aaron Lennon, a former wearer of the Spurs No. 7 shirt. The quicksilver winger hasn't been much seen in the blue of current club Everton this season, so in case you missed the news, last Sunday police were called to Salford where Lennon was detained under the Mental Health Act amid concerns for his welfare.

The thorny issue of asking heated rivals to set aside their rivalry for a greater good is made thornier by the lack of detail about Lennon's condition and the peculiarly 21st-century obligation to pay tribute to everything. Mental health issues, so long pooh-poohed by mainstream society, are rightly in the headlines these days. Nevertheless, the notion of a public display of sympathy for a multi-millionaire footballer in good physical health remains farcical to many.

The fabled 'football family' recently came together to commemorate the life of Ugo Ehiogu and it was notable that nobody had a bad word to say about the 'gentle giant', yet still most grounds deemed it appropriate to ask supporters to observe a minute's applause rather than the once-customary minute's silence. The power of silence is that it's uncustomary, especially in a crowd of pumped-up football supporters, and allows for serious contemplation. Applause, by contrast, is relatively run of the mill (insert your own joke about the legendary Highbury library or the London Stadium's own subdued atmosphere). It's the easy option that sadly reaffirms the stereotype of football fans as yobs, incapable of showing respect.

The fad, at least as far as British football is concerned, began in 2005 with the passing of George Best. In memory of this playboy provocateur – responsible for one of my all-time favourite quotes: 'I spent a lot of money on booze, birds and fast cars. The rest I just squandered' – a rowdy celebratory atmosphere seemed entirely appropriate. For a life tragically cut off in its prime, rather less so.

Because they can't be easily and boorishly broken as silence can, it's become fashionable to orchestrate applause at meaningful junctures during the flow of a match, sometimes for reasons only tangentially linked to sporting achievement … a pair of season ticket holders are celebrating their golden wedding anniversary, let's give the cute old couple a cheer in the 50th minute! The intrinsic problem with this is that the match doesn't come to a standstill. The only way to guarantee that Hammers join in this evening's organised clapping is for us to score in the sixth or seventh minute, which would rather spoil the desired effect. More pessimistically, if a player from either team were to suffer serious injury at the prescribed time, then the ovation would become grievously misplaced.

Far better, surely, for individuals to give sober thought to Lennon's predicament, and in highlighting his plight the conspirators behind the proposition have already done the job of putting him in our thoughts and creating debate around mental health, even if it's invited mirth from some insensitive souls. Footballers' salaries perhaps make them less worthy of sympathy than those without a pot to piss in, but some diseases don't discriminate. Indeed it could be argued that young men who are lionised and led to believe that they have the world at their feet are prone to depression and anxiety when their careers hit the buffers. True to form, the *Daily Fail*'s headline led with his wage and implied an element of criminality by referring to a 'stand-off with police'.

Lennon should be assured that the thoughts of many are with him and a spontaneous chant of 'One Aaron Lennon' from the fans of his erstwhile employers, courteously not drowned out by the home supporters, would be equally as powerful in making this point as a coordinated clap.

Ironically, Merseyside is united in adoration of Lennon, J. but little love has been shown in Liverpool for Lennon, A., so it's commendable that Spurs fans want to show a former favourite that he's not forgotten. In whatever form, in the words of his namesake: 'All you need is love.' Even footballers. Especially, it seems right now, Aaron Lennon. I'm not a fan of the minute's applause but I also hope that if it happens it's not marred in any way. I can wait until a few minutes later when emotions have settled for our first goal. [West Ham 1-0 Tottenham, Lanzini scoring in the 65th minute]

Let Me Take You Back a Decade

16 May 2017

The 2006/07 season was one of great expectations, based on the over-achievement of the previous season that had seen us impressively consolidate our top-flight status and be cruelly denied FA Cup glory by the brilliance of that Scouse **** Gerrard, then raised by some ridiculously high-profile squad reinforcements who generally flattered to deceive. Remove the words 'ridiculously high-profile' and I could be describing this season, a steady succession of abject performances that dampened the hope and enthusiasm we set out with.

Alan Pardew paid the price that season for our mystifying loss of form and was replaced by Alan Curbishley, who similarly struggled to maintain upward momentum and parted company with the club after less than two years. Some fans will vehemently disagree but positives I'm taking from this disappointing season include Slaven Bilić's survival, the belief that we still possess the foundations of something more spectacular than we're accustomed to, and the fact that our Premier League standing hasn't been taken to the wire thanks to the performance of the season (by players and fans alike) against Spurs.

Which brings us back to that sunny afternoon of 13 May 2007. The season on the whole was a miserable one but does the memory of that against-the-odds Old Trafford escape act compensate for it? The cult-hero status of Carlos Tevez, who spent the first half of the season making Marlon Harewood look a world-beater, would suggest so. I'd definitely argue that it does. Play-off finals aside, last-gasp survival is the closest I've come to the ecstasy of actually winning something, which goes a long way to glossing over or even erasing the agony of the preceding 37 matches. More serene seasons have sailed past without a single moment committed to the memory bank. This is not to dismiss such seasons as worthless – they might provide the sure footing for future success (or, more likely in our case, the calm before the storm) – but personally I prefer the unforgettable ones.

The season that's christened our new home was one to remember mostly for the wrong reasons, perfectly summed up by the last outing at the London Stadium against Liverpool, which was certainly not good but nor was it quite as bad as the scoreline might suggest [West Ham 0-4 Liverpool]. Slav and the board simply can't legislate for record signing André Ayew (lively in recent weeks, still with the potential to live up to his inflated market value) missing the very definition of a sitter by twice hitting the post from a yard out, or for the referee ignoring a combined elbow/handball that should have given us a lifeline rather than Winston Reid picking himself up to find that Liverpool had raced down the other end of the pitch to make it 0-3. Lady Luck has gone missing as often as our back four have!

I won't write a detailed review of 2016/17 because it wouldn't reflect well on anyone. However, I take heart from our penultimate home match, which proved that the players are capable of competing with the (second) best and that the stadium comes alive on such nights. Memories are there for the making, although on top of everything else this season I'm quite relieved that Sunday's trip to Turf Moor isn't poised to be another noteworthy curtain-closing nerve-shredder!

Time now to hit the reset button.

Year Two – 2017/18

If

19 July 2017

If the board don't hurry up and buy a striker we're going to become relegation fodder. But there's still six weeks of the transfer window remaining. Maybe their prudence has something to do with the fact that there are no obvious upgrades readily available. If they think a loan deal for a goalkeeper is better use of funds than paying £140,000-a-week wages to Javier Hernández, then they're off their trollies. But the inconsistent form of our goalkeepers last season was a major contributor to the leaky defence. Maybe Joe Hart's superior organisational skills will shore things up at the back and it's clear we still want a goalscorer in the shopping trolley too.

If Gold and Sullivan have taken the club as far as they can, then it's time to sell up to a mega-rich Arab. But there aren't as many altruistic billionaire investors out there as some people seem to believe. Maybe businessmen have finally learned from the shortcomings of Randy Lerner, Ellis Short and Venky's, among others, that football club ownership isn't an untapped gold mine.

If fans so desperately want us to follow in the footsteps of Manchester City then why is there quite so much bitching about the acquisitions of Joe Hart and Pablo Zabaleta?! It's all ifs, buts and maybes ... maybe I'm alone, but I'm finding the frenzy of conjecture swirling around the Premier League increasingly distasteful and alienating.

If 'The World's Gone Mad!' sounds like a screeching *Sun* headline, it's actually more representative of my own personal feelings. The tabloids, on the other hand, treat sums such as the £300,000-a-week reportedly demanded by Alexis Sánchez as perfectly ordinary, with the expectation that the club pay it an unspoken endorsement of a free-market economy gone wild. I'll never dispute that our national sport holds a significant, maybe even immeasurable national value, but events surrounding the recent General Election seem to have led to a recalibration of national principles from which football can't be immune. Sánchez is a quality player but the privilege of watching just him, fitness permitting, play for 90 minutes a week would cost each attendee at the Emirates Stadium £5. To put into perspective what else could be done with that money, it could pay a mid-level teacher for a decade. As an annual salary, it would have been enough to totally reclad Grenfell Tower in the more expensive fire-resistant material, thereby potentially saving 80 (at a conservative estimate) lives. And a man kicking a ball is supposedly worth more than this? The thoughts of Arsenal's local Islington North MP would be priceless!

If money makes the world go round then we need to find another form of global propulsion, fast. Inflation in the football world certainly needs bringing under control before the bubble bursts. Adding to my general disinterest in all the off-season shenanigans, thoughts have been otherwise occupied by the culmination of a compensation claim for a life-changing motorcycle accident. Supposed to cover the disruption of my career and up to five years loss of earnings, the settlement sum could pay one of West Ham's current highest earners for a week. In times gone by it would have bought Alan Devonshire 30 times over and no doubt paid a weekly wage to the entirety of the '86 squad. Where do we go from here? People balked at Trevor Francis becoming the UK's first million-pound player in 1979. Less than 20 years before that my compensation would have been enough to smash the world transfer record. Twenty years further on, £30m was needed to buy the world's best. Now £50m will buy a defender who's defensively suspect [Kyle Walker] and the £100m barrier could be broken any day.

If you're looking for an antidote to the egotism that generates obscene demands for astronomical pay packets, then England take on Scotland in the women's European Championships tonight. The women's game is growing ever more professional but, without being bankrolled by Sky money, we're talking pre-1990s levels, when the love of the game conquered all financial quibbles. Fara Williams, England's most capped lady, divulged in 2014 that she'd spent the first six years of her international career homeless; only recently has she earned enough to live off the game. Compare the joy she takes from playing to the attitude of her handsomely remunerated counterparts at last summer's Euros. Sport should be, above all, pleasurable … competitive, yes; nail-biting, yes; affecting, yes … but if, ultimately, you don't derive pleasure from it then it becomes an unhealthy diversion, a cancerous pastime.

If you remain cynical about the standard of women's football, I myself admit to having once compared the skill level and spectator value to pub football, with miskicks and howlers aplenty. But on recent evidence I stand corrected. Mistakes are still made, as they are at all levels, but there are many women now who boast talent and tactical acumen that I'm truly envious of. I've had the pleasure of playing alongside a young lady from Arsenal Girls and when, in the warm-up, she arrowed a left-foot shot into the top corner, it was apparent that she possessed finer skills than any of the fully grown men.

If it weren't for old-fashioned male chauvinism, the standard of women's football today would probably be higher still. The illuminating documentary *When Football Banned Women*, screened last night on Channel 4, revealed that on Boxing Day 1920 a crowd of 53,000 paid to watch Dick, Kerr Ladies FC take on St Helen's at Goodison Park, with a further 14,000 turned away at the turnstiles. Post-First World War, football and feminism were thriving, to the extent that a year later the FA felt 'impelled to express their strong opinion that the game of football isn't for females and ought not to be encouraged'! Women's teams were banned from playing on FA-affiliated grounds, a ban that wasn't lifted until 1971.

If half a century of progress hadn't been snatched from them, who knows what the women's standing in the game might have been. Would there be greater parity between the attendances of men's and women's matches and therefore less discrepancy in their salaries? The market forces exerted by a successful women's game might have tempered the excesses of the men's game. I've reached the point where I really don't care if West Ham are on the verge of breaking the club transfer record. If Marko Arnautović, a 28-year-old man for whom Stoke paid Werder Bremen £2m four years ago, is now worth in excess of £20m, then football has officially lost it.

'If you can keep your head when all about you are losing theirs … you'll be a Man, my son.' But maybe the football world could do with being more feminine.

Reasons to be Cheerful, Team Two

11 August 2017

Swamped by social media negativity and the malady brought on by spiralling salaries making average Premier League footballers ever further removed from the average supporter, I'm trying to muster some enthusiasm for the season ahead.

What I don't buy into is the idea that the fans have been short-changed this summer. All supporters like to have a new signing that sets pulses racing but there are a few misery guts who you sense would have found reason to grumble even had we gazumped PSG for Neymar! I also don't buy into the idea that we should be buying players for the sake of it – there's an obsession these days with padding out the squad … but newsflash: there's no European football this season (and even when there has been in recent seasons it's only added a couple of fixtures to the schedule!) and should we go deep into the domestic cup competitions, then that should be a reason for celebration, not concern. A normal league fixture list necessitates no more than a squad of 22, two players per position providing ample cover and any more than that breeding disillusion and disharmony among those sat on the sidelines.

So here's my reserve team as things stand, which I fancy to be one of the best I've known in my time supporting the Hammers, but not so fancy that it contains prima donnas who would threaten squad unity if they weren't first choice …

GK Adrián
Prone to the odd ricket but decent ability combined with personality and commitment make him a cult hero.

RB Sam Byram
Still don't think we've seen the best of him in a Hammers kit – oozes potential but needs confidence to go with it.

LB Arthur Masuaku
Looked better than reports from Olympiacos led me to believe; some even thought he performed better than Cresswell last season.

CB José Fonte
A 2016 European champion and lynchpin of a Southampton team that have finished above us for four consecutive seasons.

CB James Collins
See Adrián.

MD Mark Noble
Demoted only because of the strengths of Obiang and Kouyaté; still a solid all-round midfielder.

MD Edimilson Fernandes
One of the few players to emerge from last season with credit; should get better yet, given opportunities.

RW Sofiane Feghouli
Came from a club who've enjoyed Champions League football; we might have mocked the Algerians for

hero-worshipping him but many of them swear blind he's better than Riyad Mahrez.

LW Robert Snodgrass
His performances for Hull in the first half of last season were the equal of anything produced by those wearing claret and blue.

CF André Ayew
An African Footballer of the Year, £20m is probably fair value in today's market.

CF Andy Carroll
To trot out the classic cliché, on his day he's unplayable.

Then there's a bench made up of academy prospects who need to be given opportunities to shine, although it's unclear who those clamouring for them to start regularly (not always the same people who deem the squad threadbare) think should be dropped:

Nathan Trott; Reece Burke; Declan Rice; Josh Cullen; Nathan Holland; Domingos Quina; Toni Martínez.

As a first team, I think that lot would just about steer clear of relegation. Note that many of them have performed better at other clubs where they've enjoyed support. A little positivity goes a long way, so come on lads, let's make this season a good one.

Odds-On

22 October 2017

[West Ham 0-3 Brighton]

My beloved West Ham have treated me to some breathtaking displays of incompetence down the years so it's hard to decide whether Friday's abject display against Brighton plumbed new depths or it's just the rawness that makes it feel that way. I suspect it's the latter but, either way, Bilić looks increasingly like a dead man walking.

I've been an ardent supporter of his, just as I was (to a slightly lesser extent) of Allardyce, but have come to believe a parting of the ways is desirable if only because the atmosphere around the club has become so toxic. That's the result of, well, results partly, but I've known the club survive plenty of worse periods. As the man himself stated post-match, he bears responsibility for on-the-pitch matters. That doesn't absolve the underperforming players in a squad that, on paper at least (which of course is not where football matches are won or lost), is one of the best we've ever had. The million-dollar question is why players worth so many millions underperform so badly? Perhaps the most damning assessment of Bilić and his coaching staff is that not one player appears to have improved under their tutelage.

I expect, though, that handing Bilić his P45 would be a mere placebo. Those who do the hiring and firing hold more sway over the culture and direction of a football club, and a lot of anger is being directed at the board, who must shoulder the blame for unrealistically raising expectations and for providing too many unguarded, media-friendly soundbites. Pre-match, David Sullivan's televised remark about the 'morality' of honouring a contract 'unless things are desperate' seemed a reasonable and indeed laudable justification of not being trigger-happy; post-match, however, it only added to the ire of the many who had already reached the end of their tether. The fans undoubtedly feed off what's happening at higher levels, although I'd also contend that the masses, more than any other influencing factor, have it in their hands to determine a milieu's ambience and the fans too must take a long, hard look at their role in stirring up a noxious atmosphere in and around the London Stadium.

Censuring fans who dedicate a vast amount of time and money to their team isn't the intention here. Everyone is entitled to express an opinion but I'd ask that we be wary of the impact that expression has and also whether or not it's a fair opinion. Is it any wonder that confidence is shot when the team is frequently pilloried and individuals virtually lynched? The wave of contempt shown towards our own seems to be strangely symptomatic of our dyspeptic modern society. I'd prefer instead that we unite to kick against the prevailing culture of entitlement and instant gratification that appears to state that if a team fails to produce Harlem Globetrotter performances à la Manchester City October 2017 then they're fair game to be booed from the pitch or slated on social media. I stand guilty right there of hyperbole similar to that which I bemoan, yet the dissatisfaction that envelops approximately half the Premier League is undeniable and makes it miraculous that they continue to successfully market it as a coveted product. In the chimerical quest for self-improvement, short-termism rules and managers rightly or wrongly bear the brunt. Even at Leicester City, where there's still a relatively healthy dose of goodwill left over from the miracle of 2016, they've parted company with another manager despite having no obvious succession plan.

So who's our Bilić replacement? Is there anybody out there whose appointment would see the poisonous fug that surrounds East London dispersed by rays of optimism? Those who pine for Sam Allardyce clearly have short memories; despite his obvious strengths, he never presided over a happy camp. And much as I'm in favour of appointing insiders, it's even more alarming to see odds being quoted for Harry Redknapp (freshly sacked by Birmingham), Glenn Roeder (managerial advisor at Stevenage after a seven-year hiatus) and Frank Lampard (presumably Junior, a high-profile candidate but one that would probably meet with less fan approval than his old man coming out of retirement).

Six weeks ago you'd have got odds of more than 100/1 on Ronald Koeman, a cultured purveyor of total football with a decent track record and not long installed as boss of big-spending Everton, yet he now finds himself ahead of Bilić in the sack race. The Premier League is fast becoming the graveyard of ambitious managers; for example, Frank de Boer, winner of four successive Eredivisie titles with Ajax but sacked after four games at Crystal Palace.

At shorter odds, even if we could entice any from their current positions, I'm not sure there are any candidates that I'd wholeheartedly endorse as an upgrade. Roberto Mancini seems to have the most grassroots support but I wasn't overly impressed by his attitude or his achievements with Manchester City, where he had vast wads of cash at his disposal. Rafael Benítez has spurned us once before and would likely bring a safe but dour brand of football. I prefer the style of the other ex-Liverpool boss, Brendan Rodgers, but there are question marks hanging over his regeneration in the Scottish wastelands. Maybe it's a case of better-the-devil-we-know and focusing on what's in our power to change, namely our attitude and the atmosphere that we create for what remains, for now at least, Super Slaven's Claret-and-Blue Army. Despite the malaise that's taken hold of British football, a limited Leicester team showed two years ago how far confidence and positivity can carry you, just as the likes of Brighton bounce up from the Championship before becoming paralysed by the fear of relegation from the land of milk and honey.

Demanding a new manager is considerably easier than picking a winning one. Hopefully Gold and Sullivan have got the inside track on someone capable of doing a Foinavon but, more likely, they'll hit the hurdle named after that most famous of dark horses! Whoever our next whipping boy is, bear in mind that it would be easier for each of us to turn our frowns upside down than it is for one man to put smiles on thousands of faces. Whoever's in charge, we need to unite to bring the good times to the East End.

Two-Nil Down …

25 October 2017

[Tottenham 2-3 West Ham (League Cup fourth round)]

- Hands up if you switched off at half-time …
- Hands up if you thought Bilić had lost the dressing room …
- Hands up if you've been lambasting André Ayew as a waste of space …
- Hands up if you think we'll get knocked out by Bristol City in the next round …
- Hands up if you'll ever get used to being a West Ham fan …!

[Next match: Crystal Palace 2-2 West Ham; threw away a two-goal lead and conceded a 97th-minute equaliser]

Does Arnautović Dream of Electric Sheep?

6 November 2017

Writing anything about West Ham at the moment is a hardship. I console myself with the thought that our self-combustion is intentionally designed to heap further embarrassment on Spurs for their unexpected Carabao Cup capitulation at the hands of an otherwise spineless bunch. Seriously, if I didn't laugh, I'd cry.

So to alleviate the torment of being a Hammer, and inspired by the televisual double-whammy of *Philip K. Dick's Electric Dreams* and the fourth season of *Black Mirror*, the theme of this week's episode is alternate realities …

Match report archive

West Ham 4-2 Watford, 10 September 2016

> The natives grew restless when Watford pegged back an early two-goal deficit, disturbing in-fighting breaking out in sections of the home support just before half-time, but a resurgent second-half performance from West Ham meant that the rebranded Olympic Stadium was reverberating to the sound of 'Bubbles' by the time the final whistle blew and this trophy stadium is already beginning to feel like home to football fans.
>
> Things could have been so different. West Ham and Dimitri Payet, starting for the first time this season following his eye-catching Euro '16 exertions, began in scintillating fashion. The equally impressive Michail Antonio gave them the lead when he met a Payet corner in the fifth minute. The same player doubled the lead shortly after the half-hour mark, stooping to head home an audacious Payet rabona cross that

had the home fans in raptures. And in truth, it could have been more.

So it was a shock that, within 15 minutes of their goal of the month contender, West Ham had imploded. A tame Odion Ighalo shot that took a kind deflection off James Collins reignited this as a contest. Collins' afternoon went from bad to worse in first-half injury time when a breakdown in communication saw the Wales international head the ball over the onrushing Adrián, and Troy Deeney picked up the loose ball before curling home.

Cue unrest amongst the Hammers faithful, who were no doubt fearing the worst after their dismal Europa League exit at the hands of Romanian minnows Astra Giurgiu. The stands during the break were as lively as the home dressing room must have been because West Ham came out for the second half with renewed vigour.

Debutant Simone Zaza, who'd released Antonio with a delightful overhead kick with just his second touch in English football, restored the lead in the 53rd minute, emphatically meeting an Antonio cross. And the game was won ten minutes later when man of the match Dimitri Payet teed up Zaza for his second.

After that it was olé football from the boys in claret and blue. Bilić even had the luxury of resting his star men, a triple substitution of Payet, Antonio and Zaza departing to a standing ovation in the 80th minute. It's been a stuttering

start to life in their new home, with the loss to Astra threatening to puncture fans' enthusiasm, but that's two wins out of two in the Premier League and performances like this suggest it won't be long before East London is hosting more glory nights.
(cf. http://www.bbc.co.uk/sport/football/37263970)

Watford 3–0 West Ham, 19 November 2017

Marco Silva can't have known he was signing up to the circus when he first came to the Premier League less than a year ago. Having almost tamed the Tigers, this erudite Portuguese manager then jumped on the managerial merry-go-round himself to become Watford's sixth 'permanent' manager in the space of four years under the Pozzo family. Now performing magic tricks with Watford looking genuine contenders to finish in the European places, his team's systematic dismantling of a shambolic West Ham team has hopefully reminded their owners of the ringleader's significance.

In the Vicarage Road stands, David Sullivan wore a familiar look of befuddlement. In fairness, when he parted company with the dignified Slaven Bilić less than two weeks ago, he surely couldn't have foreseen what was to come either. The swift appointment of David Moyes, relegated last season with the freefalling Sunderland but once the hand-picked heir to Sir Alex Ferguson lest we forget, met with a ferocious backlash that included fans burning season tickets outside the London Stadium and a series of disruptive protests organised at the Rush Green training ground, causing the grave Scotsman to quit inside of 48 hours.

Repeatedly knocked back by other candidates, no doubt cowed by the fans' vitriolic response to the appointment of a respected peer, Gold and Sullivan's pioneering answer has been to hold an *Apprentice*-style audition of internal applicants, with the winner ultimately selected by a fan vote.

Pity poor Terry Westley, first into the lion's den. The off-field palaver threatened to make what was happening on it a sideshow but thankfully Watford rose above the chaos. Brazilian forward Richarlison continued to enhance his reputation with a fine first-half strike, before Isaac Success and Nathaniel Chalobah ended the contest – such as it was – early in the second half.

It's safe to say that the West Ham fans weren't as impressed as they perhaps hoped they would be by their academy director's trial match. Next up: U21 manager Steve Potts versus Leicester.

Send in the clowns … oh, hang on, they're already here.

East London United 0–0 Antwerp, 1 August 2026

The brave new world promised a decade ago hasn't quite come to pass for the East End contingent but they're still in with a shout of Europa League football this season after grinding out a nil-nil draw against classier Belgian opposition in this preliminary qualifier at the 中信集 Stadium.

The big-name purchases of Ross Barkley and Gylfi Sigurðsson following the Gold-Sullivan fire-sale and the CITIC Group takeover was supposed to herald bigger and better things … Barkley has certainly got bigger if not better, and his testimonial next season is likely to be sparsely attended, even given the rarity of such long-term service these days.

Despite the vilification of chairman Chang Zhenming, he's no more or less culpable for the gloom surrounding East London United than his predecessors. With West Midlands United simultaneously taken over by a Chinese consortium with even deeper pockets and both clubs failing to make sufficient progress before the big six pulled up the drawbridge and made the Champions League a closed shop, a place in the Europa League is the best that fans of any other club can realistically hope for now.

East London kept that hope alive with a dogged defensive performance but they rarely threatened the opposition's goal. Bereft of creativity, this was confirmation, as if any were still required, that the fabled 'West Ham Way' died along with the name.

An army of fans are expected to travel to picturesque Belgium for the return leg in a fortnight but they'll need to see a vast improvement if fortune is ever to come out of hiding.

West Ham 1-0 Leyton Orient, 6 November 2049

The last meeting between these two local rivals took place more than 60 years ago, with West Ham triumphing 4-1 at the Boleyn in a replayed FA Cup tie. Separated by three measly miles, the closest they've come to meeting between then and now was in court, with Orient threatening action over the proposed legacy of the Olympic Park that sat on the doorstep of both clubs but eventually became home to Tottenham Hotspur in 2016.

That same year probably represented the biggest divergence between the two clubs. While the Hammers were enjoying their last stint as a top-flight club, having failed to grab their golden ticket, the O's gilded pass to the next level up turned out to be anything but, their purchase by Italian businessman Francesco Becchetti resulting in two relegations in three seasons under 11 different managers. 2016/17 witnessed an ignoble exit from the Football League for the first time in their history. Having festered for a quarter of a century in non-league, during which time they plummeted as low as the sixth tier of English football, their phoenix-like rise back to the third tier is a relative success story. Neither club were in the mood for celebrating their reunion, however, not with London property developers continually circling their crumbling old stadiums.

Against the historical backdrop, this mid-table clash seemed inconsequential but West Ham's first £100m player proved the match-winner, Luisio's goal giving at least one set of fans value for money. Further points of nostalgia: following the hyper-inflation of the 2020s and '30s, André Ayew, West Ham's record signing in 2016, would today be worth £20bn, and a Leyton Orient match ticket from that season would cost a paltry £2k in today's money.

At the end of the match both sets of fans marched on City Hall in a coordinated campaign to save traditional football stadia.

Tonight we stand at a potentially pivotal crossroads in the history of West Ham United [David Moyes appointed: take one]. But whichever turn the scriptwriters take, the fans will always have a big part to play.

Cue *Eastenders* cliff-hanger theme ...

West Ham UNITED Football CLUB – Détente

8 November 2017

DAVID MOYES? What the fuck are they thinking?

He'd better turn it around and quick because he is not going to get more than one chance! The fans are already on his back and #moyesout is ALREADY trending!

The online comment above, expressed more mildly than many of the anti-Bilić, anti-Brady, anti-Gold, anti-Sullivan and even anti-Noble sentiments that have been trending in recent days, tells part of the story of why we're unable to attract a better (read more glamorous) manager. Fans are cursed with a non-revocable lifetime membership but, seriously, who in their right mind would actually want to be part of our club right now?

David Moyes isn't a dream appointment, nor is he the travesty that many are keen to paint him as before a ball has even been kicked in anger. My personal views closely mirror those of Sky's Adam Bate, who I find to be a consistently astute commentator in a hyperbolic media climate: 'West Ham appear more upwardly mobile [than Sunderland] and there is plenty for Moyes to get his teeth into ahead of winnable fixtures against Watford, Leicester and old club Everton.'

Less respected is missing link Martin Keown, writing in the pernicious *Daily Mail* ('West Ham fans need to stop moaning and get behind the team! They are like a 12th man ... for the opposition'). No love is lost between Keown and the Hammers, nevertheless he makes some valid points that the terrace agitators calling for revolution should heed and realise that, despite the impression conveyed by Sullivan's alarming choice of headgear, we're not in Soviet Russia … Gold and Sullivan are more Gorbachev, ushering us painfully into a new epoch; Terence Brown was probably closer to Stalin and, following the same analogy, I suppose that would make Eggert Magnússon our Rasputin!

A Hopeless Romantic

28 January 2018

[Wigan 2-0 West Ham (FA Cup fourth round)]

I still believe in the romance of the cup, even when we're on the receiving end of it. A contingent of nigh on 5,000 evidently believe that the FA Cup remains meaningful enough to travel to Wigan and, given that the north-west is now my home, I was making plans to be among them until I regrettably realised it clashed with my niece's first birthday party.

In the event, I'm glad not to have gone. However, what dismays me equally as much as the result is the attitude that Premier League survival is the be-all and end-all. I haven't uttered 'Moyes Out' except to malign those who were shouting it before he was even appointed, and I won't be turning on the 'Moyesiah' (give me strength, if it's not one extreme it's the other!) any time soon. Given our lengthening injury list, I thought he picked a respectable team, especially in these days of wholesale changes. An away tie against the team top of League One, who had already claimed Bournemouth's scalp, was always a veritable banana skin; however, if the writing was on the wall from the moment Lanzini, Arnautović and Carroll added to our deepening injury woes, then it was scrawled ten feet high in neon ink when Moyes told everyone pre-match that 'the priority is staying in the Premier League'.

Now, I understand that for all those on the payroll, the Premier League is their bread and butter (or should that be champagne and caviar on their salaries?). Even lifting silverware doesn't make a manager immune from the sack if the balance sheet is blighted by relegation, as Moyes depressingly acknowledged with the assertion that 'the finances [involved in staying up] are far greater than anything we'd get for winning the cup'. Balance sheets, though, aren't displayed in the trophy cabinet and no fan will recall fondly the year that their club's profit margins were at their healthiest. Moyes's claim that 'if you went back and asked the Wigan people, they'd have said they would rather not win the FA Cup [in 2013] but stay in the Premier League' was laughable. Opposition manager Paul Cook called it for the baloney it was, countering, 'You live for those moments. You remember them for ever. Nowadays money has overtaken football memories. If that's the case going forward then it's not great for the game, is it?' No Paul, no, it's not.

The date 13 May 2006 is etched in my memory. In the end, cup final day sent me into a week-long depression but the transformation of the East End into a quixotic sea of claret and blue that magical morning in May will abide with me longer than anything else that West Ham have served up in my lifetime.

As I approach my 40th birthday, we prepare to mark the ruby anniversary of our trophy cabinet being opened. Younger fans reared on the riches and the PR bluster of the Premier League might be convinced that mid-table mediocrity is a prize to be treasured but you're not kidding me; I might not have tasted success but I at least got to savour its residue, when a cup run still equated to dreams of glory rather than anxieties of burnout. As marvellous as some of Coventry's relegation escape acts were, 1987 remains their high point, and Wimbledon's 'Crazy Gang' may have been consigned to the annals of history but their 1988 upset still stands tall. The memorable achievements of relative minnows overshadow the fact that West Ham were actually the last club from outside the top division to lift the famous trophy. Indeed, the beauty of the FA Cup is that it makes a mockery of league positions.

How to Lose Friends and Alienate People

1 February 2018

Forming an opinion the day after a transfer window closes is frequently ill-advised (see my verdicts on the business of January 2016 and the summer of 2017). Hindsight provides clarity and is indeed a wonderful thing. Moreover, mid-season is rarely the ideal time to hit the sales. Moyes, whether the board's mouthpiece or not, is right to declare that there's no point in buying players just to make up the numbers. Even though numbers are severely depleted right now, I take the view that our injury threat level can't remain critical forever, even if it does seem to have been at severe for longer than the interminable war on terror has been waged.

In this context, yesterday's dealings do rather beggar belief with an injury-ravaged squad being made lighter still. The sale of two international strikers, to be replaced by a relative nonentity at a third of the price, reeks of parsimony. That's not to lament the loss of Sakho (a quality player with a questionable attitude) or Ayew (never hit his stride following an unfortunate debut injury), nor to disparage new boy Jordan Hugill. I don't want to fall into the trap of judging players by media profile or, even worse, those FIFA power rankings that get shared online as if they were conclusive scouting reports. The lad seems genuinely excited to have gone from Seaham Red Star to Premier League superstar; good luck to him, there's a lot of untapped talent in the lower leagues and he might surprise us. With the best will in the world though, his modest track record is nothing for fans to get excited about.

In contrast, our one other new recruit João Mário seemed to make a promising first impression on his home debut against Crystal Palace [1-1] and, as a champion of Europe with Portugal, has decent pedigree. He didn't exactly light up the 2016 Euros (to the extent that I had to google his name) but he evidently did do enough to earn a move to Inter Milan, even if he hasn't done enough since to still be wanted by the *Nerazzurri*. We remain unassuming enough that we could make a cast-off from Serie A's top brass our next record signing.

And there's the rub. The Deloitte Money League 2017 places us in 18th, one spot ahead of Internazionale, with the prediction that we should climb higher! Which is kind of what we were promised – the fabled next level that the move to the Olympic Stadium would bring. So why is it that, with Upton Park sold to developers and an independent auditor rating us higher than Sevilla, Napoli, Monaco and numerous other Champions League teams, we're still in hock to 'the dildo brothers', as disgruntled fans have unaffectionately christened them?

Mário, like Moyes, could perform superbly for the remainder of this campaign and still not be a Hammer next season because the option to buy, for a reported £26m, might not be exercised. David Sullivan's penchant for loan deals exasperates a lot of supporters but the 'try before you buy' approach seems prudent when for every Lanzini there's a Zaza. On the other hand, loan signings have a low-rent reputation and don't offer the stability that needy fans crave. What loan deals are symptomatic of and really does annoy me is the apparent lack of foresight and long-term planning being shown. In fairness, Gold and Sullivan join just about every other club owner in being guilty of this. Every transfer window it amazes me how much seems to be done at the last minute. In what other line of business would bulk panic buying be tolerated, never mind the norm?!

Unlike those calling for the board's heads, I think this window was demoralising rather than devastating, troubling rather than terminal. To place things in perspective, Mike Ashley manages to make them look like munificent benefactors. Where we've at least broken our club transfer record in each of the past two summers – as have most clubs in these days of hyper-inflated fees – Newcastle's most extravagant outlays remain yesterday's men: Michael Owen (£16.8m in 2005) and Alan Shearer (£15m in 1996). What Hammers fans long for and were led to expect was the ambitious level of expenditure displayed by the Geordies a decade ago. Instead, the self-made porn barons aren't doing anywhere near enough to counter the popular stereotype of them as sleazy barrow boy spivs out to make a quick buck.

On the face of our current recruitment policy, it doesn't take much of a wag to suggest that the alleged discriminatory remarks for which director of player recruitment Tony Henry has just been suspended were the least of his crimes. (On African players, he said 'We find when they are not in the team they cause mayhem.') If proven, here's hoping that he's not rewarded with a handsome pay-off and that the Davids replace him with someone who encourages them to put their hands in their pockets a bit more.

How the Other Half Live

16 February 2018

Shamefully, having spent the past five years living just a mile away, last night was my first visit to the Swansway

Stadium to watch Chester. Well, not exactly Chester. Chester Select XI versus Murray's All Stars. As in Colin Murray, presenter of Channel 5's *Goal Rush*. The affable Irishman's connection to Chester is far from clear-cut, but his recruitment of Michael Owen, Ian Rush and others is nonetheless valued.

The purpose of the occasion was to raise funds that would prevent Chester Football Club from sharing the fate of its predecessor, Chester City FC, which was wound up in 2010. The phoenix club, formed by a supporters' group, seemed to be a roaring success with several successive promotions taking them quickly back to the same level they'd occupied prior to financial ruin. The news, therefore, that £20,000 was needed in a matter of days and a further £50,000 required in the short term just to keep the club afloat was a shock to the system. Fortunately the SOS brought many such as myself out of the woodwork and last night's event added £25,000 to the £50,000 already donated.

A ceremonial kick-off saw Owen Jnr (born in Chester) pass to Owen Snr (who spent the bulk of his career with the club, which included their historical high point, beating league champions Leeds 3-0 to reach the League Cup semi-final in the mid-70s). The on-pitch entertainment was minimal, the first-half highlight being Murray's animated reaction to an atrocious penalty miss from former Hammer Neil Mellor. But the 2,000 who braved the arctic February conditions hadn't turned up to be entertained by pulsating football; we simply want our city to have a football team.

That a jocular complaint from one of the All Stars that it was much too cold to be wearing shorts was audible in the back row of the stands was semi-revelatory. I've been a staunch defender of the London Stadium but it makes for a very different – and in many ways better – experience when the back row of Chester's stands is almost as close to the pitch as the front row of ours is. Placed in a different perspective, West Ham and Chester might only be four divisions apart but they're a world away in terms of assets. The loose change put in a bucket probably means more to Chester than a renewed season ticket does to the WHUFC box office. It's disgraceful that a club's very survival is dependent on what an average Premier League player now takes home in a week. The distance from the pitch at the London Stadium can therefore be read as symbolic of the emotional distance we feel from those who are meant to represent us. That's not to say I now dislike our new home; it's more an observation that top-level football, for better or worse, has evolved into an entirely different beast from the levels below and I've been given a reminder of how refreshing it can be to feel a valued part of a small community rather than a faceless consumer. However, the dire straits that Chester find themselves in also serve as a reminder that community-run clubs with small but passionate fanbases aren't the utopian models they're cracked up to be and administrators at least need to demonstrate a degree of commercial acumen, following a business head rather than a supporter's heart.

There must, though, be room in our football landscape for both the big beasts and the small, so next Tuesday I'll take to the Harry McNally Terrace and stand behind the goal for my first taste of competitive Blue-and-White Army action against Leyton Orient (it's pure coincidence that the match I'd earmarked to be my first comes so close to my actual debut). Should Chester survive in the National League (indeed should they survive full stop), then the intention is to take in Orient, plus the other non-league Eastenders, Dagenham & Redbridge, and Chester's cross-border rivals Wrexham next season, at the combined cost of West Ham's lowest-category Premier League match, tickets available on the gate.

I began by ruminating on my new-born son's future allegiance. I still want the first live match he ever sees to be at the London Stadium and for it to have a lasting impact on him, but if we end up bonding on the terraces of our local football club instead, then that remains infinitely preferable to a day out at the Etihad, Anfield or Old Trafford.

Beware the Ides of March

8 March 2018

To march or not to march? That is the question. It's a purely hypothetical question because I have no intention of travelling 200 miles to add my size 9s to the footfall stomping on Stratford in a fairly indeterminate protest against the club's custodians. In another sense it isn't hypothetical, though, because, whether I lived in Chester or Chafford Hundred, I know that I wouldn't march.

I have some sympathy with the dissidents, not least because their commitment to the cause is commendable. On the other hand, the hackneyed chant of 'sack the board' causes me to roll my eyes in wonder at what exactly that cause is beyond general frustration and how little they seem to understand the machinations of corporate employment. The board does the hiring and firing so who exactly is this chant aimed at?!

I get that leaving Upton Park was a wrench and that the Olympic Stadium hasn't been the Shangri-La that we were led to anticipate. 'Broken promises' is a regular refrain but quite frankly it makes the dissenters sound like gullible cry-babies. The head-turning pledge to deliver Champions League football within five years should always have been taken with a pinch of salt (plus it's not even been two years) and basic geometry told us that retractable seats around an oval athletics track would never get right behind the goal. That accusatory adjective 'gullible' would probably be thrown straight back at me for retaining some faith in the board, but I prefer the term 'pragmatic'.

A season ticket-holding friend recently sent me the fanzine *Knees Up Mother Brown*'s version of the minutes from a meeting between the Real West Ham Fans Action Group (check the condescending moniker and its implication about fans who don't hold the same opinions) and board representatives. Karren Brady has since sent an open letter expanding on some of the issues raised. First point of note should be that the board obviously feels a moral obligation to engage with fans, because it's under no contractual obligation to do so. We're customers, not shareholders (although I prefer to think that our emotional investment makes us stakeholders, and credit to the board for seeming to recognise as much when many dictatorial chairmen completely close their ears to fans).

Of course it would be poor business practice to ignore the views of customers and I personally detest the corporatisation of football so I fully endorse the classic customer right to vote with our feet. The problem is that so many of the issues are antithetical. We're easy to take for granted because football supporters are a captive audience

– we won't abandon our team for any of its competitors and in many cases abandonment only makes the achievement of shared goals even less likely. At the same time, we're very difficult customers! On the one hand we criticise board members for their candidness in the media, on the other we demand transparency. On the one hand we complain of corporatisation, on the other we demand investment that only comes from following corporate strategies. Modern-day football is caught between a rock and a hard place.

West Ham right now are stuck in a quarry with granite of all shapes and sizes blocking us in every direction. To my mind, one of the biggest stumbling blocks is the LLDC. The fact that we don't own our stadium is far from ideal but I can live with that in an economy that practically bars the next generation from becoming property owners; we have a secure long-term lease that's the equivalent of renting a mansion for the cost of a studio flat. As tenants, what we don't want is to be in regular dispute with our landlords. The hollow guarantee that most concerns me regards the capacity, which was supposed to increase by 3,000 on the attainment of rudimentary safety certification, with the planning application for a further 6,000 seats taking capacity to 66,000. The antisocial behaviour of some of our own initially blocked this and we're now locked in a potential lawsuit with the LLDC over what's contractually stipulated and who shoulders the costs. Whether the fault lies with the LLDC or our board, something that blocks a sizeable number of fans from gaining entry to the matchday experience barely merits a mention from the RWHFAG. Instead, the difficulty in getting a pie and a pint and going to the toilet during half-time is on their original list of five action points. Presumably they don't want an extra 9,000 fans for fear that those things will become harder still.

Third on that list is the club badge. This strikes me as a pebble-sized issue but that might be because I like the current club badge that was voted for by 56 per cent of the fans in a consultation on different designs (I wasn't among those consulted, nor were members of the RWHFAG, so maybe the process needed widening but the lack of an outcry when the design was first unveiled suggests that this is just another stick to beat the board with rather than the abomination that Leeds fans recently knocked back). The traditional crossed irons were good enough to adorn the shirts worn by Bobby Moore; the castle was a slightly garish addition that paid homage to the history of the Boleyn site but would be incongruous now we've moved. I don't have an issue with the appearance of the word 'London' since that's our home city and seems to me a relatively smart and subtle concession to the financial benefits to be gained from appealing to an international market; if the addition of 'East' appeases people and enhances our local identity then I hold no objections, even if it strikes me as small thinking in a big wide world. Each to their own. I like the fact that fans are actively unionising to put their points across. Equally I like the fact that the club provides avenues for voices to be heard, even if they're unable or unwilling to act on everything that's said.

My main criticism of the march is that now isn't the time. If there's another summer of underinvestment followed by a disappointing start to the season, I might be inclined to lace up my walking boots by October. As it is, defeat to Swansea has left us in a perilous position (some would argue that's reason itself to protest, although wins against Swansea and Burnley would have put us within touching distance of European places); right now the team needs our support. Performances aren't affected by the club badge or by the queues for half-time refreshments; they're affected by the behaviour and attitude of supporters. At the same time as criticising the march, I defend the marchers' right to protest, only I hope the negativity is left at the turnstiles. Even better would be if it galvanises everyone to produce the vociferous atmosphere that should be standard. #SupportTheTeamNotTheRegime is fine so long as the first clause is adhered to.

What I sincerely hope we don't witness are scenes similar to those that have embarrassed supporters at our last two away matches. Our travelling support is largely amazing. I certainly can't knock the devotion shown by those who've accumulated enough points on the ticket scheme to earn their place in the stands at Anfield and the Liberty Stadium, and I wholeheartedly agree with point one of the RWHFAG: that the full allocation of away tickets must be taken up by the club. This seems like a no-brainer and wasn't on the agenda of the aforementioned meeting so is hopefully already resolved.

Then again, I'd suggest revoking a few points from the dullard responsible for the sign on show at Liverpool, tactlessly claiming that Brady, Sullivan and Gold had done more damage to the East End than Adolf Hitler! Emotions run understandably high after consecutive 4-1 defeats (Swansea and Liverpool away) but minus points also for the vigilantes who ambushed 82-year-old David Gold's car and subjected the lifelong Hammer to verbal abuse, recorded their maltreatment of a pensioner and sent the video viral (seriously, have these imbeciles attended the same PR course as Sullivan Jnr?). That Gold had the nerve to confront them only raises him higher in my estimation and intimates that a rowdy procession is going to make little impression.

We've suffered the winter of discontent. At times it's been unclear whether it's a comedy or a tragedy that's being played out. However, call me daft, but I hold firm in the conviction that all's well that ends well.

Brain Drain

12 March 2018

[West Ham 0-3 Burnley]

$OLD A DREAM, GIVEN A NIGHTMARE: this slogan spotted in Saturday's crowd could just as easily reflect how lifelong Hammers fans Gold and Sullivan feel about taking the club on. Think supporting a football club is challenging? Try running one. Running a football club is draining. In an emotional and a financial sense.

I wrote recently of Chester FC's troubles. At an even lower level, the average Sunday league team operates hand to mouth and survives only thanks to good people giving up their time and/or money. My mum harangued my dad into keeping my youth team going when I was 17 and, although lifelong friends (some of whom I might not have made had he not acquiesced) still mock his management style of reading the Sunday paper, I also saw him give up his Sunday afternoon to administration. There's often more to running a football club than meets the eye. At the other end of the scale, the eye-watering sums of Premier League life seduce us into believing that the streets are paved with gold when in actuality nearly all are built on credit. If and when the bubble bursts (and West Ham fans are programmed to believe that bubbles inevitably will), the results are likely to be cataclysmic, but the game will survive because ultimately it's a game first, not a business, and there will always be people passionate or daft enough to put their time and money into it.

Putting their time and money into West Ham is exactly what Gold and Sullivan have done. Yes, they're taking money back out – whether in dividends, salaries or interest – but they're not siphoning it on the sly; so far as I can tell, everything they're doing is standard business practice. They're also running it as a transnational venture. Naturally this rubs up against the supporters' perception of football being a sport rather than a commercial operation but I'm afraid that, until the whole Premier League goes pop, if we want to remain competitive at a high level then it's imperative that we see it as both. I accept that the disturbing scenes against Burnley were fuelled by legitimate concerns and it was a little disingenuous of me in my last entry anticipating unrest to describe fan protest as 'indeterminate', although I do still consider it nebulous, so here's a closer look at some of the complaints.

Where has all the money gone? Players' wages. We reportedly have the seventh-highest wage bill in the country, which I suspect (given the pre-eminence of the Premier League but without having access to the figures to prove it) would place us higher in the wages-paid table than our standing of 17th in football's global rich list. According to a study by Brazilian sports economics firm Pluri Consultoria, during Sam Allardyce's tenure he was the 13th-best-paid manager in the world, pocketing significantly more than Vicente del Bosque of Spain's all-conquering national team. In short, the books aren't balanced and there's still a sizeable debt issue.

The sale of Upton Park bought us Marko Arnautović. I told you he was overpriced but I hadn't calculated at the point of purchase that a hit-and-miss Premier League player could cost the same as prime East End real estate. Some fans would have happily paid money to be rid of him after a few matches, although right now he looks our most saleable asset. On the topic of which, isn't it nice that in recent years we've not sold off our better players, the exceptional case of Dimitri Payet aside. Selling André Ayew back to a resurgent Swansea might not prove the smartest transaction ever but it's telling that the Swans broke their transfer record for a bit-part player maligned by most Hammers fans. Broadcasting revenue might have sky-rocketed but transfer fees and salaries have done so commensurately, which is why Ayew was our own record acquisition before Arnautović and why his ostensible replacement (although Hugill's playing style is markedly different) merits an eight-figure price tag despite being untested at the top level. And yet poor Hugill, who hasn't had an opportunity to show us what he's capable of yet, still symbolises things being done on the cheap, although if you were nearly £100m in debt you probably wouldn't be shopping at Harrods either. The haphazard nature of our purchases is more damning but unfortunately there's no such thing as a sure thing, as Ayew and Arnautović attest.

The Olympic Stadium isn't fit for purpose. Nor is the Stadio Olimpico in Rome (home to Roma, Lazio, Italian athletics and Italian rugby, host of the 1960 Summer Olympics, the 1987 World Athletics Championships, the 1990 World Cup Final, two European Cup finals, two

Champions League finals and numerous concerts). It's a soulless bowl, incapable of generating any atmosphere, detested by any right-minded football fan. Ditto the Olympiastadion in Berlin, home to Hertha Berlin and the German national team. And the thing that everyone remembers from 1966 is that fans were miles away because the Wembley pitch was flanked by a greyhound track. Oh no, hang on, that's a load of shit.

Just because it wasn't purposely built for football or specifically for West Ham United FC doesn't automatically mean that it's not fit for purpose. Compromises have had to be made and further modifications wouldn't go amiss (the Stadio Olimpico has undergone several renovations but retains the athletics track, minus retractable seating) but don't try telling me Upton Park was perfect.

Granted, the Boleyn was 'home' and our new domicile is very different to Upton Park, but that's not automatically a bad thing either. It's laughable the number of people bemoaning the death of the East End spirit, almost invariably beginning their laments with 'I lived in ...' (note the past tense). Basically it's okay for people to move away and better themselves but gentrification of the East End is to be sneered at, as if rationing and bunking in air-raid shelters during the Blitz were preferable to grabbing a bite to eat at the Gourmet Burger Kitchen, Westfield Stratford! Green Street represented a walk down memory lane and the turrets of the west stand loomed like an East End theme park. These self-centred critiques are concerned with the past (of which we should be mindful but not chained) and have little bearing on the future of West Ham United, especially if we want to remain competitive in the hyper-commercial climate of 21st-century football, which much of the carping about lack of investment suggests we do.

Had our owners passed up the once-in-a-lifetime opportunity to move to the Olympic Stadium, they probably would have faced parallel accusations of killing the football club. As countless other clubs moved onwards and upwards, we were in danger of stagnating. Anyone who thinks we could have easily rebuilt within Zone 3 of the London Underground need only study the protracted history of Chelsea's £1bn development to find that this isn't the case. Spurs might be in the process of renovating White Hart Lane but in 2011 the spectre of Tottenham invading our turf was very real. Arch negotiator that he is, Daniel Levy probably would have wrested more concessions from the Olympic Legacy Committee too.

It's a bugbear that stewarding and other such custodial issues are outside the club's control. On the other hand, our identity is stamped on the stadium far more than any of the other clubs who are occupying tenants of Olympic-made colosseums. Not only do Roma and Lazio not own the stadium, these fierce rivals share the space. It hasn't stopped them becoming European giants with their own distinct character. Hertha Berlin also rent. Italy and Germany have modelled long-standing tenancy agreements between football clubs and governing bodies so let's look and learn instead of crying that it's doomed to failure and we've 'sold our soul'.

It's been said that relegation would be the death-knell of West Ham, that playing in a half-empty arena would destroy whatever spirit remains. It might therefore interest the doom-mongers to know that Roma and Lazio's average attendances last season were 32,638 and 20,453 respectively, far from the 70,634 capacity. And those clubs are famed for fervent support. The division we play in has never had any relevance to my attendance or support (the lower cost and ease of gaining entry associated with lower-level football might actually have allowed me to attend more frequently; being a relatively long-distance supporter, the reduced TV coverage of lower divisions would also incite me to make more regular pilgrimages back to the East End). It strikes me that a far better way of demonstrating passion would be to pack the stadium to the rafters in the Championship rather than creating a hostile atmosphere that increases the likelihood that that's where we'll be. It would also ram the disturbingly prescient words of Tottenham's chief architect on their Olympic Stadium bid back down his throat: 'There would be nothing worse than, five years down the line, for a failing club not being able to meet its obligations because it's not getting 60,000 fans, saying there's no atmosphere.' [David Keirle, quoted in the *Daily Mail* 13/01/11]

Back to stewarding momentarily, Saturday's events exposed it to be lax, as has been observed from the outset. The spectacle of senior players being forced to tackle pitch invaders without a single steward anywhere to be seen was surely distressing for all concerned. I can't say I've ever been to a match and paid any heed to the effectiveness (or otherwise) of stewards and security before; it's my personal view that they should be invisible because the general public ought to be civil enough to marshal themselves, but if that's not the case then of course competent stewarding and security services are required. The Southampton match will be a test of what's been learned from Saturday's debacle. Stewards have also been castigated for not dealing with interlopers; I must admit to having watched West Ham while nestled quietly among the home supporters of other teams, as well as attending numerous matches as a neutral, but ideally further steps should be taken to ensure true fans have access to tickets before anybody else, and anybody with the gall to openly flaunt their affiliation to another team should be ejected (for their own safety if nothing else).

The board are doing to us what they did to Birmingham City. In a sense, yes, they are. If what you mean by that is trying to run a football club on a budget and hopefully leaving it in a healthier state than they found it. As with Birmingham, progress isn't shown by a smooth upward curve and there are shared perceptions of Sullivan in particular being a dictatorial PR nightmare. That doesn't escape the fact that in 1993, the year they bought the club, Birmingham flirted with relegation to football's third tier and had an average attendance of just over 12,000. The worst happened the following year, plunging Birmingham back to the lowest level in the second city's proud history (also occupied between 1989 and 1992). The club was clearly in the doldrums and in an even worse state than the Icelanders left us.

By 2002, St Andrew's had been largely rebuilt and crowds of nearly 30,000 were enjoying Premier League football. When the club was sold to Hong Kong businessman Carson Yeung in 2009 (having just been promoted back to the top flight), Sullivan commented, 'The public have had enough of us. They think we should have mortgaged our houses to buy more players to compete with Chelsea and Arsenal.' The same public that were happy to see the back of him thought their new owner was their saviour. The following season they won the League Cup, a historical high point built on the foundations inherited. However, they were also relegated and Yeung was arrested for money-laundering. Under Chinese ownership since 2015, several fractious years have put them back on the brink of relegation to football's third tier with attendances dwindling below 20,000. We're welcome to Gold and Sullivan according to who exactly?!

We have a dire public relations machine. The board does blather too much, amounting to a litany of broken promises. Ironically the careless clamour that emanates from the boardroom matches that coming from the stands, precisely because the owners are also hot-blooded fans prone to braggadocio. If Sullivan were only the second-richest person in Theydon Bois rather than numero uno, it's a fair bet he'd be protesting along with others at the inability to move to the next level. So, the 'marquee signings' haven't arrived, largely because the big guns have upped the ante and £35m would probably not come close to buying the coveted Alexandre Lacazette, who's returned a pretty meagre nine goals for Arsenal so far this season.

The London Stadium isn't what it looked like in the brochure. Then again, what ever is? From an objective viewpoint, it does fulfil the criteria of a UEFA 5 Star Stadium. Sunderland's Stadium of Light was also lauded as a 4 Star Stadium capable of hosting European finals but will instead be hosting third division football next season. PR efforts can be brilliant or bollocks, it all boils down to what happens on the pitch and, if West Ham were enjoying the season we did in 2015/16, our last at Upton Park, I can guarantee the knives wouldn't be out. By the same token, if 2015/16 had matched any of the previous

13 campaigns (save perhaps 2005/06) then expectations wouldn't be nearly so high and Upton Park probably would have gone the way of all those bubbles, fading gently rather than going out with a bang.

Alhough I'm very glad it was the latter, I do wish the upward momentum and the accompanying goodwill hadn't so quickly dissipated, beginning with the disastrous loss to Astra Giurgiu for the second year running (a reminder that the Boleyn still witnessed the occasional debacle in that final season too). Imagine an alternative reality in which a floodlit London Stadium had hosted a spine-tingling performance against the likes of Roma, who topped Astra's group (not forgetting that the Italian giants, who symbolise glamour and prestige, are a couple of places below us in the latest Deloitte Money League and don't even own their own stadium, which is surrounded by a running track). A scintillating start against Watford and Payet's cheeky rabona fleetingly rekindled the spirit of 2016 but the subsequent capitulation and in-fighting signalled a definite turning of the tide and nothing since has been able to stem the backwards flow. Players and fans alike need to make memories that give the London Stadium positive connotations rather than the undertone of menace and failure it currently carries.

A further criticism of the club has been the placing in storage of memorabilia and the need to find a new home for this. Personally I think our new home already pays ample homage to our past and that heaping Boleyn relics around it would be an unnecessary albatross. The Champions statue apparently faces being bulldozed due to a restructuring of the junction on which it stands and I accept that time can't stand still, but it seems to me a far better option to construct a museum as close to the Boleyn as possible in order to create a permanent corporeal connection to what many still see as our spiritual home, thereby supporting some of the local businesses with increased supporter footfall too. It's been a dereliction of duty by both the club and Newham Council not to properly memorialise our home of more than a hundred years and its significance to E13. On the other hand, if we'd had a more auspicious start to life in Stratford then this would have been a mere footnote, the equivalent of misplacing a box of ornaments between house moves – some of them had fond associations but you need to refurnish anyway and they'll probably end up in the loft.

Any defence of Gold and Sullivan isn't intended to cast them as saintly philanthropists in the mould of the late Jack Walker, whose millions would struggle to buy Blackburn the Championship trophy these days. It's designed, however, to give some perspective, for nor are they the self-interested folly represented by Venky's. The comparison to Blackburn Rovers and earlier allusion to the plight of Sunderland and their stay-away owner Ellis Short (whose fortune was once thought to be their key to the next level) demonstrates that there are copious numbers of fans who have more right to feel aggrieved and to vent their frustrations than Hammers do. To name just another dozen:

Newcastle United

Hovering just above the Premier League trapdoor with us, it's only the hope of Rafa Benítez steering the ship into calmer waters that's preventing mutiny. A once mighty football club indelibly linked to what it means to be a

Geordie is now a millionaire's plaything for peddling his cheap and tainted sportswear brand.

Southampton

Suffered a similar fate to that which we're now threatened with. Having swapped a poky but well-loved abode for a gleaming new one that was supposed to herald bigger and better things, they promptly got relegated all the way down to League One where, credit to the fans, more still turned up to watch than were ever able to get into Premier League matches at The Dell. Having admirably rebuilt, they're staring relegation in the face again while half their team of recent years is competing in the Champions League for Liverpool and a golden generation of highly acclaimed academy products ply their trade elsewhere.

Wolverhampton Wanderers

On their way back now, albeit at the whim of super-agent Jorge Mendes, another once proud club suffered the ignominy of consecutive relegations while incensed fans clashed repeatedly with sub-standard players over inflated and unmerited salaries, although Jamie O'Hara and Roger Johnson never had to wrestle anybody off the Molineux pitch (Wolves fans would probably counter that those two would never have been able to muster the energy and effort to do so).

Aston Villa

Once members of English football's 'big six', the wealth of Randy Lerner was supposed to parachute them back to those heights. Instead they're on for top six in the Championship and a play-off place, having at least stabilised this season, little thanks to their AWOL owner.

Leeds United

At least they got to live the dream for a few seasons under Peter Ridsdale. His lavish mismanagement (Google's top predictive search is Peter Ridsdale fish!) followed by the impulsiveness of Massimo Cellino and now Andrea Radrizzani mean that Leeds has become a byword for how not to run a football club.

Nottingham Forest

It might only have been the genius of Brian Clough that propelled them to unforeseen achievements in the first place but they declined along with Old Big 'Ead and proceeded to fall even further, reaching their nadir just over a decade ago and treading water with scant optimism of a return to the big time ever since.

Hull City

As with Sunderland, consecutive relegations have seemed a very real prospect this season, the receipt of Premier League parachute payments proving once again that financial largesse doesn't directly correspond with success. That's as nothing against the obdurate owner's resolution to rebrand the club though. The city of Hull is enjoying something of a renaissance as the UK's capital of culture but, according to Assem Allam, the 'City' mark is 'irrelevant' and 'common'. Allam is granted a lot of goodwill, having saved Hull from liquidation and become a generous benefactor to his adopted home, which makes it all the more remarkable that he doesn't understand the link between football club and wider community. The proposed 'Hull Tigers' is a pretty cool sobriquet and approximately half of the fans who responded to a poll voted in favour of it, although possibly because that option came with the caveat that Allam would only continue funding the club if he got his way. A redesigned club crest was also introduced without any consultation. Dismissing supporter protest, he remarked, 'Nobody questions my decisions in my business.' Falling-outs with managers have also been a theme of his ownership.

Portsmouth

As with Leeds, stretched themselves for short-term gain resulting in long-term loss. Culprits move on, loyal supporters pay the price. They do at least have an FA Cup to show for that bout of profligacy and I'm all for prioritising silverware over Premier League survival but not to place the club's existence at risk.

Charlton Athletic

Addicks fans know what it is to be homeless, having lodged with us and Crystal Palace through the late-80s and early-90s; however, they're times of prosperity compared to the downward spiral of the Roland Duchâtelet regime, which has comprised eight managerial changes in four years, a stark contrast to the continuity of Lennie Lawrence and Alan Curbishley guiding them relatively seamlessly through two decades of turbulence. Protests have included a free alternative to the club programme, a boycott of club catering and merchandise, a funeral march and the disruption of matches by flying pigs and stress balls; they've so far proved futile but have received media praise and support for being creative and well organised.

Blackpool

Mismanagement taken to a whole new level when you lose 27 players and have a squad consisting of eight outfield players and no goalkeeper two weeks before the start of the season, as the Seasiders had in 2014. The Oyston family has taken the fans on a roller-coaster ride of ups and downs but the relationship has turned irreparably toxic. The club is up for sale after a court ruling of illegitimate asset-stripping against the Oystons. The question is, who would want to buy it now?

Coventry City

I worked on the bar at Highfield Road while at university. It was no great shakes but the majority of fans seemed to be content with their lot, which at that time meant being the top flight's annual escape act but also its fourth-longest-serving team behind only Arsenal, Everton and Liverpool.

As in so many cases, a swish new stadium was supposed to be the harbinger of future success (in the quarter century since the advent of the Premier League, 29 of the present-day Football League clubs have moved to new homes – compared to just one in the previous quarter century – so they can't all be a permanent fixture in its global success story, go figure). Instead the decline has been steady and involves a financial collapse that means they're now controlled by a hedge fund, the Ricoh Arena is owned by Wasps RFC and fans spent the 2013/14 season making a 70-mile round-trip to Northampton's Sixfields Stadium, which has less than a quarter the capacity of the Ricoh, due to a rent dispute with the operator Arena Coventry Ltd.

Leyton Orient

To think they were worried about us moving next door. As if we didn't already occupy different football spheres, the loss of league status for the first time in the O's history was brought about by the malpractice of yet another foreign investor who was supposed to represent an improvement on wide boy Barry Hearn. In fairness to the ruinous Francesco Becchetti, the rot had already set in. The last time I went to Brisbane Road, one end of it had been turned into flats and a car park; at least our custodians waited to secure a new home before selling off the old one.

In all of these tales of woe there have been demonstrations, although in the very worst cases dissent has given way to apathy. Fans should be passionate but there's a right way and a wrong way to show you care for your club and in all the above case studies of anguish, grief and affliction, zero have invited scenes as shameful as those we witnessed at the weekend. Knowing that pitch invasions and projectiles could be the tip of the iceberg for a group of fans that still cling to the notorious reputation of the Inter City Firm as a badge of honour, I'm given the sinking feeling that the vaunted West Ham Way is in fact predicated on thuggery.

It was regrettably telling on the morning of the Burnley match, in an interview published by *The Times*, that the abiding memory of Upton Park that Julian Dicks cared to share with the reporter wasn't the fans united behind the team or celebrating a trademark net-busting penalty but the intimidation he received as a 17-year-old playing for Birmingham. Much as I adore the Terminator, the pejorative nature of this comment on our fans' boorish mentality seemed to be entirely lost on him.

John Motson described Saturday's events as 'the most scary moment I've had in a football ground', which should be taken with a pinch of salt from a septuagenarian who commented on the Hillsborough tragedy, but it's pretty damning nonetheless. A mob mentality has taken hold and, although the man who attempted to plant the corner flag in the centre circle formed a singular peaceful petition designed to evoke the Bond Scheme protests, he may as well have been holding a pitchfork.

Despite its peerless ability to transcend boundaries, sport and politics aren't the most comfortable bedfellows, hence considerable disquiet at the prospect of boycotting this summer's World Cup in Russia as payback for Putin's recent alleged aggression. Nevertheless, I can't help drawing parallels between the predicament West Ham find themselves in and the ongoing Brexit saga. It's a gross generalisation but I have a sneaking suspicion that the ringleaders of our protests would have been Leave voters. While, on the whole, cosmopolitan London opted to remain, a large swathe of the disenfranchised indigenous population in outlying areas such as Havering and Ockendon were staunchly in favour of 'sticking it to the man' in the EU. In the case of both EU membership and London Stadium tenancy, the new dawns might not have been all they were cracked up to be (the comparison falls down slightly in Eurosceptics having lived with their perceived problem for more than 30 years against stadium detractors less than three) but at the same time neither Britain nor West Ham were in a terribly unhealthy state. Rather than making the best of situations, recognising systematic flaws and working proactively with all parties to improve matters, we are instead crippling progress in a fit of pique while pining after an imagined past, all the while missing the bigger picture of an unfettered capitalism riding roughshod over communities and cultures. It's a simple solution to pin the blame for everything at the door of the EU/the board. Quite frankly, if you want to protest against the route West Ham are on then the best course of action is probably to cancel your Sky subscription.

Picking apart the detritus of each of these hostile scenarios, there's a pressing need for moderate diplomats to occupy the middle ground rather than extremists on either side making false claims or unrealistic promises. The image of a forlorn Trevor Brooking, caught between his ambassadorial role in the directors' box and a bond with the angry everyman firing coins and verbal volleys in its direction, was truly poignant. Dicks, in the aforementioned interview, justifiably defended the supporters' right to protest without offering any denunciation of his erstwhile employers. It would be hugely instructive to hear the unspun thoughts of club legends such as Brooking, Dicks and Bilić, who have been heavily involved with the Gold, Sullivan, Brady administration.

I hope against hope that things have now come to a head, simply because I'm exhausted from pouring my thoughts and feelings into this drama. To cut a very long story short, I condemn the mindlessly harmful actions of a minority while attempting to provide a degree of perspective on both sides. I don't want the club I love to be associated with ugliness and disorder, and I think the protests lack rationality, although I sympathise with the bitterness that's given rise to them. For most, empathy with frustrated supporters doing foolish things comes more easily than with closeted millionaires who appear out of touch but are also liable to make mistakes in life. Much of the shock of the images beamed to the nation on *Match of the Day* and news bulletins derives from us mortals getting so threateningly close to our idols and our governors. A timely reminder that those on the football front line are fallible human beings who deserve to be treated with respect, not to be confused with unfaltering support (although that's exactly what the players need now), came today from the heart-rending admission by World Cup winner Per Mertesacker that he's never much enjoyed playing football, because of the associated stress.

Still, at least we've not yet descended into the anarchy of Greek football. Heaven help us all if David Sullivan follows the lead of PAOK's proprietor and brings a firearm to the next do-or-die match against Southampton!

Junior Hammers Newsflash

22 May 2018

Sitting in the sunshine, enjoying an ice cream after nursery pick-up.

DADDY: Hey, West Ham appointed a new manager this morning.

JAMES: What's his name?

DADDY: Manuel Pellegrini. Sounds fancy, doesn't it.

JAMES: Yeah. What's he do?

DADDY: Well, you know how in football there are two teams of 11 players. The manager picks who plays.

JAMES: So he doesn't play?

DADDY: No. He's a bit too old to play these days.

JAMES: How old is he?

DADDY: Sixty-four, I think. Nearly as old as granny was at the weekend.

JAMES: What does he do?

DADDY: Like I said, he picks and supposedly organises the team. That means he also takes the flak for their poor performances.

JAMES: But he doesn't play?

DADDY: No.

JAMES: That's not fair.

DADDY: Hmm, life isn't always fair unfortunately. Ask David Moyes.

JAMES: Who's he?

DADDY: He was our last manager.

JAMES: What did he do wrong?

DADDY: Not a lot. He was hired to steady the ship and keep us up, which he did, but the owners opted not to extend his contract. That means they didn't want him to be manager any more.

JAMES: That's not fair.

DADDY: I know but, sadly for Moyes, he didn't have the support of a lot of the fans. You see, we were promised someone to take us to the next level and no one thought that he was the man to do that.

JAMES: What does next level mean?

DADDY: I don't really know. No one does. But we think Pellegrini might be the man to take us there.

JAMES: Why?

DADDY: Because he's a winner with a strong track record. He's the only manager in our history to have won a league title.

JAMES: Will West Ham win the league?

DADDY: No, that's not what we do.

JAMES: Why not?

DADDY: Because we're not good enough. Especially not these days. These days you have to have money to buy the league.

JAMES: But Pellegrino—

DADDY: Pellegrino's a posh lemonade. Pellegrini won the league with Man City a few years ago but he was given millions to spend that he won't get from us.

JAMES: Why?

DADDY: a) Because our owners don't like to spend too much money. And b) we don't actually have that much money.

JAMES: Why not?

DADDY: It's complicated. Probably best not to get into the economics of football with a three-year-old. The important thing is that Pellegrini plays attacking football that fits in with the West Ham Way.

JAMES: What's that?

DADDY: Good question. I thought I knew but now I'm not so sure. Something to do with playing attractive football and not really caring about results, yet still caring enough to have hopes of European football and a mortal fear of relegation. It used to also have something to do with being a family and looking after our own but that doesn't seem relevant anymore.

JAMES: Why?

DADDY: Well, too many fans are quick to abuse the owners, the players, the manager and even each other. We try to hound people out rather than make them welcome.

JAMES: Is the Pelé-person welcome?

DADDY: Pelé would have been very welcome in his prime. We might be gaining a reputation as a retirement home for once-great players but Pelé would be pushing it. Yaya, maybe …

JAMES: Yaya. That's funny!

DADDY: It won't be funny if we pay him £150,000 a week and he breaks down before Christmas. Although Hallmark will be laughing if he demands 'get well soon' and then 'sorry you're leaving' cards from everyone.

JAMES: What is Yaya?

DADDY: Yaya Touré. He's a footballer who was one of the best in the Premier League but has hardly played for two years. His agent has also gifted him a reputation for being a bit of a diva. We're linked with him coz he used to be the main man under Pellegrini.

JAMES: How long will he last?

DADDY: What do you mean how long will he last?

JAMES: Pelle … will he still be the manager when I'm a big boy?

DADDY: Highly unlikely but it would be great if he was. God, I've just worked out we're on to the fourth manager already of your short life. I was into my 20s before we'd gone through four managers. Hopefully he'll last longer than the recent batch but maybe not into his 80s. Only the Queen works till that age. And maybe your generation. Do you remember the bubbles song I taught you?

JAMES: No.

DADDY: I'm forever blowing bubbles, pretty bubbles in the air, they fly so high, they reach the sky, then like my dreams they fade and die. You try. I'm forever blowing bubbles ...

Enter Mummy

MUMMY: Have you been telling him all about the new West Ham manager?

DADDY: Yeah.

MUMMY: Are West Ham going to win the league next year, James?

JAMES: [spluttering sound]

MUMMY: What was that?

JAMES: Just a little choke.

DADDY: I think he's getting it.

Wembley Way

27 May 2018

So, yesterday, I experienced the strange sensation of seeing a team in claret and blue play at Wembley. And the even stranger experience of supporting the opposition.

It was instead a case of 'Come on you Whites!' as Fulham emerged victorious over Aston Villa in the battle to make up the numbers in next season's Premier League.

Happily, this was a reversal of fortunes from the Cottagers' last trip to Wembley, way back in 1975 when the FA Cup was adorned with claret and blue ribbons, much to my dad's dismay. The ruining of his club's biggest moment by my beloved Hammers remains a source of guilt, despite the fact that I wouldn't even be born for another five years.

Yesterday represented an opportunity to experience in person the triumphant Wembley roar that I'll probably never hear from the Irons faithful. Not because I have so little faith that we will one day lift another trophy but because, not being a season ticket holder, I wouldn't get a sniff of one of those golden tickets. Even my dad, as one of the relatively small number of long-suffering ever-presents at Craven Cottage but a complete novice when it comes to Ticketmaster scrambles, nearly missed out thanks to the mathematically illogical allowance of five tickets per season ticket holder. And as a casual fan who didn't even pay for his ticket – thanks dad! – I'm not in a strong position to be complaining about the seats we ended up with. However, what was galling – and pertinent to our own London Stadium travails – was the ignorant selfishness of teenagers who insisted on standing for the entire match, necessitating all those behind them to follow suit.

Now I'm all in favour of safe standing and have signed the petition urging a rethink that probably won't be forthcoming given the government's abrupt rejection of West Brom's recent request to trial rail seating. I think that standing generates atmosphere, hence the natural inclination for virtually all spectators to rise to their feet at moments of excitement. A throw-in on the halfway line, on the other hand, carries no upstanding urgency.

Yet all polite entreaties to rest their backsides on the plastic provided fell on deaf ears. Conversely, they had the temerity to turn on septuagenarians who had waited 43 years for their day in the sun (and it was sweltering in our shadeless spot) to accuse them of lacking enthusiasm!

Fretting over the well-being of my old man was an anxiety I hadn't bargained on. Combined with the tension of defending a one-goal lead with ten men, he acknowledged that he might not have seen it out pre-heart operation. I admit to welling up at the final whistle so God help me if West Ham ever put me in the same situation. Steven Gerrard's outlandish strike at Cardiff felt like an arrow through the heart. If I'd been a hot, exhausted pensioner sitting directly in its trajectory then I honestly think it would have killed me. I've always said I'd die happy if West Ham win just one major trophy in my lifetime … it'd be sod's law if their barren run stretched from my year of birth to my senile years, finally ending with my last, relieved breath.

Year Three – 2018/19

Vive la Révolution

10 August 2018

I didn't see that coming. When news broke that Manuel Lanzini had ruptured his ACL on the eve of the World Cup, my enthusiasm for football was virtually nil. If you'd told me then that in a few weeks to come I'd have just witnessed the best World Cup of my lifetime and would have high hopes for the season ahead then I'd have suspected Russia of disseminating more 'fake news'.

First then to Moscow, where England reverted to type by falling just short when it really mattered, but not before reconnecting with fans and elevating the image of the sport in the national consciousness. That Gareth Southgate – a man no Premier League team would have touched with a barge pole when he was appointed to the impossible job – is largely responsible for the renewed positivity says a lot about the fluctuating nature of the game. And beyond the rampant patriotism, it was gratifying that fears about the host nation, the malign influence of VAR and cynical, defence-first tactics were likewise turned on their heads.

Back at the London Stadium it's become difficult to see where a fit-again Lanzini – one of the few reliable performers of recent years – might fit into this new-look West Ham team that Pellegrini and new head of recruitment Mario Husillos have assembled. As if similarly rejuvenated and love-struck by events in Russia, Gold and Sullivan have been on an unprecedented spending spree. Either that, or someone's cloned their credit cards. I'm loath to laud the new signings, having acclaimed last summer as sensible business, but at the very least they've injected optimism and cultivated the belief that our unloved bowl in Stratford might finally serve up a bit of fantasy football. Whether prompted by the petulance of fans is a moot point. The board deserves at least one full season's grace for the purchases they've gifted us – when have we ever outspent Manchester United, Arsenal and Spurs! – and their munificence suggests that the new manager is being entrusted with more than just our short-term future.

Of course it's Liverpool, the biggest spenders of all, first up and Anfield isn't a happy hunting ground so things could quickly turn sour again. Ever a pragmatist, I'll forego points in favour of any performance that doesn't entirely sink our chirpy buoyancy. I just want this feeling to last …

Long live the revolution!

[Liverpool 4-0 West Ham]

Reasons to be Cheerful 2018/19

29 August 2018

1. Fan optimism might have evaporated in a nanosecond but if you think back to this time last year Arnautović looked a waste of space. If all new signings perk up as he did then give it a couple of months and we're in for a treat!

2. Anderson's already starting to look the part.
3. There were nine changes to the team that worried Arsenal [Arsenal 3-1 West Ham] so the Wimbledon line-up was essentially our reserves and, on paper at least, it looked strong. [AFC Wimbledon 1-3 West Ham, League Cup second round]
4. Gradual improvements suggest we're getting closer to finding the right balance. A centre-midfield pairing of Rice and Obiang might have initially paid the Dons too much respect but addressed the need for fortification. Declan also looked more at home in the position than he did at Anfield, although personally I still prefer him in a back three.
5. If Pellegrini is intent on a back four then Cresswell had an opportunity last night to show that he's a better left-back than Masuaku. There wasn't much defending required and, post-injury, he's struggled to hit the heights that earned him England recognition, yet last season he still managed to demonstrate his defensive worth in a back three while also recording more assists than any other full-back.
6. The statistic of 80 per cent possession in our favour is unheard of. Granted, it was against a League One team reduced to ten men but the pattern of play was eye-catching.
7. Pellegrini's praise for calm and patience was well earned, by the players if not the fans.
8. A banana skin was avoided (and how many times in the past have we slipped?!), meaning we're still in the one competition that we have a realistic chance of winning.

9. Crystal Palace lost their first seven league matches last season and still survived with something to spare so the panic button doesn't need pressing for a while yet.
10. Allardyce remains unemployed so he can clomp to our rescue should we still be bottom at Christmas (which is only 118 days away)!

Reasons to be Fearful 2018/19

2 September 2018

1. We haven't looked like a team since the early days of Bilić, which leaves a nagging feeling that any semblance of organisation was a hangover from Allardyce, sprinkled with Payet's stardust.
2. Symptomatic of this is a lack of leaders. Arnautović's good form alone doesn't make him captaincy material. Noble and Reid, whatever their shortcomings, do try to take control of situations. The promise of Balbuena and Diop included the leadership skills expected from the captain of Corinthians known as 'The General' and the young skipper of Toulouse and France U21; these qualities must quickly become evident as they find their feet.
3. Midfield remains the biggest soft spot. That's where we need a general! As enthused as I was by the summer spending spree, top of my shopping list would have been a defensive-minded midfielder who covers the ground. Give us N'Golo Kanté and we'd be challenging the top six. Kouyaté was the closest we had, in both name and style, and although I don't think he's a massive loss on recent form, Obiang and Carlos Sánchez are more positionally astute but even more ponderous.

4. What we do have is a calamitous tendency to shoot ourselves in the foot with costly individual errors. See Sánchez's 93rd-minute dithering against Wolves [West Ham 0-1 Wolves].

5. No one knows what our best team is. This can be a strength if the manager is able to keep players on their toes but, while Pellegrini seems to know his system, he doesn't seem to know who best works in it. And given the flimsiness of our midfield, most fans would probably prefer a reversion to Moyes's 3-5-2, especially now we have a relatively capable right wing-back in Fredericks (Byram remains untried and Zabaleta, despite his willingness, doesn't have the legs).

6. We're giving maximum points to teams who should be around us in the league. Without wishing to sound defeatist, losing to Arsenal and Liverpool away is one thing but, as Pellegrini himself alluded to in yesterday's post-match interview, we should be beating Bournemouth [1-2] and Wolves at home. Wolves are no mugs and no match is a given, but we're losing ground while serial sackers Watford somehow sit joint top!

7. Fickle fans who lauded Pellegrini and his signings are already calling for their heads. As with Avram Grant (the last manager to start a doomed season with four successive defeats), I fear there's a bit of the emperor's new clothes about Pellegrini. Then again, I never had an ounce of faith in Avram, whereas I do believe that Manuel could and should come good.

8. Cancer … AIDS … child poverty … Let's keep things in context. While we want the best for our football club, relegation shouldn't really be something to be

> feared and creating a climate of fear will do us no good whatsoever. So let's assume the international break has come at just the right time and we'll be firing on all cylinders at Goodison Park in a couple of weeks.

Come on you Irons!

Crisis? What Crisis?!

16 September 2018

[Everton 1-3 West Ham]

When I clicked 'Pay Now' for the Sky Sports 24-hour pass, it was more in hope than expectation. In truth, as an armchair supporter usually having to settle for the *Match of the Day* ten-minute 'highlights' package, win lose or draw I was watching primarily with a view to gaining some insight into what's happening with West Ham. Sandwiched between a horrendous start to the season and a daunting sequence of fixtures, a winnable match away to one of our (many) bogey teams represented a judicious opportunity to take the pulse of Pellegrini's West Ham. And the good news is that, despite reports to the contrary, we're alive and kicking.

In all honesty I've harboured doubts about our urbane Chilean boss ever since he emerged as the likely successor to the stolid Moyes, largely based on his having gone down the lucrative semi-retirement route of the Chinese Super League. Would he still have his finger on the pulse? Doubts persist about his choice of full-backs but he seems to have chanced upon a successful shape at last, one that doesn't leave us with a soft middle. On paper, the trio of Noble, Obiang and Rice looked alarmingly pedestrian but they all did a job today. Noble, whatever his detractors say, still knits the team together better than anyone else; Obiang displayed some surprisingly silky skills venturing further forward in a box-to-box role; and Rice really looked the part in a holding role that I wasn't entirely sure he was suited to.

Fair dues to the chief – with hysterical sections of the media and fanbase branding this a must-win match, the composure of a serial winner such as Pellegrini shone through. Credit too to the board, which coolly dismissed talk of the sack during the international break. The performance against an unbeaten Everton – particularly the control we exerted in the second half after the classic West Ham move of gifting them momentum by conceding with virtually the last kick of the first – indicated what reasonable fans have recognised all along: it's a talented bunch of players we have.

Fabiański has been one of the big plus points and must surely keep a deserved clean sheet sooner or later; Balbuena and Diop are looking sturdier; Anderson's nonchalance was a joy to watch, although more end product is needed before he can be declared a bona fide hit; and Yarmolenko did the business on his first start with two goals and a lively display overall. All healthy additions to the squad on this evidence.

Being hypercritical, the scoreline put a bit of a gloss on things. If Everton had taken one of their chances then it could have been a different story, just as it could have been if we'd taken one of those chances against Bournemouth, Arsenal or Wolves, all of whom are sitting pretty in the top half. Even anticipating a drop back into the bottom three in the weeks ahead, I'm convinced that with our quality we should only be looking upwards. The infamous Class of 2003 testify to the truism that there's no such thing as 'too good to go down' but if the current crop are below the likes of Cardiff, Huddersfield and Newcastle after 38 matches then something will have gone seriously awry. If such a calamity befalls us then we may as well forget the manager and players and quite frankly swap the lot for a shaman to lift the Hammers hoodoo!

The Eighth Wonder

27 September 2018

[West Ham 8-0 Macclesfield]

I don't care that it was *only* Macclesfield. I'm not having it that they're bottom of the Football League and there for the taking. Okay, the first of them is an incontrovertible fact, but another is that in the 30-odd years I've been following them, the Hammers have never before hit eight!

I still recall going slightly giddy at the old BBC vidiprinter showing 7 (seven) (actually written out in brackets so as not to be mistaken for 1!) versus Hull. We've been on the receiving end more often, although even then never to the tune of eight, unless I've somehow blanked that horror show from my memory. Five is fantastic, six is special, anything more is truly extraordinary.

Even with the recent upturn in form and weak opposition, it's fair to say that no one saw that coming. A quick glance at the Sky Sports live report for the first quarter of the match is far more like what we've come to expect:

> 20:05
>
> WEST HAM 0-0 MACCLESFIELD
>
> 18: What a shock to the system that would have been! The hosts have not really got going here.

20:07
WEST HAM 0-0 MACCLESFIELD
20: Still, West Ham opt to go long, but it is not working.

20:09
WEST HAM 0-0 MACCLESFIELD
22: Really subdued atmosphere in the stadium as West Ham continue to struggle. The visitors have plenty of men behind the ball, but look comfortable.

Still, I always had faith that we'd come good. In fact, so blasé was I about this encounter that I didn't check the score again until 75 minutes in, at which point I interrupted the wife's viewing of *Grand Designs* to point dumbstruck at my phone!

If there can be a downside to an 8-0 victory then it's that there were only 25,000 in attendance to relish it. That's not a criticism of the hardcore season ticket holders who are understandably reluctant to fork out an extra 15 quid for a match that seemed to represent, at best, routine progress to round four, at worst one of those mortifying cup moments that are more familiar to us than the glory days. Nevertheless, it's the kind of match that I'd have been all over if I still lived just off Barking Road, too poor to pay for a season ticket or even Category A fixtures, left fighting it out for the general sale tickets against less glamorous opponents. Then again, having recently discovered that my old ex-council house has more than doubled in value to £375,000 in the six years since I sold up, Newham residents these days either have more money than sense or are living on the breadline just to make rent. So the fact that 25,000 souls went out of their way to watch is a success in itself.

This is one that I expect to remember for the rest of my life. I'm just envious of the folk who are able to say, 'I was there when Grady Diangana [I have to be honest, I had to look him up on checking out the line-up before kick-off] scored a brace on his debut.'

Are You Macclesfield in Disguise?

29 September 2018

[West Ham 0-0 Chelsea]

[West Ham 3-1 Manchester United]

A corner was turned against Everton but, this being West Ham, we fully expected them to stumble and fall round the bend. The Chelsea-sized speed bump was rightly approached with caution, then we accelerated into the Red Devils barrier and flew straight through it. Indeed, our first-half display was so assured that I even began thinking, 'We're only one goal behind where we were at this stage against Macclesfield the other night,' instead of worrying that in head-to-heads against Romelu Lukaku/ Anthony Martial alone we're probably on a negative goal difference.

The 'Macclesfield in disguise' dig is actually a bit cruel on the Silkmen, bearing in mind they mustered more shots on target in the first half than the Mancs managed, although Lukaku's header against the post served as a warning of the expected onslaught … which never came. On the rare occasion that he was called upon, Łukasz Fabiański produced a save of the season from Marouane Fellaini. Marcus Rashford's flicked consolation could have heralded a nervy finale. Instead we'd restored a two-goal lead and were playing olé football within five minutes. If we'd picked them off once or twice more in the last ten minutes then it wouldn't have flattered us.

Every single player performed to a high standard but special mention to homegrown talent at opposite ends of the age spectrum. There's been some serious shit spouted from the stands about Mark Noble, a man who bleeds claret and blue. I'm not sure whether the comment that he knows his way around a football pitch should be attributed to Owen Hargreaves, Paul Scholes or Rio Ferdinand – a BT Sport line-up typically weighted in favour of ManUre – but they all know their stuff and it was a spot-on appraisal more complimentary than many of our own have given of late.

Captain Fantastic was ably abetted by his natural successor (should the ongoing contract negotiations not spiral out of control). In contrast to Noble, Declan Rice has seemed at times to be given an easy ride because of his academy status. Don't get me wrong, Rice is a super player but his duck against Arsenal last season was far more quickly excused than it would have been any of our other centre-backs, and in the opening match of this season he looked a little boy lost in the middle of the Anfield pitch. Today he looked every inch the man, constantly snuffing out the threat of an opposition midfield that cost in excess of £130m (ours cost a mere £8m by the way) as well as making efficient use of the ball. I was initially lukewarm about his switching allegiance from the Republic of Ireland to England, not only because I distrust the fluidity with which modern-day sportsmen treat international borders, but on this form he'd easily oust Eric Dier from the Three Lions' holding-midfield role.

Because there's more fight in them than we saw from their insipid band of pink-shirted superstars, the bickering Mourinho and Pogba will undoubtedly hog the headlines, which will be an unfair reflection of the Irons' fine performance. We've had some mighty memorable victories against United over the years but this is the first time I recall us totally outclassing them.

Reflections

4 November 2018

[West Ham 4-2 Burnley]

A minute's silence is intended to give pause for thought. The tragedy that befell Vichai Srivaddhanaprabha and the four others aboard the helicopter that spun out of control after our match at the King Power Stadium last week put Leicester's last-minute equaliser [1-1] into sharp perspective. Yesterday the football world momentarily fell mute to pay its respects. And by 15.05 the murmurings of discontent at grounds around the country had started up again.

As inevitable as death and taxes is the football fan's prerogative to gripe and moan. It's a paradox that belligerent criticism is actually one of the pleasures that the game gives us. Even those who have pumped their blood, sweat, tears and savings into the sport can find themselves targets of those who profess to love it; the outpouring of grief in Leicester shows that Srivaddhanaprabha became well-loved and respected but he certainly wasn't immune from criticism and abuse, especially in the immediate aftermath of the cold-blooded sackings of Nigel Pearson and his even more successful and popular successor, Claudio Ranieri.

Masuaku has been my number-one scapegoat this season but if Arthur were taken from us tomorrow then I like to think I'd remember the player who ran rings around Chelsea rather than the one caught napping by Brighton [Brighton 1-0 West Ham]. More pertinently, when Arthur himself looks in the mirror, I hope that he sees a man capable of a star turn against the big boys rather than someone riddled with self-doubt over his defensive abilities and supporters' criticisms ringing in his ears. Because I know which of these I'd rather see take to the pitch.

Footballers are fallible human beings. Even if we enjoy both placing them on a pedestal and knocking them off it, we must try not to lose sight of their humanity or our own. It's fair enough to criticise but the visit of Burnley for the first time since our open revolt helped to illustrate that it can be equally unfair to write people off.

On that black-letter day against Burnley last season, Gold and Sullivan bore the brunt of our communal displeasure. A summer of unparalleled spending has partly redeemed them in the eyes of many, save at least one brain-dead sociopath who wished online that it had been our owners on board that doomed chopper. However, some of the new blood they've brought in already find themselves *personae non gratae*, while the relative success of others shouldn't automatically relegate past heroes to the status of whipping boys.

Mark Noble and Winston Reid are arguably the club's greatest servants of the past decade. Their service is reflected in their club captain and vice-captain statuses, yet this is strangely used by some as a stick to beat them with. Time catches up with us all and hanging on too long can undoubtedly taint a legacy, just as longevity can cement it.

Which wins out is determined largely by perspective: in the heat of the moment our faculties are impaired, at too great a distance the truth becomes hazy. Bobby Moore and Billy Bonds are rightly revered as legends but that's not to say they didn't have some bad games, eliciting groans from the Chicken Run.

It's a cliché to say that football is a team game, but it is, and when the stalwarts don't step up (or are suspended/injured in the case of Noble and Reid) it presents lesser lights with the opportunity to shine. Felipe Anderson is our club record signing and therefore expected to shine bright every week, yet in recent weeks has looked off the pace and been a target of fan ire. Yesterday he produced a match-winning and widely praised performance. We want to see more of this but bear in mind it's hard enough being always at your best in day-to-day life, never mind when there are highly paid and highly motivated opponents trying to stop you!

Similarly, Michail Antonio has been consistently condemned this season for his lack of subtlety; on the flip side, it was his directness that first endeared him to many of us – Antonio made things happen, even if nobody (himself included) knew in advance what those things might be. In the build-up to yesterday's fourth, he cushioned the ball deftly with that broad chest into the path of Javier Hernández, who duly gave us the two-goal cushion. Chicharito is another who's been regularly derided and hasn't lived up to (unfair?) expectations, yet showed with a neat finish that he can still be of use given the right chances. Then there's the likes of Robert Snodgrass, shipped out on loan to the Championship last season and missed by no one in particular, yet a perpetual motion machine in the middle of the park this season.

There are always two (or more) sides to every story, and that extends to the fanbase. I remain critical of supporter attitudes but that criticism isn't mutually exclusive from an understanding of the frustrations that gave rise to the scenes that blighted Burnley's last visit. Yesterday, the London Stadium appeared to be rocking in a very different sense. We're a pretty fickle bunch! Marko Arnautović quickly went from pariah to pin-up but will be as dead to us as Dimitri Payet if his agitating for a move to Manchester United pays off. But who, at the end of the day, could really blame him? After all, life's as short as a supporter's forbearance.

End-of-Month Review

30 November 2018

Last time out, we took a bit of a hiding from Pep Guardiola's free-scoring artistes. A 4-0 reverse on home soil would normally be a source of spleen-venting all round. Contrarily, a fair portion of attendees seem to have been satisfied with our display, if not the result. The reason being, we took a hiding but we didn't hide.

Countering the best attacking team in the land with an attacking approach of your own might seem foolhardy but Pellegrini's explanation of adopting a big-game mentality and not playing for nil-nils is music to the ears of Hammers fans turned off by Allardyce's regular game plan of shutting up shop from the first whistle. On paper, 0-4 is a thumping that offers no crumb of comfort to armchair fans, but paying witnesses at the London Stadium saw us contribute to an entertaining spectacle of free-flowing football. We can't match Man City but at least we tried. Total football above sensible soccer: that's a return to the West Ham Way, even if it doesn't put points on the board (and never really has).

Speaking of entertaining if ill-fated football, this month saw the announcement of Joe Cole's retirement, following a couple of years of semi-retirement in the States. I don't hold it against the player, who probably ranks second in my personal list of favourite Hammers, that he left for Chelsea, or even that he declared himself a boyhood Chelsea fan. What matters to me is that he left it all on the pitch. It's a team game so no one can be fully absolved for the calamitous underachievement of the 2002/03 relegation season, but Cole (only 21 at the time) comes as close as anyone to absolution. In a team of underperforming senior players, he was hands down Hammer of the Year. Graft is rarely paired with flair but he even took on the role of tenacious-tackling midfielder towards the end. It's just a shame that he never quite lived up to the heights promised by that 9-0 Youth Cup demolition of Coventry. But in the hard-nosed Premier League era, Cole was a bit of a throwback, his ball skills a specimen of pure joy, an example of what makes little boys falls in love with the game in the first place.

If anything, Joe lacked some of the athleticism and perhaps the gamesmanship required to reach the absolute peak of the modern era. In comparison to the way George Best strolled through matches a generation earlier, if Cole had been around in the '60s or '70s to orchestrate things then I genuinely think he'd have been endlessly eulogised and those cup-winning West Ham teams would have been even more special. Grady Diangana's sparkling cameos have been reminiscent of young king Cole and rekindle the thrill of homegrown talent bursting on to the scene and getting bums off seats, a sense of elation that's ever rarer.

Highlight of the month is the long-overdue news that the increase in stadium capacity has the green light. Although there are concerns that it opens the gate to fair-weather fans, any filling of vacant space should enhance atmosphere and I know of fans who still struggle to get tickets despite the pessimistic predictions that we'd never fill our new home. Our 60,000 equals what Arsenal can hold, soon to be overtaken by Spurs (if the new White Hart Lane's ever finished), to then be overtaken by us again once full capacity of 66,000 is rubber-stamped. Good things come to those who wait. And if it pisses on Levy's chips, all the better!

Top of the (Form) Table at Christmas

15 December 2018

[Newcastle 0-3 West Ham]

[West Ham 3-1 Cardiff]

[West Ham 3-2 Crystal Palace]

[Fulham 0-2 West Ham]

Four wins on the trot! Apparently we did it in February 2014 but it feels like uncharted territory.

Tonight's result was the most satisfying of the bunch for me. Not because my father's a Cottager – I have great affection for Fulham and hope they find a way out of their current predicament. But how 'West Ham' would it have been to have gone to the bottom club on the back of an encouraging winning streak and been turned over, gifting them their first clean sheet of the season? Instead, without playing particularly well, we were devastatingly clinical and got the job done with a minimum of fuss. All achieved with an ever-lengthening injury list. Whisper it ... is Pellegrini building a squad capable of something special?

We should remember that this is exactly the same squad that lost four on the bounce at the start of the season. What's changed? Pellegrini's philosophies are obviously starting to take effect. Most significantly, the players look like they believe in themselves, and the fans are with them – pretty much every single one of them was pilloried in August, right now they're all heroes. We'd probably forgive any one of them one bad match and because of that they're playing with confidence, not fear.

I'm eyeing seventh and the European spot that bestows should those above us also claim the cups. If it wasn't for the belief that Man Utd can't get any worse, on current form I'd even say sixth is there for the taking, which, given our lame start and the different stratosphere inhabited by the so-called 'big six', would be a remarkable feat. The winnable run of fixtures stretches into January and I'm more optimistic than I've been in a long time. Roll on 2019!

[Note: we lost our last match before Christmas 0-2 at home to Watford!]

A Farewell to Arns

12 January 2019

Having initially bemoaned spending £20m on Arnie (a snip in today's market, which became astronomically inflated by PSG's eye-watering £200m acquisition of Neymar, but still not exactly the 'peanuts' his meddling brother/agent would have us believe), it was impossible not to warm to the temperamental Austrian as he produced the best and most consistent year of his career in 2018. However, I was never entirely comfortable with the acclaim, bordering on hero-worship, showered on him by sections of the fanbase. He's a cult figure at best and, despite the endearing proclivity to celebrate with the trademark crossed arms, those heavily-inked biceps are never likely to have an Irons tattoo added to them.

While it's true that players don't share the loyalty to a badge that us fans do, I find it hard to accept the prevailing modern-day argument that they're just employees and that any one of us would leave our job in a flash if a rival company came calling with the offer of a higher salary. Firstly, a Premier League footballer's salary can't be weighed against that of the average employee; many of them earn in a week several times the average annual national salary and it would take only a modicum of financial prudence to never have to worry about money again. Secondly, I take umbrage at the suggestion that the world is full of mercenaries. The band of brothers spirit that helped propel underdogs Leicester to Premier League glory and formed the backbone of all the best teams I ever played in has no truck with money-grabbing egotists. I wouldn't begrudge a team-mate or workmate the opportunity to better themselves but would hope that they said their goodbyes having first considered the range of factors that contribute to contentment – family, friends, job satisfaction, status, legacy – and not just counted the digits on their payslip.

It looked today [West Ham 1-0 Arsenal] as if Arnie was saying his goodbyes. I won't go as far as saying 'good riddance' – I'd rather a West Ham team with him in it – but there are several players I'd miss more. Top of that list right now is Declan Rice, a young man who has his career ahead of him, grows in stature every match and who was the difference between us and Arsenal. Oh, and Arnie, that look on Dec's face when he scored the winning goal – that's priceless.

The Iron Ladies

8 March 2019

International Women's Day seems an appropriate time to pay respect to West Ham Ladies. Experiencing their first season in the Women's Super League, they too have taken their fair share of batterings but are on course for a seventh-place finish that the men would be envious of, as well as having the quarter-final of the Women's FA Cup to look forward to later this month. I can't pretend their winning will ever be as meaningful to me as a men's victory but they're part of the West Ham family, so I wish Gilly Flaherty, Kate Longhurst and Alisha Lehmann all the best.

A couple of months ago I don't think I'd have been able to name a single player but *Britain's Youngest Football Boss* has brought them into my living room and has proven a fascinating watch. Casting the ladies as Sullivan Jnr's playthings didn't seem the most auspicious starting point but, in fairness to young Jack, he comes across as a decent, well-meaning lad who's capable of dislodging the silver spoon that's made him managing director of the ladies' team at the tender age of 18. Even if the motivation was to remove Jack from meddling in the men's transfer dealings, we're ahead of the curve in being part of the 11-strong

Women's Super League, which includes Yeovil Town but not Tottenham or Manchester United, although gone are the days when Doncaster Belles were the biggest rivals to Marieanne Spacey's Arsenal – nowadays Manchester City and Chelsea join them in making up a top three that's even more entrenched than the men's top six.

Bung a bit more money the ladies' way, though, and they could make a real splash. Between them, West Ham, West Ham Ladies, England and the Lionesses have to win something one day. I'm happy to spread my support that wide. And watching *Britain's Youngest Football Boss* on my lap has been four-month-old Daisy, who has quite a kick on her and seems more entranced by it than her older brother. So just as my hopes of glory now span several teams, my hopes for a successor are invested in two children. It's great that there are girls' teams springing up all over the place, so Daisy will be as welcome to lace up her boots as James. I hope that the professionalisation of the women's game learns some constructive lessons from the men's, and if their earnings could meet somewhere in the middle, then should either child ever make it, that provides me with two potential pension pots. How's that for equality?!

[2019 FA Women's Cup Final: West Ham 0-3 Man City]

We've Had Our Fun; Put 'em Away Now Lads!

28 April 2019

[Tottenham 0-1 West Ham]

In light of the recent furore surrounding an infamous chant and banning orders issued to those singing it on public transport, is it reasonable to suggest that 'We'll be running round Tottenham …' probably received a few more airings last night? Michail Antonio's suggestive goal celebration might even have put a new slant on such puerile shenanigans!

Yesterday's result was indeed celebrated as if it was our 'cup final', although the fact that the hosts had recently moved out of Wembley and hadn't previously tasted defeat at the new White Hart Lane obviously gave it greater import. As with being the first team to inflict defeat on Arsenal at the Emirates, the boys created a slice of history to be cherished. But let's not get too carried away. The performance, to a man, was superb and, coupled with outplaying Manchester United the other week [Man Utd 2-1 West Ham], bodes well for next season. However, those scalped were possibly distracted by an impending Champions League semi-final. Furthermore, setting aside tribal allegiances, their shiny new home is quite something … those three points feel good right now but, in the grand scheme of things, they're relatively meaningless and most of us would still swap places with Spurs in a heartbeat, in terms of current stature if not heritage and culture.

If we're to instil the 'big-club mentality' that Pellegrini has consistently referenced, then it's time to stop whipping our willies out every time we beat the Lilywhites.

Year Four – 2019/20

The Poor Relations

9 August 2019

Sandwiched between the close of the transfer window and the Premier League curtain-raiser, this morning's sports news should have been eye-catching for a variety of reasons. Yet it was something more humble than the £1.41bn spent this summer or the predictions of glory/grief that stood out above all else and managed to elicit both disappointment and pride in this reader.

Perhaps it's not, strictly speaking, sports news. However, if the sport and the clubs that pay extortionate wages wish to continue espousing the idea of a football family then the amount paid to stewards, cleaners, kitmen and the like is of far greater significance than Everton splashing £35m on an Arsenal squad player. I feel no natural affinity or enmity towards Everton but they rise above Arsenal in my estimation simply for the disclosure that they're one of only four Premier League clubs paying all their employees the living wage, a shameful situation that gave rise to my disappointment. That another of the four is West Ham is the source of pride, albeit muted pride given that paying £9 per hour (£10.55 in London) to service staff is no grand distinction for operations spunking £100,000 per week on middling players. I'm not saying Betty the tea lady is as valuable as Javier Hernández but she quite possibly does more to earn her wage in the average week. Even if Hernández was superhuman, working every hour that God sends and banging in a goal a game, would he really be worth the £863 per hour that his reported salary works out at? If we accept training as work then, being generous, his per-hour pay is probably more like £4,500, which would cover the cost of more than 400 Bettys.

While everything is geared towards what happens on the pitch and giving the top earners the opportunity to showcase what makes them worth so much, would the Premier League superstars flourish if left to clean their own boots in dirt-ridden changing rooms? And would the matchday experience suffer if toilets were filthier and queues for a pint longer still? A single mum slicing pizza is not obviously comparable to a flair player slicing open defences but it could be argued that they're working to the same overall objective: to bring pleasure to supporters and enhance the standing of the football club.

Players are (rightly) praised for championing community projects but few would happily volunteer pay cuts in the event of demotion, leaving the disposable catering staff to pay the price when a minor cut in playing costs would go a long way elsewhere. In what's supposed to be a team game, it would be refreshing to see remuneration linked to team success rather than a source of bragging rights that can lead to splits in the dressing room. How can people at stark opposing ends of the social spectrum possibly be expected to feel part of the same family?

Frankly, if I were a Betty subsisting on minimum wage, I'd frequently feel inclined to spit in the tea of a sulky star striker.

False Start Rather Than Snuff Movie

13 August 2019

[West Ham 0-5 Man City]

Textbook West Ham. Closely match the champions for half an hour, only to run out heavy losers. It was a chastening experience that didn't just dampen new-season optimism, it doused and extinguished it. For the third season running, we prop up the Premier League table after the first round of fixtures.

Optimism giving way to pessimism is par for the course, yet these many precedents should also tell us not to overreact. Outdoing last season's drubbing was certainly not the hoped-for sign of progress and the same weaknesses – an overrun midfield, individual errors, tactical naivety – were worryingly in evidence again. However, Manchester City are likely to take six points off all but a handful of teams so aren't a particularly useful yardstick. With 11 vs 11 from the same elite division, it can seem a cop-out to say that the opponents are on a different level but Manchester City truly are.

Even after repeatedly breaking our transfer record, I'd suggest that only Fabiański, Rice and Diop would realistically merit a place in the Citizens' second-string. Saturday was reminiscent of the treble-winners' swatting aside of Watford in the FA Cup Final [6-0] – neither West Ham nor Watford played abysmally but they were made to look distinctly third-rate, which I guess befits the relative standard of player. The Premier League used to be extolled for its competitiveness but, when Liverpool can finish runners-up having lost one solitary match, it's time to dispel any notion of meritocracy.

Ask again after four matches what the season holds and we'll have a clearer picture. As ever, my personal dream is silverware, based on the hope that the Big Six prioritise the pursuit of Champions League riches over cup glory. However, given that Liverpool and Spurs crave domestic success to further validate their A-list status, the chances appear slim. It's not that long ago that Tottenham's top-four aspirations were mocked and now they're Champions League finalists; Chelsea, Arsenal and Manchester United are all in a state of flux so there's a potential opportunity for a well-run club to gate-crash the upper echelons of the league table but there's no doubt ourselves, Wolves, Everton or Leicester (or any of the other ten) would all be content to be crowned 'best of the rest' and take the prize of Europa League football that almost invariably accompanies seventh spot. Given the uneven playing field, I'd settle for entertaining football and the continuing belief that a cup win is within reach if fortune finally reveals itself.

Déjà Vu

1 January 2020

Pos		Team	P	GD	Pts
15	▼	Southampton	20	-14	**22**
16	▶	Bournemouth	20	-8	**20**
17	▶	West Ham	19	-11	**19**
18	▶	Aston Villa	20	-11	**18**
19	▶	Watford	20	-18	**16**
20	▶	Norwich	20	-19	**13**

Everything changes while some things are eternally monotonous. Such is the paradox of life as a West Ham fan and of life in general. The familiar face returning to the dugout today is less familiar than the ennui of yet another season that's reverted to type by dashing our hopes and expectations before the new year was upon us. Leading Crystal Palace 1-0 in October, we were headed for third place. Then we stopped playing [West Ham 1-2 Crystal Palace]. And we've only restarted in fitful bursts, such as the typically unexpected victory at Stamford Bridge [0-1] that deferred Pellegrini's fate.

I never like to see a manager sacked. Despite being as ambivalent about the Chilean's arrival as I now am about his replacement – who's neither the 'Moyesiah' nor a 'yes man' but deserves some credit for past achievements and was rather shoddily treated by both board and fanbase last time out – Pellegrini's unswerving playing style combined with unprecedented investment managed to raise my expectations until that unfaltering blueprint became his fatal flaw. As with Slaven before him – who's looking quite super again with the Baggies – he was a dead man walking once the atmosphere turned toxic.

And that brings us back to the crossroads, with the fabled 'next level' pointing one way and relegation the other, and David Moyes back in the driving seat. My worry with Moyes is that he's an understudy, filling time before we return to exactly the same point in another season or two. Because we're West Ham, and that's how we roll.

Although the London Stadium appears a false dawn, perhaps we've covertly ascended to the next level already. By tradition we're a yo-yo club, with our place at English football's top table never to be taken for granted. Misplaced or not, would the pre-season talk of top-six contenders ever have been generated without the clout of a 60,000 capacity? We look on enviously at 'lesser' clubs such as Leicester and Wolves currently challenging the big boys but they've each had to suffer lower points than us over the decade. And the secret to their success now? Well, if we knew that then this football management lark would be a doddle. The alchemy between boardroom, dugout, pitch and terrace sadly cannot be bottled.

Right now this season seems a write-off, Premier League survival the only prize. It almost makes me nostalgic for the days in the Championship when things were only just hotting up in January. Relegation, should it happen, really wouldn't be the end of the world. But I genuinely don't think that it will happen because of the quality in our squad; without wishing to utter those famous last words that we're too good to go down, we bloody well should be! The biggest indictment against Pellegrini in recent weeks is that Anderson, Diop and many others were a shadow of what they've been. That's an indictment against the players too but Pellegrini seemed incapable of motivating them in the way that I hope the more workmanlike Moyes can.

And the season's not over yet. Just as I'm reserving judgement on Moyes, I'll reserve judgement on the season when we're only at the halfway point. Although I'd accept the track to mid-table mediocrity, the next two matches could signpost what's in store. In a heavily congested league (Liverpool aside), a morale-boosting win against Bournemouth could be the start of a rapid climb up the table. More importantly, the FA Cup third-round tie away to Gillingham is make or break in ensuring there's a tangible reward to play for. As unlikely as it may seem – especially given our woeful record against lower-league opposition, which both Pellegrini and Moyes are culpable for – FA Cup glory could be the tonic that cures the West Ham curse of fading bubbles and, against all the odds, makes this a season to live long in the memory. That would be so very West Ham.

40 Years and Counting

29 January 2020

[West Ham 0-1 West Brom (FA Cup fourth round)]

Hey ho. Another year down, another hope dashed. And it was terribly obvious from the moment that the draw paired us with Slaven Bilić's Championship-topping West Brom, made even more obvious by their slump (six without a win) since the fourth-round balls were drawn. Need a confidence boost? The Hammers will be happy to oblige!

But who's gonna give us a confidence boost? Bournemouth did their bit by being the only team more out of form than us and gifting us a rousing 4-0 victory on Moyes's return but the new-manager bounce has been otherwise imperceptible. The third-round vanquishment of League One Gillingham was uncomfortable but businesslike [0-2], VAR cruelly denied us an undeserved point at Bramall Lane [Sheffield Utd 1-0 West Ham] and then it was business as usual in the midweek surrender to Leicester: sluggish, careless, uninspiring [Leicester 4-1 West Ham].

Bilić, Pellegrini, Moyes … maybe it's not the manager. Popular theory is that it's all about the people at the top and there's certainly some truth in that. They appoint the manager, they hold the purse strings, they set the tone.

But they don't kick any balls. Ultimately the players have to take responsibility for what happens on the pitch.

Notwithstanding his apparent ineptitude, Carlos Sánchez has 88 caps for Colombia, who always give our nation's finest a stern test. It seems like he's stealing a living on a ridiculous £70k p/w. Seriously, he doesn't look worth it even if you removed the k! So why don't we just pluck someone from the stands to make up the numbers, or at least play the youth team? Believe it or not, there's no such thing as a bad Premier League footballer. But there are plenty of misplaced or dispirited ones.

Take Lanzini. Our 'diamond' hasn't become a bad player overnight but has contributed next to nothing this season and looks a lightweight. Having first excelled and then floundered under both Moyes and Pellegrini, it's impossible to pin the blame on the manager. Form is temporary, class is permanent goes the old adage. But bringing it to the surface? It seems we need an expert in diamond mining.

Pressing the Pause Button

24 March 2020

We live in unprecedented times. That's not to compare coronavirus to a world war or the bubonic plague, merely recognition that modern society – of which the Premier League's global mass-market operation is painfully representative – has never encountered disruption on this level.

Planning for the future feels like a fool's errand given the surreal rapidity with which life has changed since the first match cancellations happened, to the chagrin of many blissfully ignorant fans. I admit to having quickly segued from wry amusement at the prospect of Liverpool being denied the title in the cruellest fashion imaginable to concerned bemusement at what this all means for the sporting calendar. Reality truly kicked in when it became inevitable that my Euro 2020 tickets were going to become void! Football's problems obviously pale into insignificance against those of wider society but the point has been made countless times that football is both a barometer for the world we live in and an antidote to our daily travails. So, what are the solutions to the fix we find ourselves in?

Closed Doors and Cancellations

Baroness Brady was typically outspoken in asserting early on that the current season should be expunged. 'Self-interest' cried many, and rightly so. No matter how much she dresses it up as the right thing to do under the guise of health and safety concerns – and happy as I'd be for a dire 2019/20 season to end with the Hammers sat in 16th place – it's just not cricket, it's more like the type of playground football that ends when the tetchy owner takes their ball home! She's correct to note the original timescale for football to return as one of false hope but to cancel a season at this stage would bring litigation on an industrial scale. There's no love lost between West Ham and Sheffield United but the Blades' dream season would be blunted by a premature conclusion, making them just one of the many losers who could launch legal challenges that would make the Carlos Tevez affair look like chicken feed, with only the lawyers getting fat.

In the eventuality of the season being declared null and void, the floated notion of no relegation and a 22-team top flight incorporating Leeds and West Brom

– the leaders of the Championship but by no means mathematical certainties for promotion – seems more appealing from the insular viewpoint of the Premier League (especially if more fixtures = more broadcasting revenue) but becomes considerably messier as we move down the footballing pyramid.

For Paul Merson (always a finer footballer than thinker), the only problem with shutting down as things stand is Aston Villa's game in hand, as if a trip away to Manchester City were the same as a home match against Norwich. Outcomes are always subject to the vagaries of the fixture list but to relegate a team with nine (or in Villa's case, ten) matches remaining negates all the 'great escapes' of the past.

Gary Neville has suggested a 'festival of football' to raise the nation's spirits, with the season concluded at the earliest opportunity in a short two-week burst. Now, Nev is one of the more engaged and engaging pundits so can surely see the contradiction between arguments for a winter break to avoid burnout (ironically granted in this of all seasons) and the madness of making rusty athletes play every other day by squeezing a quarter of the season into a fortnight. The majority of fans might revel in the return of the people's game but if a fortnight of poor form comes to define your team's season then it's going to feel considerably less festive! It's also weighting things further in the favour of those with a wealth of resources who are able to field reserve teams stronger than another club's first XI.

Then there's the issue of playing behind closed doors. For many this seems to be a necessary evil that could be alleviated by having every match televised. While such a move would be a boon for the broadcasters, we know from watching behind-closed-doors matches such as Bulgaria versus England that they're soulless affairs. Locking fans out is supposed to be a punishment so it doesn't seem the best way of welcoming back the Beautiful Game. Liverpool fans would understandably do whatever it takes to see (or not see, as the case may be) the season completed. But what's the worth of victory with nobody there to celebrate it? Concluding the season in this artificial environment compromises the integrity of the competition and sets the worrying precedent of treating the 12th man as disposable. In my opinion, it's a solution that should be resisted at all costs.

Extra Time

What strikes me about all these 'solutions' is the race to return to normality, to reassert the status quo at the earliest opportunity. As if, once the 2020/21 season begins, the current turmoil can be forgotten. Instead, isn't this a prime opportunity to recalibrate? The 92 of the Football League are already down to 91 thanks to the demise of Bury, and the inequality between the Premier League and the rest grows ever wider. When the Champions League is made as redundant as the Leasing.com (formerly LDV Vans/ Johnstone's Paint/Checkatrade) Trophy, surely it should prompt a rethink?

With current forecasts suggesting that a semblance of normality is unlikely to return before August, something has to give. Although loaded with obstacles – lapsed contracts, broadcasting terms, etc. – my priority would be to finish the current season in as fair a way as possible and then do something different with what would have been 2020/21. Limited movement will have become commonplace so let's make a virtue of it. Regional leagues could offer a more egalitarian approach, the likes of Blackpool and Bolton in the north-west rejuvenated by fixtures against the Manchester clubs, all gate receipts and broadcasting revenue split evenly. Would City and United fans turn out for the visit of Tranmere Rovers? Depends how much they've missed their football. The reverse fixtures would certainly be sell-outs. And when practically the whole of society has been hit in the pocket by coronavirus, reduced ticket prices and travel costs wouldn't go amiss. After an abridged league season, the top teams of each region could enter a knockout format to declare a national champion and a return to the standard league and cups the following season would hopefully be accompanied by a new sense of perspective.

It's a solution that involves those with the deepest pockets acting selflessly but the current situation throws into stark relief the relative insignificance of wealth when survival is at stake. Is it realistic to expect the balance sheets of Football League clubs to supersede the ego of the Premier League? Well, I never thought I'd see the day my old man cancelled his Sky Sports subscription but, with no action for the foreseeable future, that's already happened. Unprecedented times indeed.

I Haven't Felt That Good Since ...

2 July 2020

[West Ham 3-2 Chelsea]

You know that scene in *Trainspotting* where Renton compares an orgasm to Archie Gemmill scoring against the Netherlands in 1978? I think Andriy Yarmolenko may be my Archie Gemmill.

Di Canio's volley was a better goal but nobody saw it coming (not a great analogy for consensual sex) whereas Yarmolenko's winner had that steady build-up to the climax … Diop wins the header … drops to the edge of the D … up goes Souček … gets something on that and then Rice hooks it clear to Antonio … who chests it down and plays in Fornals … who gives it back to Antonio … and Yarmolenko might be through here … and Yarmolenko's been found on the edge of the box … just Rüdiger to deal with … here's Andriy Yarmolenko … and he's SCORED for West Ham United in the 89th minute!

Perhaps not when Chelsea equalised but when Rice hooked it clear we could all see this one coming – Yarmolenko penetrating the acres of space and, once it was on his left foot, only Rüdiger seemed unaware of the explosion to follow as Andriy stroked the ball home.

Unlike Gemmill's solo effort, all those names in the mix risk giving the impression of a gang bang, but that's not entirely inappropriate given that Chelsea have been our bitch this season, from David Martin teasing them (a little bit sadomasochistic, not to mention incestuous with his dad watching on) through to Yarmolenko's cum scene in last night's second blue movie, the fact that we were all watching in the privacy of our own homes only adding to the air of impure vice.

It looks like we're safe so let's hope and pray that the squeals of delight that accompanied the big (Yarmolenk)O weren't premature ejaculations of relief.

Year Five – 2020/21

Diang-Goner

5 September 2020

How many of the young players we've let go in recent years have actually gone on to achieve anything? I preface this entry with that question not to defend the sale of Grady Diangana but to put it in perspective.

Reece Oxford? A reputation and ego built on an excellent but overhyped debut. Reece Burke? Attracting little attention in a relegated Hull City team. Domingos Quina? Increasingly looks as if his career peaked at U19 level. Toni Martínez? A goal machine for our U23s but couldn't cut it at Oxford United. Jeremy Ngakia? Another afflicted with delusions of grandeur after a couple of good first-team appearances.

The point is, how many of these do we regret moving on? It's always hard at the time because of a reluctance to accept that they've not lived up to expectations, like ending a relationship with somebody you once thought could be 'the one'. But we wouldn't take any of them back, with the possible exception of Ngakia, if you could forgive his roving eye. So what makes Grady different? More than the player himself – a promising winger who might dazzle at West

Brom but might just as easily fade into obscurity – it's what he represents. And, more pertinently, what his sale represents to the academy products left behind.

When Moyes stated that he wanted to build a team around hungry young players, eager to reach the next level, it was music to the ears of fans who've had their fill of overpaid has-beens and foreign imports. Looked at objectively, there's logic in selling a winger who spent the past season in the division below for a fee that could amount to £18m, especially when Antonio, Bowen, Anderson, Yarmolenko, Lanzini, Fornals and Snodgrass can all fill a similar berth. The difference is that nobody wants to take any of those players off our hands, at least not on the same terms that we're paying them.

Taking our two record signings by way of contrast, Anderson is blessed with talent but looks fragile and apathetic. If we sent him on loan to the Championship, rather than looking a class above I'd expect him to sink without trace. Diangana's loan spell fulfilled the brief in giving him experience and strengthening him up; he proved himself in an unforgiving testing ground. That's not to say he's going to tear up the Premier League but he looks ready to have a go. Haller runs Anderson close in the apathy stakes (some would say it's the only running either of them do), yet seemed to have struck up an understanding with Grady in pre-season, praising the youngster who provided two assists for his hat-trick against Ipswich. Connections such as this can make or break players, hence Haller, Jović and Rebić all looking shadows of the three who formed Eintracht Frankfurt's magic triangle.

Diang (as he wished to be known) could have been just the tonic we needed. Now it feels as if that tonic's been thrown in our faces.

I'm still not ready to clamber aboard the #GSBOut bandwagon: a) because I don't believe that anyone makes money out of owning a football club; b) for that reason there's not a queue of billionaires lining up to take over; and c) while I can get behind the 'support the team not the regime' mantra, it still adds to the toxicity that seems to constantly surround the club. Much depends on how the transfer window pans out. If Declan Rice leaves, then things will go nuclear. Fans want to see that players care about the club, that they have a connection to it beyond the weekly BACS transfer, which is why academy players are so valued. Noble's honest but possibly ill-considered tweet resonated with many: 'As captain of this football club I'm gutted, angry and sad that Grady has left, great kid with a great future!!!!!' Let's hope Rice's liking and then deleting the tweet doesn't foreshadow his own cutting of ties.

The pledge in the official club statement is that the funds from Diangana's sale, not to be sniffed at in the financially straitened times of coronavirus, will be reinvested in a more balanced squad. Defensive reinforcements are certainly needed and Burnley's James Tarkowski would be a welcome addition. However, the reported offer of a couple million more than we stand to make on Diangana for an England international in his prime at an established Premier League club does little to dispel Sullivan's reputation for having deep pockets but short arms. Messi's complaints of mismanagement at Barcelona ring hollow compared to some of the transfer business we've been subjected to!

Even with last-minute winners against Chelsea and Antonio's four-goal haul against Norwich, it's been a struggle to muster much enthusiasm for football post-lockdown. I was looking forward to watching Diang and, although I doubt his presence would have made much difference to today's embarrassing 3-5 submission to Bournemouth [Betway Cup], that result combined with the reaction to Diang's departure make me less optimistic than ever for the season ahead. Nevertheless, a single signing or goal can make a world of difference and I cling to the hope that pre-season results rarely reflect a season's outcome. And it's faintly possible that Emmanuel Longelo, Jamal Baptiste or some as-yet-unheard-of starlet will have us all saying, 'Grady who?' come May.

A Change in the Narrative

5 October 2020

[West Ham 4-0 Wolves]

[Leicester 0-3 West Ham]

The stories we tell ourselves are powerful. Tell yourself you can do something, you're more likely to achieve it, and vice versa. Take, as a prime example, the uncanny ability of Alex Ferguson's Manchester United to score late winners: he told them it would happen, they believed it, and so did 76,000 people inside Old Trafford. On the unhappier side of the coin, our inability to hold a lead last season was exacerbated by becoming part of the wider narrative.

These are some of the other stories we've been telling recently about West Ham:

1. Moyes is a clueless dinosaur.
2. The squad is threadbare.
3. The owners are bleeding us dry.

Needless to say, there are two sides to every story:

i. He's twice overseen a general upturn in our fortunes and serial underachievers don't get the opportunity to manage Manchester United.

ii. There was £100m of talent among yesterday's substitutes.

iii. The fees paid for the aforementioned aren't loose change. If they were really in it for the money then Rice would have been sold by now and, quite frankly, good luck to anyone trying to make money from football in the current climate.

The truth, invariably, lies somewhere in between.

Every transfer window, the big stories revolve around the comings and goings, the new blood. Starved of stories, supporters feel starved of oxygen, yet it needn't be this way. Granted, new arrival Vladimír Coufal provided quite a story – knocked out of the Champions League on Wednesday, signed on Thursday, spanking the early-season form team on Sunday – but his solid performance was only a footnote in a team that played as if it was full of new signings compared to the sombre opening-day performance against Newcastle [0-2].

It's sadly true that familiarity breeds contempt and I'm happy to admit that I'd have jettisoned Angelo Ogbonna and Arthur Masuaku at the end of the 2018/19 season. However, reinvented as a wing-back (or perhaps finally played in the only position that really suits him), Masuaku looks quality and for the past six months or so Ogbonna has looked better than the one we signed from Juventus. The search for a centre-back continues but, as part of a back three, the much-derided Cresswell has never looked out of place; his ability to step into more advanced positions and deliver deep crosses like the one that Antonio dispatched against Leicester would have us purring if he'd just been sold to us as a multi-million-pound *libero*. Likewise, Antonio has rightly been earning rave reviews but there are still some who carp that he's not a natural centre-forward; if Haller were only able to scare defences in the way that Antonio has been, no one would even think of quibbling over the £45m price tag of our 'out-and-out striker'!

The story that Haller needs to be telling himself (and Anderson, Lanzini, etc.) is that they have the quality to supplant those who look undroppable right now. Form is temporary, class is permanent, yet football is such a confidence game that even the classiest of performers can start to look like donkeys if there's a constant feed of negative stories around them.

Of course, stories don't come from nowhere. #GSBOut is trending because mismanagement has been rife and overpaid prima donnas have given us a fair few shitshows. However, stories can be full of twists – in the space of a week, the narrative for the season has gone from being a fight for survival to something far more optimistic. The story of our first seven matches was supposed to be set by the corresponding fixtures from last season, which would have left us with zero points come November. As it is, we can afford to lose the next three and still be significantly better off than many expected. But there I go again with the negative plotlines. Why should we lose to Tottenham, Manchester City or Liverpool? The narrative has been significantly disrupted by Covid-19 – where, once, teams went to Old Trafford and Anfield telling themselves they had no chance, the removal of 50,000-plus storytellers is beginning to make a mockery of home advantage. The mood-shifting performances and results against Wolves and Leicester only amount to a couple of paragraphs but, if the players can write a full chapter, maybe fans will start to believe that legends can be made and not just bought.

There's No Business Like West Ham Business

17 October 2020

During the Diangana hoo-ha I said that I'd reserve judgement until our transfer business was concluded. And the verdict now that it has been: underwhelmed, if I'm honest. But that's not necessarily a bad thing. West Ham fans tend to react badly to raised hopes, despite the inevitability of disappointment being clearly communicated by 'I'm Forever Blowing Bubbles'. On the flipside, whenever we're not expecting much, the team tend to be capable of springing pleasant surprises. So, to business ...

Coufal looks a solid purchase at a bargain price but I remember opining that Sam Byram, after an assured debut, could prove our right-back solution for the next decade, so any judgement after a single match is hopelessly premature.

Which means I'm in no position to judge Saïd Benrahma less than 24 hours after he put pen to paper. I will, though, admit to being sceptical. His stats from the Championship are undoubtedly impressive and many before him have shown that the step up isn't as big as many make out. However, the one time I watched him for Brentford, in the play-off final, he made zero impact against a Fulham team that look like being this season's whipping boys. Then again, his highly rated strike partner

Ollie Watkins equally drew a blank that night but managed a hat-trick against Liverpool last week [Aston Villa 7-2 Liverpool]! Fingers crossed he'll be a Riyad Mahrez rather than a Sofiane Feghouli.

In fairness, the other reservation I have over the Benrahma signing has nothing to do with the man himself. Nor with the last-minute renegotiation to a loan deal with an obligation to buy should the concerns raised by his medical come to nothing. Rather, it's to do with our general transfer strategy. The Diangana sale was reasonably explained by our surplus of wingers but, having then dispensed with our star signing of yesteryear in Felipe Anderson, it's fair enough to question the logic of offloading players with stronger credentials than the one brought in at greater expense. Benrahma might prove to be twice the player but it would once have been thought eccentric to expect more of a lower-league Algerian than a Brazilian international! And it makes me sympathise more with Diangana over his ejection. After all, he'd impressed intermittently in the Premier League when given the chance and delivered for West Brom who, despite the plaudits afforded to Brentford and Benrahma, actually won promotion. The penny-pinching allegations made against Gold and Sullivan don't add up but the accusations of mismanagement certainly do.

So the money raised from the Diangana sale, earmarked for a centre-back, was blown on a direct replacement. And at centre-back we get on loan somebody who's been relegated in successive seasons. While not holding him accountable for the failings of West Brom and Watford, I wouldn't exactly call Craig Dawson a good-luck charm either. More worryingly, some Watford fans were pleased to see the back of him, but he has a general reputation as a 6/10 player who will hopefully provide solid back-up.

The one that got away, I fear, is going to be cheering on the enemy tomorrow. Joe Rodon is the Championship youngster we should have gone for and were heavily linked with before Tottenham made their move. Every signing is a gamble to some extent but we could have got this guy for less than we received for Diangana. Unproven but with huge potential, I like what little I know about him and think he has the quality to have easily usurped James Collins as our favourite Welshman and been a fixture at the back for the next decade. Then again, I said that about Byram.

Black Lives Matter

'We were the Three Degrees six years before the West Brom trio' (google it) is a recommended read for anyone who wants an idea of what our club and community stand for. The reason that Clyde Best, Clive Charles and Ade Coker aren't as famous as Cyrille Regis, Brendon Batson and Laurie Cunningham is that, in typical West Ham style, they weren't as good! Clive's big brother John, though, should be recognised as a pioneer, a quality footballer who partnered Bobby Moore and would have been an FA Cup and UEFA Cup winner were it not for injury, and a thoroughly decent bloke to boot. There have been better players but, all things considered, a mark of honour wouldn't be out of place.

On the topic of black history though, as far as taking the knee goes, I'm with Sir Les – it's become a hollow virtue-signalling gesture that means less and less the longer it goes on. The return of fans would be a litmus test of its reception from the general public but I fancy that it will be conveniently disregarded in time for that equally seminal moment. Although I sympathise to some extent with the under-representation of BAME faces in boardrooms and dugouts, this is a reflection of society that will evolve in time, just as players of all colours and creeds are now the norm. Yes, we can use things like the Rooney Rule to give progress a nudge but any form of tokenism is largely self-defeating. And sport is (even taking into account financial doping) the most meritocratic of arenas – with a 'win at all costs' mantra, skin colour is secondary to skillset and a black Jürgen Klopp would be in demand just as much as the white one.

Scenes!

18 October 2020

[Tottenham 3-3 West Ham]

Well that was probably the most Spursy game we've ever had the pleasure of watching!

> **spursy** adj.
> To consistently and inevitably fail to live up to expectations. To bottle it.
> *My team only got to the last 16 – they're a bit spursy.*
> #fail #soft #frustrating #crap #losers

Careful not to rub it in too much, though, because the West Ham Way is almost a synonym for Spursy. Some people will say it was a game of two halves that saw the best and worst of both teams. While that might be true of Spurs, perhaps the most heartening aspect for me was that I thought we performed quite consistently. That sounds absurd when we were 3-0 down within 15 minutes and scored all our three in the last ten. However, by the time they scored their second, as early as it was, we'd already created four chances. It's difficult to judge a football match as a contest when the scoreline is as one-sided as it was here for 81 minutes but it impressed me that the players stuck to their task. Granted, I wouldn't have been publicising that if it had remained 3-0, although in the more promising days of the Pellegrini reign I said something similar after we were thumped by Man City.

It remains as true as ever that goals change matches and today we got our just reward – both players and the fans who stuck it out when they'd have been tempted to switch off in the 16th minute. As disheartened as I was then, though, I've seen us play far worse than we were at that point. The defending could have been better but sometimes you have to hold your hands up and say we were being dismantled by a world-class performance from Harry Kane. Yet it's notable that, commentating for Sky Sports, Jamie Carragher praised Kane's defensive contribution when naming him man of the match in the 89th minute. I wrote recently about the significance of narratives and Carragher's narrative was that West Ham were awful in the first half and better in the second. Although I'm wary of stats, they don't entirely back this up. Be wary too of overly simplistic narratives.

And hopefully this is the start of a new chapter for Manuel Lanzini. Our 'diamond' has been looking blunt for quite some time but there's no better polish than a goal-of-the-season contender in such dramatic circumstances! Manu's problem is that even that's not a route back into a team that should be buzzing after recent results and performances. Yet all our subs proved their worth in the short time Moyes gave them today; that's all anyone can ask and the whole squad seemed to have bought into the lesson that football continuously teaches us: keep the faith! It's a pity the celebratory scenes on the pitch weren't reflected in the stands but be patient, our time will come.

KEEP OUT!

27 November 2020

Having expressed deep reservations about the return of football to empty stadiums, surely it would be perverse to be equally sceptical about the return of fans after a nine-month absence? On the contrary, my anxieties spring from the same source, namely the compromised integrity of the competition.

On the face of it, being the first Premier League team to welcome supporters back into the stands, as we'll be when we host Manchester United on 5 December, should be a boon. So why am I left joyless by the prospect? Kicking off before us that weekend are Aston Villa vs Newcastle, Burnley vs Everton and Man City vs Fulham. All played out in empty stadiums because of the geographical tiers that the home teams find themselves in. Is that fair? I certainly wouldn't think so if Newham was placed in tier 3 and our rivals were able to welcome back fans but we weren't. And the arbitrary nature of the government's tier system is a whole other issue; when Manchester has an R rate under 1 and falling but is locked in tier 3, whereas London has an R rate above 1 and rising but is conveniently classed as tier 2, one could cynically suggest that our capital is being shielded out of capital interests!

It's strange to find myself siding with Gary Neville, especially in a debate with West Ham vs Man Utd at the centre of it, but then it's a topsy-turvy time: quarter of the way through the season and we somehow, despite a torturous-looking fixture list, find ourselves above Man Utd, Man City and Arsenal. As the lesser team, maybe Man U do need all the help they can get! Sympathy is naturally limited for the Manchester clubs, who hold enough of a financial advantage over others, but, in seriousness, the likes of Burnley, Sheffield Utd and West Brom could do without having the odds stacked further against them.

It could be argued, in mitigation, that 2,000–4,000 fans won't make much of a difference anyway. Which may well be true. Although Turf Moor (capacity 21,944) would seem fuller than the London Stadium. To think we used to fuss about 2,000–4,000 empty seats! The latest press release about ticketing ignores the rumoured guidelines about not singing, chanting or shouting, which, if true, is an absolute nonsense and would make me question whether it's worth having anyone back under such circumstances anyway. Don't get me wrong, I desperately want fans back, but only under the right conditions, not as zombie spectators.

Having bemoaned the perceived (dis)advantage of (not) having fans present, West Ham (typically) could be an exception to the rule! Data from the matches played during the enforced absence supports the hypothesis of the 12th man, with away teams faring significantly better than usual. In West Ham's case, though, particularly in recent years, the 12th man can sometimes weigh us down. The players seem to be much better drilled since Lockdown

1.0 but they also appear unburdened, the hostilities and anxieties of 60,000 supporters lifted from their shoulders.

West Ham fans can be brilliant: I still remember the 1991 FA Cup semi-final when Keith Hackett played as Nottingham Forest's 12th man but we out-sang their supporters even at 4-0 down. It was a formative experience in my early years of football watching and it made me proud to be a Hammer. When we're united, there's no better bunch. But the antagonism towards our own can also go unrivalled. Maybe it's two sides of the same coin, passion imprinted in different forms, but we're currently faring better without them, so from an entirely selfish perspective – especially given the unfettered TV coverage I can enjoy up north – I say again, all fans should stay home!

How Do You Solve a Problem Like Séb Haller?

31 December 2020

Is Sébastien Haller any good? Anyone watching the highlights wouldn't be able to square what they see with the negativity they read in online comments sections. One can only assume we bought him on the basis of a highlights reel rather than any thorough scouting report. For there's no denying that Haller has some ability – as proven by his record at Eintracht Frankfurt and some brilliant goals for us – but the problem is fitting him into the West Ham Way.

The big fella's not helped by any comparison to the injury-stricken Michail Antonio's rich vein of form either side of the season restart. Our recently converted No. 9 isn't always the most cultured or prolific but, whatever position he's played, his effort can never be faulted. In many ways Haller is the anti-Antonio. Lacking mobility, lacking speed, lacking strength, his industriousness pales in comparison. Antonio lacks four inches in height against Haller yet is far more potent in the air than a goliath who appears to turn aerial challenges into a charade by feigning to jump. I've heard Haller termed 'trampoline feet', which unfortunately refers to his inept hold-up play rather than a mighty spring. The wonder strikes against Sheffield United [0-1] and Crystal Palace [1-1] would go some way towards masking his overall lack of contribution if Antonio hadn't been offering the full package.

There's an old axiom that it's better to be an exceptional scorer of goals than a scorer of exceptional goals. British fans will generally take either to their hearts, so long as the goals are accompanied by effort. We appreciate workhorses like Vladimír Coufal – man of the match against Palace – who wear their heart on their (rolled-up) sleeve. By contrast, Haller's moody listlessness is classically French (even if he's given up hope of a senior call-up to Les Bleus and defected to the Ivory Coast) and wins him no admirers in the East End.

And How Do You Solve a Problem Like VAR?

I'm equally losing patience with the VAR virus, whether it's going for us (Ollie Watkins' late disallowed 'equaliser' for Villa) or against (Man Utd's out-of-play equaliser or Leeds' retaken penalty). It was easier to take the rough decision-making with the smooth when it didn't make such a pretence of being perfectly precise.

The crux is, do we want matches to be refereed forensically or with a human touch? I'd sway heavily towards the latter: sometimes it seems fairer to judge an innocuous edge-of-the-area challenge as undeserving of an odds-on opportunity to add to the goal tally, even if it would be a foul anywhere else on the pitch. Similarly, I prefer referees to have a word rather than reach straight for the cards.

In a fairly feeble defence of VAR, Gary Neville made an analogy to the fractions and fine margins that can decide other sports, such as a 100m race. While it's true that small gains make a big difference at an elite level, to compare individuals running in straight lines for ten seconds with a team contact sport lasting an hour and a half is disingenuous at best. Football is messy and chaotic; the ability of coaches and players to turn that into something approaching an art form is where much of the appeal lies.

I agree with Neville that technology still has a part to play. Nobody would dispense with the Hawkeye technology that's been almost 100 per cent accurate in determining whether the ball has crossed the goal line or not. The problem with VAR is that it's become too intrusive, as always feared, and ceased to be about correcting clear and obvious errors. The miscarriage of justice now occurs when goals are chalked off for minor infringements that nobody on the pitch has noticed – you know it's gone too far when it's not just fans at a distance but the players on the pitch who are bemused by decisions.

My own solution would be twofold. Firstly, put the onus on the players, as those with the best feel for the game, to question decision-making. As with cricket and rugby, this would give greater tactical responsibility to captains. However, there's no doubt that some appeals would amount to a tactical ploy to slow down and disrupt. As with tennis, recourse to VAR would therefore be limited to three appeals per team per match. Secondly, speed things up by sticking to the clear and obvious. Do away with all the arbitrary line-drawing for offside and stop looking at fouls in slow motion from multiple angles; if a mistake isn't immediately apparent in replay then the original decision stands. Linked to this, increase transparency by making the decision-making process audible. As in rugby, there will remain an element of subjectivity but players and fans will accept an official giving a reasoned explanation of how they see it and why. Pundits don't always agree but they can disagree respectfully and see the others' point of view. Then again, the *Times* correspondent from the Leeds match [Leeds 1-2 West Ham] awarded Haller a higher player rating than Rice, which reveals either the highly subjective nature of the game or someone doing an even more half-arsed job than Séb!

Mid-Term Report

26 January 2021

WHU has made significant progress this year. Effort and attitude show marked improvement, with the conscientiousness of newcomers having a positive impact on the collective. Squad fitness has contributed to consistency but there's also sufficient cover in most key areas. The usual aberrations have been largely eliminated from performances, leading to strong results that place them above some of the usual high achievers. Keep it up!

- ★ Professionalism is evident in a cup run that balances optimism with pragmatism.
- ★ Raised standards and resilience embedded.

- ⊙ Could be more assertive and forward-thinking against inferior opponents, e.g. Brighton.
- ⊙ Use a proven goalscorer to convert chances.

Moyes Versus Manuel

5 February 2021

Manuel Pellegrini received a warm welcome from fans and the relationship grew ever frostier. With David Moyes, the reverse has been true. And I know which way round I prefer.

Succeeding Moyes, Pellegrini seemed like a step up. A Premier League winner. A class act. He was the big name that fans craved, even if there was a sneaking suspicion that the Chilean returning from China had already settled into semi-retirement. He brought a big-club mentality, setting out his stall by focusing on our style of play and not conceding any ground to the opposition. This was an approach I praised even after a heavy home defeat proved that Pellegrini's old club, Manchester City, were in a different class to us.

Wednesday's impressive victory [Aston Villa 1-3 West Ham] highlighted a stark contrast between the approaches of Pellegrini and Moyes and, in hindsight, it's clear which works best.

After the passive performance against Liverpool last weekend [West Ham 1-3 Liverpool], there were groans when the team selection was announced and Jarrod Bowen had been sacrificed for Ryan Fredericks: ignoring the fact that the lightning-quick Fredericks is a converted winger and Bowen, for all his endeavour, hasn't been as effective of late, two right-backs suggested a defensive stance. The point, of course, wasn't to sit back but to nullify Jack

Grealish on the left-hand side, through whom all Villa's good stuff goes. And it worked a treat, largely thanks to a terrier-like performance from first-choice right-back Vladimír Coufal but ably assisted by the man he's usurped. Meanwhile, the rest of our players went about dominating the rest of theirs. It was never a case of parking the bus as Allardyce was and is still prone to do. Pellegrini, I think it's fair to say, wouldn't have afforded Grealish the same level of respect and would have attempted to outgun the opposition, which isn't to say the result would have been any different but it's no coincidence that the commentators assessed it as an off-day for Villa, which I think did our players and manager a disservice. Similarly, it's no coincidence that our own off-days are ever more rare; this season, for the first time in a long time, every player seems to know what their job is and is confident in doing it.

Moyes has sensibly talked about changing the mentality and building gradually, comparing the club to a tanker that needs turning. Gold and Sullivan hoped they could hand control to Pellegrini and he'd sail it as smoothly as he did the Man City ship but Moyes seems to understand more clearly how the tanker handles. The big-club mentality is still there but Moyes has a go-slow, safety-first approach to it. That doesn't necessarily make him a better manager. It's more about right manager, right club, right time.

Ditto the Players

My first impression of Jesse Lingard when he made his breakthrough at Manchester United was that he was an irritating little prick. But the testimonies of coaches who know him much better say otherwise. Still, I'll be honest, I wasn't sure where he was going to fit with us and he didn't seem to represent what we needed. For whatever reason, his face doesn't fit anymore at United either but there's undoubted quality in his boots and the big question for me was whether we were getting Jesse Lingard the footballer or JLingz the promoter. That seems to have been answered in one impressive debut. He definitely looked to be on the same wavelength as Antonio, who could also be misconstrued as a pain in the neck, but misdemeanours like crashing a Lamborghini into someone's wall while dressed as a snowman are forgiven as long as he's performing on the pitch.

Reputations can be easily won and lost. It's only two seasons ago that Lingard was part of a popular England team that reached the World Cup semi-finals. And now we're turning our noses up at him. Links to another member of that team, John Stones, were scoffed at in the summer but he's now the defensive heart of a resurgent Manchester City and looks nailed on to reclaim his England place after a prolonged period out in the cold. We got excited about Anderson and Haller yet thought we were scraping the barrel with the surprisingly brilliant Craig Dawson. Turns out that both transfers and managerial appointments obey William Goldman's disconcerting observation of Hollywood: nobody knows anything!

Life's Good (When Your Team Is)

16 February 2021

Team	P	GD	Pts	Form
Man City	23	32	**53**	WWWWWW
Man Utd	24	19	**46**	LDWDD
Leicester	24	16	**46**	DLWDW
Chelsea	24	16	**42**	DWWWW
West Ham	24	9	**42**	WLWDW
Liverpool	24	13	**40**	WWLLL

If you'd told me before a ball was kicked that we'd be above Liverpool in mid-February then I'd have assumed Covid had struck again to curtail the 2020/21 season. And even that would have stretched credibility given the daunting start to our fixture list! So right now is a bit of a 'pinch yourself' moment.

I was vocal in my opposition to Project Restart and I still think that the Beautiful Game has an awful long way to go to sort its priorities and get its house in order. It does, however, retain its power to divert and entertain and, boy, has such leisure been in short supply over the past year. Then again, there are welcome and unwelcome diversions. Televised coverage of every Hammers match has been a boon, yet in previous seasons I probably would have considered it a slog. I'll support them through thick and thin but it's not always, or even often, fun; even though hope springs eternal, I'm accustomed to expecting the worst when I switch on and that's why I respect anyone who spends a chunk of their hard-earned income on the 'privilege' of having a seat for every match.

This has been one of those rare seasons when 90 minutes of West Ham generally raises the spirits. If, however, it were the typical relegation-threatened season then I'm not sure I could face that on top of everything else. My sympathies therefore lie with supporters of Sheffield United, West Brom, Fulham, Newcastle and Burnley, all of whom have little to cheer besides desperate survival. Worse still, in the lower leagues literal survival is on the line, with the National League North – which my local team Chester belong to – having just been cancelled because clubs can't meet running costs without fans. But let's not dwell on the bad, let's focus on the good …

First things first, we're already safe from relegation! Not mathematically perhaps but, given the travails of others, I think it will take closer to 30 points to stay safe this season rather than the magical 40 mark that we surpassed last night [West Ham 3-0 Sheffield Utd]. Still, I'm not going to get carried away with dreams of the Champions League, not only because the Champions League represents the corporate greed that's taken a wrecking ball to domestic leagues (though don't get me wrong, I wouldn't turn down a ticket to the San Siro or Camp Nou!). Maintaining our pre-eminence over Chelsea, Liverpool and Spurs is highly unlikely. Chelsea duly knocked us out of the top four after a matter of hours but that's hardly a cause for brooding when you're more used to battling with Crystal Palace and Watford for capital bragging rights than sitting atop the lot.

Regardless of the final outcome, what's really made this season refreshing is the atypical consistency and control displayed, to the degree that I don't think I've ever witnessed its like before. Case in point, last night's handsome victory was a mediocre, workmanlike performance, and that's not to damn the boys with faint praise but to marvel at their efficiency, typified by the engine room of Declan Rice and Tomáš Souček. We've coped admirably without other key players such as Ogbonna and Antonio but should either of these two face a period on the sidelines – as threatened by Souček's risible red card against Fulham – then we could quickly fall away from European contention, especially given the congestion of places 4 to 10.

The shame of such a promising season is that, while fans such as myself have enjoyed it remotely, there's no one cherishing it in the flesh. I've written before that fans would take the stadium to their hearts more easily if we made some more favourable memories there. The paradox is, would the players be displaying the calm and control that's brought such success if there were 60,000 previously disgruntled supporters present?

Noble to the End

10 March 2021

noble *adj.*

1. belonging by rank, title or birth to the aristocracy.
2. having or showing fine personal qualities or high moral principles.

Back in early 1993, my old man gave me a bollocking (and justifiably so) for disrespecting the memory of the late, great Bobby Moore. The context: I volubly complained about local newspaper *The Post* carrying yet more back-page headlines on the recent passing of Moore. My excuse: I was only 12 and Bobby Moore seemingly belonged to another, bygone world. That and the fact that, in those days, the only sources of team and transfer news were newspapers, Ceefax and the premium rate phonelines advertised in the aforementioned freesheet. Shamefully, I was more interested in the fitness of Trevor Morley than the death of a legend. Luckily, Dad's not even a Hammer and was, with Bobby, on the losing side of the 1975 Cup Final so has less rosy memories of the man whose memory he defended, which perhaps saved me from a literal kick up the backside as well as the metaphorical one that got meted out.

My petulant, far-from-noble gripe stemmed from a preoccupation with the here and now. And Mark Noble's open letter to fans reminded me of that parental correction. He doesn't, thankfully, display the same anger – that would be unnoble – but in subtly reminding everyone of the bond he has with the club he's hopefully stemmed the vitriol and disrespect shown to him from some quarters. And that disrespect comes from the same place as my own to Moore: revering the present at the expense of the past. The implicit admission from the man himself that he's been usurped by better players and a recognition of his own shelf life should stop everyone disparagingly pointing out that he's lost a yard of pace, which was never his strong suit in the first place. With an end-date attached to his West Ham playing career, the contract extension has suddenly gone from a stick to beat him with to a long goodbye in which the focus has switched from his shortcomings to a recognition of his significance.

On the topic of those perceived shortcomings, let's be clear: Noble is a consistent, adaptable midfielder who continues to make the most of his varied but limited talent. Legends come in different guises. He hasn't attained the level of Bobby because he hasn't won a World Cup, FA Cup or European Cup Winners' Cup. But I'd place him in the same bracket as Paolo Di Canio and Julian Dicks as someone who's given his all and set high standards over a meaningful period of time. Billy Bonds bridges the two tiers thanks to his appearance record and FA Cup medals but there are certainly similarities between Bonds, Dicks and Noble in their lack of international recognition and committed style – we don't think of Noble as a 'hard man' but he takes no nonsense from either players or extremist fans!

Let's also be clear that the contract extension isn't some eked-out retirement gift. Rice and Souček are above him in the pecking order and squad upgrades will probably be sought in the summer, especially if there's a European campaign in the offing, but Noble remains valued as a player and leader, with a key contribution to make, *especially* if there's a European campaign in the offing. There's little room for sentiment in the modern game, which makes Noble's durability all the more impressive. Football is a game of opinions and a player's fortunes can twist and turn with managerial comings and goings but eight permanent managers now have made him a pillar of the first team – that's almost half the managers in West Ham's history who've recognised a value that shouldn't diminish with age. The open letter stops short of announcing retirement; even if he feels that a playing career can be prolonged elsewhere, it's imperative that – unlike Bobby Moore, who was slighted by the West Ham and FA top brass as well as my 12-year-old self – Mark Noble always has a place at West Ham United.

Hammers of the Year

12 March 2021

Although I wouldn't wish to denigrate any former Hammer of the Year as the best of a bad bunch, it probably is fair to say that the higher-quality winners tend to pick themselves. This year, however, must be the most hotly contested award I've ever known. There's still time for heroes and villains to emerge but, with nearly three-quarters of the season gone, these are the contenders and the odds I'm giving …

Łukasz Fabiański – 10/1

2019's Hammer of the Year has been dependable but nothing special; has made the saves you'd expect him to, which is no bad thing as a decent team shouldn't be relying on regular heroics from their last line of defence.

Angelo Ogbonna – 4/1

Last year's runner-up was an absolute rock until injury struck, and it's only our continued solidness in his absence that undermines his cause.

Aaron Cresswell – 5/1

2015's winner has been much-maligned in recent times but he has more assists than any other defender in the Premier League and his ability to switch between full-back and centre-back has been key to Moyes's tactical plans.

Vladimír Coufal – 3/1

Would walk the award for Bargain of the Season, but walking's not Vlad's style. The upturn in the season pretty much coincided with his arrival; he's not had a bad match and has had several stonkers, most notably his taming of Jack Grealish. A cult hero in the making, if he could add goals and assists to his forays upfield then we'd have arguably the world's best on our hands.

Craig Dawson – 4/1

Didn't make his debut until 29 December but that man-of-the-match performance against Southampton has been followed by one after another. Everyone would have laughed at the suggestion of an England call-up at the start of the year and some are still laughing now, but I can't believe there's been a more in-form centre-back in 2021.

Declan Rice – 5/1

The incumbent hasn't let his standards drop. If anything, his passing has become more expansive and his driving through midfield reflects the team's forward progress. The only demerit is that this is no less than we've come to expect from our own Captain Marvel.

Tomáš Souček – 3/1

Being fêted as the best box-to-box midfielder in the Premier League and linked with Barcelona. His pairing with Rice is spot-on. Plus, he brought us Coufal.

Michail Antonio – 5/1

Reinvented as a centre-forward over the past two years, his skillset is integral to our style of play. If only those hamstrings would hold up!

Jesse Lingard – 8/1

Even more of a latecomer than Dawson but another whose current form has prompted talk of an England recall. If he can be the spark that cements a European place then there could be more honours to follow for Manchester United's cast-off.

Punching Down

21 March 2021
[West Ham 3-3 Arsenal]

In a season of overachievement, it would be churlish to criticise the management or players. On the other hand, squandering a three-goal lead is always a bitter pill to swallow. Especially when it's self-inflicted by a pattern of play that's become depressingly familiar against the so-called bigger clubs.

Asked by an Arsenal-supporting friend how excitable I'd been during the 90 minutes, I summed it up thus:

0–30 Ecstatic

30–60 Nervous

60–90 Irritable

In that first period we gave them no breathing space. We played on the front foot, with an intensity that the Gunners couldn't live with, although the lethargy of the opposition played its part – it's worth remembering that both teams contribute to the flow of a match. The nervousness kicked in because, even at 3-0, I know better than to take victory for granted!

Protecting what you have is often instinctive, but it's this mentality that fans have the right to bemoan. Last week against Manchester United we tried to protect a nil-nil and were only undone by an own goal. It wasn't pretty but, as Jamie Redknapp astutely observed from the commentary box, the approach would be judged purely on the result. What was frustrating today was the inability or reluctance to get back on the front foot; instead, we surrendered ground and invited pressure. Even in victories against Burnley, West Brom, Sheffield United, Crystal Palace, Aston Villa and others, I've been uneasy for the last 20 minutes, but I put that down to being a particularly anxious armchair viewer; for the most part, we've been impressively controlled and seen out matches with relative comfort. But when the opposition boast players of real pedigree and can bring a £72m attacker off the bench, sitting back is a fool's game. The defensive substitutions irritated because, although understandable, they handed all impetus to the opposition for the game's climax.

Arsenal's mid-table position isn't a true reflection of their talent, as shown by their recent dismantling of Leicester and Spurs. Unfortunately, aside from the blistering start, we played like a team who believe that their superior league standing is also a falsehood.

We're On Our Way to Europe

6 April 2021

[Wolves 2-3 West Ham]

Team	P	GD	Pts	Form
Man City	31	45	**74**	WLWWW
Man Utd	30	25	**60**	DDWWW
Leicester	30	19	**56**	LDWWL
West Ham	30	11	**52**	LWLDW
Chelsea	30	16	**51**	DWWDL
Spurs	30	19	**49**	WWLWD

I think it's fair to say that last night's hard-earned three points was the least I've ever enjoyed a 3-2 victory! Why? Following straight on from the submission to Arsenal and its uncanny similarities, it was a little more than the heart could handle. And also because of what's on the table ...

I make no pretence that we are or should be a Champions League team but, on the other hand, we're where we deserve to be after 30 matches, and that's currently in a position to qualify for next season's premium competition. It's all very congested so we could have ended yesterday anywhere between fourth and eighth; I'd happily take the median position.

Whatever happens, we're on course for one of the best league finishes in our history and amazingly some fans are still overly critical – of tactics, of management, of individual players or performances. Even in the best of seasons, there will always be bumps in the road. No team has achieved perfection, even the record breakers of Manchester City and Liverpool who we're now mixing it with. Personally, I consider any of those rare occasions where we can boast a positive goal difference to be a season of triumph, and we'd have to capitulate far beyond what even ardent Hammers expect for that not to be the case come the end of May.

Expectations were understandably dampened by Declan Rice's injury suffered on England duty – damn you again international gods of wounded fate who have already stolen Dean Ashton and an in-his-prime Manuel Lanzini from us! There's no ready-made replacement for our star player but we'd have been incredibly lucky if his formidable partnership with Tomáš Souček had lasted every minute of every match. Mark Noble did a solid job replacing the man who's replaced him as regular team captain. And perhaps, especially on recent form, Declan's injury will be a blessing in disguise in making attack our best form of defence.

As against Arsenal, we were devastating for 30 minutes at Molineux. The opening goal in particular was exquisite; widely credited as a solo effort by red-hot Lingard, it owed plenty to Coufal's composed defending, to Fornals' deft flick and to the movement of a rampant Antonio. Fingers crossed that he and some of the other walking wounded who held out to the final whistle are fit to go again against Leicester.

Hopefully back for that match will be Angelo Ogbonna, and it's testament to our squad togetherness and depth that we did take victory last night, despite the mental demons of surrendering three-goal leads and despite being without our best centre-back, best midfielder and, once Antonio went off, best centre-forward.

I've seen it said that any European qualification would be a curse because the squad is too thin to cope! This strikes me as a fairly limp stick with which to beat the board: let's give them the chance to strengthen, if necessary, before we go wishing ourselves out of Europe. Credit to Moyes for his rather more pragmatic outlook. I dream of the Champions League and the associated riches; I'd cherish a Europa League adventure and the chance to build on what look like very solid foundations; I know next to nothing about it but I'd also happily take entry to the Europa Conference, which I think comes with seventh place and that we'd presumably have the most realistic chance of winning … inaugural winners of a European trophy would be quite something, assuming it carries more prestige than the much-maligned Intertoto Cup, which was our dubious reward for a heady fifth-place finish back in 1999.

Last Man Standing

11 April 2021

[West Ham 3-2 Leicester]

Come season's end, our trilogy of 3-something thrillers could be seen as an entertaining high point. Or it could just be a last hurrah. Certainly, had I known today's final score at kick-off time then the unfolding of the next two hours would have been far more enjoyable … Issa Diop's (rightly) disallowed fourth and Mike Dean's uncharacteristic leniency when Leicester's Ndidi could easily have been given a second yellow would have been laughed off rather than seeming like portents of doom. It's reached the ridiculous point that I really don't want to take another 3-0 lead this season!

Credit to the lads for hanging on again, even if injury time nearly lived up to its name by giving scores of fans a cardiac arrest. Leicester are now looking over their shoulder as much as we are, but I hope we both hold on in there because it's brilliant to see two relative minnows disrupting the top four. I'm anti-Champions League only because it's an elite cabal that generally increases the divide between the rich and the rest. The group fixtures haven't interested me for years; it's just going through the motions for most of those involved. For West Ham, however, it could be a game-changer: the step up to the next level that could bring some serious squad investment. And boy, do we need it, looking at what might be available for Newcastle next week …

Proving again the benefit of hindsight, I fully intended to write a pre-match analysis highlighting the quality of our line-up even in the absence of lynchpins such as Rice and Antonio but worried about tempting fate. Moyes utilised his players sensibly, 3-4-3 offering the most balanced system available, and the only alteration I'd have made was Benrahma for Fornals, despite the latter's strong showing against Wolves, simply because I thought Benrahma would cause the Foxes more problems and it has to be the

Algerian's turn to step up at some point and vindicate his hardcore band of admirers. Shows what I know, thinking our issues would be in attack rather than defence!

Lingard is deservedly getting the plaudits right now but this is definitely not a one-man show. And it will need to be a proper squad effort to make that Champions League dream a reality. Having been ready to acclaim today's team sheet, the next one might not make such good reading if Cresswell and Noble don't recover. Assuming the worst-case scenario that none of today's absentees are ready for next week, then how do we line up at St James' Park?

Just as our players are dropping like flies, Newcastle's key men are back. Hence I'd have Coufal drop into the Cresswell centre-back role and the speedster Fredericks helping to deal with Allan Saint-Maximin, just as the same pair nullified Jack Grealish. My biggest concern would be a probable Diop–Masuaku pairing on the other flank. That's a potential recipe for disaster. And Callum Wilson has an irritating knack of scoring every time he plays us so it's bad news that he came off the bench today, even if he did play second fiddle to Saint-Maximin in the Geordies' comeback win at Burnley. Souček has notably sacrificed his box-to-box instincts in the absence of Rice as a midfield anchor but he might have to sit even more without Noble by his side.

It would be so West Ham to lose twice to a team that's struggled around the relegation zone all season. But that's the old West Ham, isn't it? I'd have a decent degree of faith in this team to keep us buoyant. Then hopefully we'll be closer to full strength for the visit of Chelsea. One match at a time, but if we can manage four points from the next two then I really will start believing ...

The 400 Club

Today's match was also notable for Noble notching his 400th Premier League appearance.

Life didn't begin with the Premier League but, given how much football culture has changed since, it's a useful watershed for various metrics. Loyalty allegedly went out of the window around the same time as its inception so these days it's rare for players to reach a century of performances with one club. Kudos then to Noble for joining Ryan Giggs (632), Jamie Carragher (508), Steven Gerrard (504), Paul Scholes (499), John Terry (492), Frank Lampard (429) and Gary Neville (400) on reaching the 400-match landmark with a single club. Not bad company to keep, in terms of ability if not personality!

Those guys won multiple trophies and international caps so Nobes is perhaps more on a par with Jason Dodd (329) and Gary Kelly (325), particularly in that they all stuck with their clubs outside the top flight. It's easy to be loyal when you're a star player with an extensive medal collection. It's often said that Noble's loyalty has never been tested because no big club has ever come in for him but there's no doubt that there would have been interest from other Premier League clubs had he shown any inclination to jump a sinking ship in 2011 or any of the other times we've been relegation-threatened in the past decade and a half.

Prediction Time

16 April 2021

Seven months ago the talkSPORT 'supercomputer' had us finishing 19th, which exposes the senselessness of making predictions and proves that our current situation is beyond everyone's wildest expectations, making it sage of Moyes and Noble to talk of enjoying it rather than feeling the pressure.

Nevertheless, with seven matches to go, I'm going to make a prediction. The belief in the group and the momentum they have is reminiscent of Leicester's miracle workers who just kept winning against the odds. We can do it too, albeit at a level below. On the other hand, we're West Ham and the other time I'm reminded of is 2006. We're doing well, better than expected, I'm just starting to believe, then the underperforming Scousers throw a last-minute spanner in the works. You heard it here first folks: put your life savings on Liverpool to nick fourth!

Hello Disaster, My Old Friend

17 April 2021

[Newcastle 3-2 West Ham]

Can a season hinge on one poor touch? Rationally speaking, no, but try telling that to Steven Gerrard. Dawson's mis-control is never going to rival Gerrard's unfortunate slip, credited with handing the title to Manchester City, for import. Its hapless calamity rating, on the other hand, was peerless thanks to the accompanying red card and then Diop and Fabiański getting in on the act to gift Newcastle what turned out to be – just about – an unassailable lead.

Having regularly flirted with calamity over the past month, West Ham are used to being architects of our own downfall but the three minutes in which we somehow contrived to shoot ourselves in the foot three times took things to a whole new level! The question was, how would we respond?

Getting #GSBOUT trending.

Making memories (and hoardings to accompany them). ©WHUFC

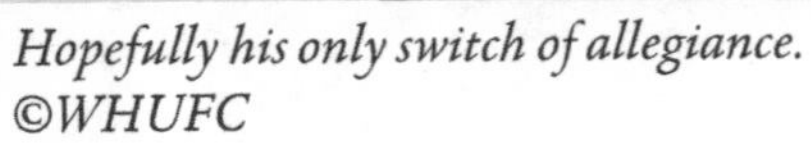

Hopefully his only switch of allegiance. ©WHUFC

Priceless. ©WHUFC

'Busting it out' to celebrate being the first opponent to score (and win) at the new White Hart Lane. ©WHUFC

Ain't nobody… in the stands, or like Lanzini for hitting a last-minute screamer against Spurs. ©WHUFC

Twist and shout. ©WHUFC

400-up for Mr West Ham. ©WHUFC

My Junior Hammers.

Stadium tour.

Setting standards as sweeper.
©WHUFC

Game on: next level accessed.
©WHUFC

Balmy nights in Lyon.

Eintracht Frankfurt away end. ©WHUFC

Where this chapter ends.

At half-time, my thinking had already turned to next week. 2-0 would have been getting off lightly based on the first-half performance. I held out no hope of a comeback; recent events may have taught us that it's not over till it's over but I didn't honestly expect that to work both ways. So credit to the lads for giving a response sooner than expected. The levelling of the scoreline may have had as much to do with Newcastle's own weaknesses as our strengths but it was, nevertheless, gratifying to watch us dominate the half despite being a man down.

Newcastle's eventual winner only served to remind us that the 'Bubbles' lyrics encapsulate what we're all about. It felt oddly reassuring to watch us crumble after the unnerving victories against Wolves and Leicester that saw us hit giddy heights. All in all, the character was impressive. Although the result was less favourable, we've clearly come a long way since the visit to St James' Park around the same stage last season when we were fourth from bottom rather than fourth from top. Having thrown away the chance to go third and match the boys of '86, we also showed we're still some way off 8-1 victories and Alvin Martin hat-tricks. I will, however, settle for the calamitous hat-trick of errors we did get if it's now out of our system and we push on with the form and attitude shown outside of those farcical few minutes.

Does This Mean We Might Actually Win Something?

19 April 2021

Imagine a league without the self-appointed Big Six … with pleasure. Strip their fixtures out of this season and we'd be best of the rest, on course for a first league title in our 125-year history! Not that I'd want to taste glory in such unedifying circumstances – there's already enough self-interest evident in last night's controversial European Super League (ESL) statement – but I wouldn't be at all averse to a reset brought about by avarice.

The assumption that their absence would leave a gaping hole in the game is what the ESL founders are banking on but I actually think it could reinvigorate the domestic footballing pyramid. How much interest and enthusiasm would be generated from fans of Everton, Villa, Wolves, Leeds, Newcastle, etc. if they went into a season with the belief that they could actually be champions and not just 'best of the rest' with an outside chance of qualifying for Europe? Promoted clubs would have similarly raised aspirations, even if the prospect of Norwich 2022 being a repeat of Nottingham Forest 1978 remains a long shot. It would equally revive domestic cup competitions. Saturday's drab FA Cup semi-final between Chelsea and Manchester City was a glimpse of what ESL fixtures might be, demonstrating the complacency of two teams accustomed to success, having each featured at the semi-final stage in four of the past five seasons. And I'm sure Benfica, Ajax, Steaua Bucharest – all great champions of the past – won't be crying any tears at the prospect of European football actually being a more level playing field once again with every Champions League finalist since 2004 (bar the French and Germans who, credit to them, seem to have some principles left intact) removed from competition. What makes the Premier League more bankable than La Liga, Serie A, Bundesliga and the rest? Apparently it's the unpredictability, which should make the established competitions more bankable than they've been in a long time.

In contrast, where's the interest in watching the same teams play each other again and again and again, even if they're supposedly the best? Familiarity breeds contempt. Glamour fixtures played weekly quickly become run of the mill. Former players have already opined that they wouldn't want to be part of a closed shop, even for richer rewards. Only time will tell, and modern footballers certainly have a reputation for following the money rather than their hearts, but I think there would be a drain of talent from the ESL into the 'normal' leagues as new clubs and players rise to prominence. Equally, the initial reaction from fans suggests that many aren't inclined to follow. Tribal allegiances should never be underestimated but many supporter groups are already suggesting that the clubs they loved are dead, their souls brokered to the highest bidder. Should the ESL commence, more phoenix clubs will rise with unprecedented levels of backing. FC United of Manchester have got a head start thanks to fans who saw where things were going with the Glazers. Expect record crowds to be watching the Northern Premier League Premier Division next season!

What do I say to the Hammers who feel we sold our own soul by moving stadium? Firstly, the stadium is only one aspect, albeit a significant one, of our identity and the locale remained true to our community roots, even if it felt heavily gentrified. Secondly, yes, we were looking to better ourselves, to try to rival the ESL clubs, and the increased revenue was necessary to give us even a sporting chance of competing. Does this make our owners mercenaries who would jump ship to the ESL if invited? I'd like to think not because, for all their faults, they really are fans and not *just* money men like the Glazers and Fenway Sports Group.

Finally, my main justification for moving was to let more people in, whereas the guiding principle behind the ESL is to lock others out. If a Tottenham Hotspur phoenix club wanted to use the London Stadium for Isthmian League fixtures, I'd welcome them doing so, and not just out of ironic mockery.

Divisions will inevitably open up in all leagues but, while Spurs and Arsenal (unable to merit a Champions League place but kidding themselves they're part of Europe's elite) will be stuck at the bottom of a closed shop, clubs in the English pyramid will continue to evolve. A hundred years ago, it would have been Huddersfield and Blackburn leading a breakaway; pre-Premier League, Nottingham Forest would have had a big say in things. Things change. That's part of the beauty of competitive sport. Tradition and history can't always stand in the way of modernisation but the change being discussed now is driven by pure greed and misses the essence of what makes sport captivating. In the United States, NFL and NBA succeed with teams treated as business franchises but that's how they've always been organised and they do have the draft and salary caps to help ensure a degree of balance, so comparisons are invalid.

I say call their bluff, let them go. Kick them out of FA, UEFA and FIFA competitions as threatened. It could be the reset the game needs and a salutary lesson to the champions that follow.

Stick or Twist?

22 April 2021

It's supremely irritating that much of the discourse around Declan Rice focuses on Chelsea rather than West

Ham. Journalists perpetuate the lazy assumption that he's destined for Stamford Bridge based primarily on his boyhood connections. In fairness, I could see the appeal to Declan himself: the chance to prove that he's good enough for them after all, like a jilted lover trying to confound their ex; the chance to play alongside his best friend, Mason Mount; the chance to win things. Superficially speaking, it seems a good move. Just as it no doubt seemed a good move to Ross Barkley, Danny Drinkwater, Victor Moses and many other forerunners. Anyone who thinks they're good enough to buck the trend should remember that this is the club that chewed up and spat out Kevin De Bruyne and Mo Salah!

So, stick or twist? Continue on an upward trajectory as the heart of a middling team, a guaranteed starter with a secure place in the national team and legend status ready to be conferred should you ever lift a trophy? Or step up a rung to intense squad competition, having to prove yourself all over again and silverware being an expectation rather than an aspiration? Without wishing to sound unambitious, it never ceases to amaze me how many players opt for the latter. Money can of course be a contributing factor and Dec undoubtedly deserves a pay rise, but I'm taking remuneration as a secondary consideration, given that no Premier League player should ever be short of a few bob. If anything, salary turns into a status symbol within squads and Rice's next option should be top earner at West Ham or average earner at a more successful club.

It's been reported that, while on England duty, Rice also sounded out Harry Maguire and Luke Shaw on life at Old Trafford. If he needs to discuss options with anyone, may I suggest Jesse Lingard. Working in reverse,

JLingz knows how it feels to be a little fish in a big pond. Many don't survive when they're chucked into a different ecosystem, so credit to Lingard for what he's achieved in West Ham's smaller pond. Now he's looking a big fish and other predators are hungrily circling, the big pond might want him back. Does he stick or twist? Well firstly, which option's which? Contractually he's still a Manchester United player, they're his club, but sticking with them is actually a leap into the unknown – will there be a change in his circumstances thanks to the heroic exploits in East London, or is he back to being premier benchwarmer? The same goes for a move to Real Madrid, Inter Milan or any other 'super' team he's been linked with. West Ham is the 'stick' option in terms of knowing where he stands; anything else represents a gamble with the remainder of his career.

And the ESL ...?

What now? Much as it pains me to side with a 24-carat imbecile like Florentino Pérez, I don't think it's dead in the water. These same clubs will continue to plot how to press home the competitive advantage that they currently enjoy. The ESL's speedy demise will only be a victory for ordinary fans if regulations are put in place to limit the power and wealth accrued, as opposed to the existing Champions League reforms designed to appease the elite. The worst possible outcome will be carrying on regardless. As a commentator on BBC's Livefeed sarcastically put it, 'So glad to read the news about the ESL this morning. Back to the egalitarian structure which has seen the Big Six win 20 of the last 21 major domestic honours and one team from outside the group finish in the Premier League top three in the last 20 years! Bury fans rejoice.'

Repentance will probably save all the English clubs from strict punitive measures such as demotion or points deductions, which is fair enough since the backlash has been predicated on the idea that sport should be decided on the field, not in the boardrooms or corridors of power. That said, it's in these places that change needs to happen. UEFA needs to stop kowtowing to the guilty parties and look at alternative Champions League reforms that aren't weighted towards the most powerful. Problems began with the value being loaded into one competition (the Champions League) rather than spread across three (the European Cup, the Cup Winners' Cup and the UEFA Cup), so the most obvious step seems to be to disband the Champions League and rethink European football. I suspect, however, that money still speaks louder than words.

Join Our Club …

The funniest/saddest thing Pérez said was, 'As for signings like [Erling] Haaland or [Kylian] Mbappé, they won't exist without the Super League.' Which must come as news to Bryne FK, Molde, Red Bull Salzburg, Borussia Dortmund, Monaco and Paris Saint-Germain, all of whom have been involved in transfers between the two said players but none of whom were involved in the ESL fiasco.

Surely it's a good thing that a handful of clubs can't hoover up the world's best players? And if the Champions League riches aren't enough to sustain Real Madrid's business model then that model's clearly kaput.

Given the PR disaster of the ESL and the clubs' tarnished reputations, those who can still afford to will doubtless attempt to distract and mollify fans with galáctico signings. Which is exactly where players such as Rice, Lingard and the superstars more sought after than them have a duty not to be taken in by pound signs and the size of a trophy cabinet. Clubs should have a value beyond fiscal measures and trinkets. The likes of West Ham can compete by making compelling sales pitches that aim for glory but prize other things besides, including community, fans and ethics.

GSB have taken a kicking in recent years because of their vainglorious attempts at playing Levy, Woodward and the rest at their own game. As fans who've made their fortune and already entered their dotage, they can have no serious hope of putting much more in or taking much more out of the club. Cynics will now point to their reported asking price and the terms that deter a sale before 2023. However, as the saying goes, you can't take it with you. David Gold is 84 and David Sullivan is 72, with net worths making them and their families more than comfortable for life; what's their incentive for further profiteering? As Pérez implies, even at the top end, money is more easily lost than made in club ownership; although the ESL sought to maximise income, their greater greed was ring-fencing and protecting it at the expense of others. If, as I've always optimistically believed, our owners really do have the best interests of the club at heart, they're in a prime position to lead the way into a German 50+1 model of fan ownership by gifting a portion of their shares to club members. Think of it as an heirloom more valuable than any cup. It might not bring fans closer to the pitch but it would bring them closer to the club.

Project Big Picture

24 April 2021

[West Ham 0-1 Chelsea]

As Gary Lineker put it on *Match of the Day*, we've seen everything now: a player sent off for kicking the ball.

VAR has enabled more laughable decisions than it's corrected. But is the problem with the technology itself or the robotic application of the law by the officials using it? I don't know whether referee Chris Kavanagh or Stockley Park bureaucrat Peter Bankes ever put down jumpers for goalposts but it's hard to disagree with Moyes's withering assessment that the decision to send off Fabián Balbuena was 'made by somebody who has never played the game'.

Now, I've no desire to see Gary Neville refereeing Manchester United versus West Ham. Players who've kissed the badge on Sky Sports can't seriously be expected to be impartial. We can see that in much of the commentary! But retired pros from further down the pyramid could surely do a better job of reading the game and sensibly applying the rules than the current PGMOL (Professional Game Match Officials Ltd) crew. One of the urgent reforms needed is fast-tracking ex-players into officialdom in place of the automatons ruining the game. Although I wouldn't necessarily ditch VAR altogether, the forensic elimination of contact and risk is symptomatic of where the game has long been headed, as with the ESL.

If I didn't love football so much, I'd have long since fallen out of love with it. Every time the VAR officials start drawing lines or the man in the middle is sent to the monitor my heart sinks a little further. Even in a sensational season for Hammers, it's getting harder and harder to watch.

Will I ever give up on it? West Ham till I die? The problem with that old adage is that it gives clubs and other institutions licence to take the piss. Although I think the transition to the London Stadium has been overstated, I respect the right of fans to say, 'This isn't the matchday experience I cherished, I'm off down Dagenham & Redbridge.' The ESL has given fans of the Big Six pause for thought and many feel an ethical line has been crossed that's left a void in their hearts.

That said, fidelity works both ways and it's also a piss-take when fans turn against the team after two narrow losses in extenuating circumstances. Next weekend's social media blackout is being held on grounds of racism but stupidity doesn't discriminate – it's evident in one form or another on practically every social media thread. There will be an element of disappointment if, nay when (this is West Ham remember), we fail to reach the Champions League, simply because the rare opportunity is tantalisingly within reach. But recent events should help us see the big picture clearer than Project Big Picture ever did. If we attain European football of any level then it will have been a stonking season.

The Upside Down

4 May 2021

[Burnley 1-2 West Ham]

'Every game's a cup final. We probably need to win them all to give ourselves a realistic chance.' (David Moyes)

Such appraisals sound familiar from our past great escape attempts but the prospect of winning matches is met with pessimism when you're in the losing habit. At the other end of the table, it's a different story. It's been observed that we have a kind run-in: every match is eminently winnable, yet it's hard to shake the feeling that they're very losable too! Burnley away, on the back of two defeats and a litany of injuries, was a good litmus test. And we passed with flying colours.

Most pleasing of all was the attacking intent. Moyes is known as a pragmatist but the team selection indicated that he's ready to throw caution to the wind. Manuel Lanzini being deployed as a deep playmaker set the tone and our interplay as an attacking unit was a joy to behold, even if the lack of killer instinct meant another nail-biting finale. Saïd Benrahma has skills but needs to develop composure. Still, we looked capable of scoring every time we went forward, against a Burnley defence with a miserly reputation. It was only the laxity of our own defence, specifically Issa Diop's worrying inability to deal with balls over the top, that kept things interesting for neutrals.

The expected return of Declan Rice and Angelo Ogbonna should shore up the rearguard and provide an even firmer basis for taking the game to Everton, Brighton, West Brom and Southampton.

Whatever happens in the rest of May, to be sitting above Liverpool, Spurs and Arsenal at the start of the month is the stuff that dreams are made of. Even if the bubble bursts and we fall just below one of the dotted lines denoting European qualification, it's still a far cry from relegation. Champions League? Stranger things have happened.

Faded but Not Dead

14 May 2021

Team	P	GD	Pts	Form
Man City	35	46	**80**	WLWWL
Man Utd	36	28	**70**	WDWLL
Leicester	36	21	**66**	WWDLW
Chelsea	36	22	**64**	DWWWL
Liverpool	35	20	**60**	WDDWW
West Ham	35	10	**58**	WLLWL
Tottenham	35	20	**56**	LDWWL
Everton	35	4	**56**	DWLWD

The Champions League is a long shot. But wasn't it always? The fact that I'm mildly disappointed to be overtaken by Liverpool with just three matches remaining says it all for the season we've had. We were 34 matches in and above a team that conquered all before them last season. Does this mean that if we had a fit Virgil van Dijk we'd be title challengers? I knew he was worth a punt when he was at Celtic!

The worst part of losing to Everton [West Ham 0-1 Everton] is that it put any form of European football in jeopardy. The blue Scousers are back in the hunt, whereas if we'd won our six-pointer (not the sort that we're used to!) then seventh or higher would have been virtually guaranteed. As it is, someone's going to finish eighth and miss out altogether. Our realistic ambition all along has been disrupting the top six (Europa League rather than the new Conference League) and a Premier League record points haul (63+). Oh, and finishing above Spurs. Even with three winnable games remaining, I'd settle for the table as it stands now.

Having been everyone's second team in 2016 – the last good season we had, funnily enough – my other hope is that Liverpool don't catch Leicester. Our transformation from relegation candidates to Champions League challengers has been remarkable enough but Leicester's leap from bottom three to champions was nothing short of miraculous. No one can claim that freak event was the product of good planning but the Foxes have pretty much been the model of a well-run club ever since. Having fallen at the final hurdle last season, their daunting finish to this season could precipitate another collapse. I sincerely hope their bubble doesn't burst because their success is a prototype for others to follow.

Manager of the Year

20 May 2021

European football all but secure. A record Premier League points tally. Above Spurs. It's okay to be disappointed at missing out on Champions League football having flirted with the top four so late in the season but any fan who thinks this group of players bottled it or in any way underachieved needs to f*** off to one of the 'Super League' teams.

You could say we made hard work of it against West Brom last night [West Brom 1-3 West Ham] but that implies victory should have been easy. That may be the case for Manchester City, but even they were comprehensively outplayed by Brighton (who we should also have comfortably dispatched last week according to some [Brighton 1-1 West Ham]), albeit in the extenuating circumstances of ten versus eleven for 80 minutes. If matches were won on paper then there would be no need to play half of them and we may as well just have the Big Six compete among themselves.

Although we didn't hit top gear, the most impressive aspect of that decisive victory at The Hawthorns was the character shown. The earliest missed penalty in Premier League history and trailing to an own goal all seemed so very West Ham; to turn it around, especially with home fans-only cheering on the opposition, so very not. David Moyes has never been the most glamorous of managers but if the resilience and grit displayed this season is due to a team playing in its manager's image then I for one am quite happy to have a grizzled Scot at the helm!

Morning-After Reflections

12 July 2021

[European Championship Final: England 1-1 Italy (2-3 pens)]

Am I happy to have finally reached a major tournament final? Of course. Have this England team brought me great joy over the past month? Not exactly. The thrill of progress was tempered by largely underwhelming performances; even the uplifting Germany and Ukraine victories would be more accurately described as 'good' than 'great'. Greater things were expected than in 2018 and we've indeed moved up a gear, but there's no escaping the feeling that there's another gear still to be found.

In summary, we should be semi-proud of their achievements. This England team has character and much to admire about them, including their social activism, although it's rarely helpful to mix that up with their on-pitch accomplishments. They deserve our applause and support. Only, I hope they're not as content to be 'unlucky losers' as much of the nation seems to be. The 'win as a team, lose as a team' mantra is spot-on, so the abuse (racist or otherwise) received by individual players is disgusting. However, it's fair to question and critique overall performance, in particular the manager's decision-making.

Now, Gareth Southgate is undoubtedly a fine man and role model, and I can't think of anybody better suited to nurturing a talented group of young players. Is he a fine manager though, a coach and tactician capable of guiding them to the zenith of international football? That's still open to debate. Everyone has an opinion and I admire Southgate's ability to ignore outside noise, to have faith in his own judgement. But that comes back to him being a fine man as much as a fine strategist. As the man himself stated at this morning's press conference, 'You make hundreds of decisions day in, day out, during the tournament. Some you get right and some that you don't. You have to get more right than wrong. So I take responsibility and take the criticism that comes with that.' Refreshingly frank and self-aware, he knows better than the armchair pundits what it takes to succeed at this level, while admitting he doesn't know it all. Most big matches are decided by fine margins and penalties epitomise that truism – Rashford was the width of a post away from changing history.

In a parallel universe, England teams of the last 55 years have tasted the same triumphs as Italy, Germany, Spain, France, the Netherlands, Portugal, Denmark and Greece. Why, in this universe, have we not? Well, it's said that you make your own luck. Sir Alex Ferguson's Manchester United were famed for their late 'Fergie-time' goals and propitious penalties but neither were pure luck, they were the embodiment of a relentless forward drive that sprung from the manager's mindset. Southgate shares Ferguson's protective paternal instincts (albeit informed by more 21st-century attitudes) but is a naturally more conservative manager. Italy's equaliser was scrappy – some might deem it lucky the way the ball rebounded to Bonucci – but it had been coming, the embodiment of Southgate's cautious approach that saw England sit deep and concede ground to the *Azzurri.* For all his talk of being brave, Southgate's teams consistently adopt a safety-first approach, which has ultimately, and ironically, been their undoing.

There's a logic to the defensive base: Southgate has name-checked the relatively unfancied Portugal and Greece as having triumphed at the Euros by being hard to beat. Again though, this highlights a critical flaw in Southgate's thinking. While it's commendable that he looks to learn from the past and from other nations, it shouldn't be at the expense of what's in front of him. To go alongside its creditable character, this England team now needs to forge an identity of its own and stop fixating on others. The flexibility of systems that Southgate has developed since our midfield was overrun by Croatia in the World Cup semi-final has helped us through different tests in this tournament and should generally be taken as a positive but it does leave us playing second fiddle: rather than being proactive and dictating play, we've been reactive, so preoccupied with nullifying others that we effectively nullified our own threat – see last night's second half for evidence. From Trippier at left-back in the Croatia rematch, to a 3-4-3 formation to complement Germany's, to a similar wing-back system against Italy, team selections have flattered the opposition rather than ourselves, to the extent that English fans still have no idea what Southgate sees as his best attacking unit.

The Greek and Portuguese defensive models were formed out of necessity – Greece had no other options, while Portugal relied on the talismanic genius of Ronaldo to pull them through. We, on the other hand, seemingly play Mount and Saka as much for their defensive attributes as their offensive ones, while Grealish, Foden, Sancho and Rashford stagnate on the bench. Declan Rice unsurprisingly won more tackles than any other player on the pitch against Italy. Shockingly, he also went on more dribbles than anyone else! The match was there to be won in extra time and Southgate's reluctance to unleash the attacking talent at his disposal was a factor in our downfall.

An ugly win would have more than glossed over such misgivings; it could also have instilled the belief necessary to start playing on the front foot and reap further reward. Ironically, for a nation accused of arrogance, we routinely demonstrate an inferiority complex, probably because 'it' hasn't come home for 55 years (and counting – take out the uplifting clarion call of 'It's coming home' and 'Three Lions' rivals our own 'Bubbles' for melancholic defeatism). No team at a major tournament should be treated lightly and all-out attack against serial winners such as Italy would be foolhardy but this generation needs to strike a finer balance between wariness and recklessness if it's to flourish at Qatar 2022 and beyond.

Sir Alex was criticised for not adapting to the different challenges of European football but Manchester United did conquer the continent twice under his tutelage, each time with a healthy dose of 'luck' … in another parallel universe, Bayern Munich held out in 1999 and Chelsea won on penalties in 2008. Sir Gareth Southgate has a nice ring to it and he has the makings of a knight; now he just needs to find the bravery of one so that we can all dare to dream again.

On a Personal Note ...

It's not just me that I want to be inspired by the Three Lions. The small boy continues to show little interest in the national sport but he did stay up until the 66th minute of the final, departing for bed seconds before Italy's equaliser. It's an omen. Just as I appear to have hexed West Ham's fortunes since coming on to the scene in late 1980, I'm taking that quirk of timing as a signal that our footballing fortunes are bound up with James's enthusiasm for the game. So, there you have it: success next year rests on Southgate producing the style of football that will hold the attention of an eight-year-old!

Year Six – 2021/22

All Hail Antonio

1 September 2021

Being West Ham's all-time top scorer in the age of the Premier League is roughly the equivalent of being Newham's top tourist destination in the age of Tripadvisor, but the inadequacies of McCarthy, Mido, Zaza and countless others shouldn't detract from the fact that Michail Antonio has turned into a formidable No. 9 who now deserves to be bracketed in the upper echelons of Hammers strikers, joining Ashton, Tevez and Di Canio from the past 30 years and other club legends from the pre-Premier League era.

The shame of it is that it's taken this long and £40m spunked on Sébastien Haller to discover that we've had a top-quality target man in our ranks for the past half-decade! Without wishing to sound hyperbolic, Antonio has got it all. He has pace, he has power and, contrary to the reputation he gained as a raw winger with a slightly heavy touch, both finishes against Leicester [West Ham 4-1 Leicester] showed that he's developed a good deal of finesse. And he's a character who brings a lot to the dressing room. If we were scouting around for a replacement, we'd expect to pay about ten times more than the £7m it cost to take him from Nottingham Forest!

Whether or not 25-year-old Antonio could have made it as a solo striker straight away is a matter of conjecture but, like Arnautović before him, Moyes's conversion of Michail from wide man to main man has been a masterstroke. It makes one wonder why nobody saw it before but we can be too quick to pigeonhole players into positions, hence the vitriol aimed at Bilić when he saw the makings of a right-back in the same player. Okay, that didn't work out quite so well but credit all round for trying.

The question now is whether he can sustain it. If he reaches 100-up in the next two seasons then we can begin speaking in terms of all-time great. He's not exactly the new Harry Kane but when Dominic Calvert-Lewin is next in line for the national team, England's loss looks like Jamaica's gain.

P.S. The league table shouldn't be taken seriously until at least six matches in but I'm leaving this here for posterity's sake anyway …

Team	P	GF	GA	GD	Pts
West Ham	3	10	5	5	7
Chelsea	3	6	1	5	7
Liverpool	3	6	1	5	7
Everton	3	7	3	4	7
Man City	3	10	1	9	6
Tottenham	2	2	0	2	6

Priorities For Me: Cups, Then League

23 September 2021

The less said about Sunday's late drama [West Ham 1-2 Man Utd] the better, save for the fact that it made last night's reversal [Man Utd 0-1 West Ham, League Cup third round] all the more satisfying. That reserve centre-backs Dawson and Diop were the standout performers indicates the type of match it was, but for all the complaints about our lack of strength in depth going into a European campaign, beating a Manchester United second-string that still boasted 11 internationals speaks volumes for the rude health that West Ham currently find themselves in.

And our reward for winning at Old Trafford? To be drawn against Premier League champions and recurrent League Cup winners Manchester City! We may never have won it but the unfancied League Cup still represents our best chance of a trophy at the beginning of each season, thanks largely to it being bottom of everyone's priority list. In contrast, I think Moyes should now place it top of our list. With European football providing a bye through to round three, it's only a five-match run to glory! That we've drawn the two Manchester giants in the first of those matches, while Chelsea and Liverpool have been granted relatively kind passages to the latter stages, lengthens the odds considerably. Still, as daunting as any of those teams are, we've shown ourselves a match for anyone. Beat City and the fans will really start believing that our name's on this year's trophy.

Sacrilegious as it is to question the supremacy of the Premier League, I'd happily trade three points for a better shot at actually winning something. Therefore, the other priority this year should be the Europa League. The litany of big names – Lazio, Napoli, Monaco, PSV, Leverkusen – should hold little fear, as shown in our proficient dismantling of Dynamo Zagreb [0-2] in the first round of group matches. The Europa League's big-hitters are generally at the level of Leicester and Tottenham. Come the knockout stages, the quality will approximately resemble what's left in the League Cup – true, there will be no one as weak as QPR, Preston or Sunderland, but (bar catastrophe leading to early exits from the Champions League) there will be no one as strong as Manchester City, Chelsea or Liverpool either.

It would be nice to cement our status as a top-six club and qualify for Europe again next year but Arsenal and Spurs fans would attest that there's limited satisfaction in eternally qualifying for something that you never actually win. As the most attainable trophies, the League Cup and Europa League have to take precedence over the Premier League.

Viva East London

24 October 2021

[West Ham 1-0 Tottenham]

If the remarkable turnaround at the Tottenham Hotspur Stadium almost exactly a year ago was the catalyst for an inspired season, then today's unremarkable victory at home to our bitter rivals cements the turnaround in West Ham's identity. Fourth in the league, sailing in Europe, Manchester City to come in the Carabao Cup … nothing to see here, keep calm and carry on. That seems to be the mindset these days under Moyes. The players have totally bought it and if the fans are still a little over-excitable it's only because composure and self-control isn't part of our DNA!

The new-found equilibrium is evident in different components stepping up and finding a way to win when others aren't firing. After a promising start to the season, Saïd Benrahma was a passenger today, but we don't have many of them anymore and others comfortably took the strain. Although Rice looks capable of carrying the team on his shoulders, the player who's perhaps most indicative of Moyes's West Ham Way is Pablo Fornals – he rarely sets the world alight but he's tidy and tenacious, with hints of real quality. A winning blend of Spanish flair and East End resilience … who would have thought it back in the days of Kepa Blanco?!

Shoulda, Woulda, Coulda

5 November 2021

[Europa League group stage: Genk 2-2 West Ham]

We *should* have beaten Genk. But football rarely follows the expected patterns, which is why xG stats don't actually count for anything and why the sport is consistently enthralling. From a neutral perspective, last night's match was an end-to-end thriller; from a Hammers perspective, particularly after our recent controlled performances, it was shockingly sloppy.

Oh well, in his 1,000th game as a manager, Moyes is well wise to the fact that you can't win 'em all! Let's face it, if anyone had offered us ten points and a four-point lead at the top of the group with two matches remaining then everyone involved at the club would have bitten their hand off. We've already qualified for the knockout stages but we need to finish top of the group to bypass the first stage and we *would* have had that sewn up were it not for Souček's outrageous slice of misfortune (87th-minute flying OG). The frustration is that, while we continue to fight on three fronts, unlimited players could have been rested in those matches against Rapid Wien and Dinamo Zagreb, but that's not now a risk worth taking.

Drawing away to Genk is only disappointing in that it breaks a peerless run of five wins on the trot. The ongoing European travails of Leicester and Tottenham also put it in perspective. It's disappointing for a team that *could* potentially win the Europa League.

The Next Next Level

7 November 2021

[West Ham 3-2 Liverpool]

'We are massive' is the buzz phrase around the London Stadium. Who would have thought it?

Some of the scenes around the club in recent years and the cries of broken promises didn't point towards growth. While this piece is no apologia for Messrs Gold and Sullivan, who have made multiple missteps, there can now be no denying that the move away from Upton Park has indeed taken us up a level. Even if the winning formula has been found by luck rather than judgement, the club is now on the most solid footing I've seen in my lifetime. Let's face it, we've been, since the late 70s, a yo-yo club, relegated five times. Only twice before in the club's history have we enjoyed a longer stretch in the top flight. And although we know from recent experience how quickly fortunes can change, we don't look like being relegation candidates any time in the foreseeable future. That, I'd say, is a step up from our traditional status. And, without wishing to get carried away with fanciful talk of title challenges, for the first time in my spectatorship we look like serious contenders for silverware and Champions League places. That, to my mind, is another level still and, although the owners were rash in promising it as a justification for leaving our spiritual home, regular

60,000-plus crowds provide the foundation for a bright new future that wouldn't be in the offing if we'd hung around Green Street.

Smut and erotica vendors may never make model citizens or ideal owners but, in their defence, Gold and Sullivan are genuine football men who've never sought to rename either of our stadiums the Daily Sport Arena. Although piggybacking the Olympic gold rush isn't pure, organic growth, our way of doing things appears preferable to the cash injections of Chelsea, Manchester City and, now, Newcastle United, which brings the contempt of neutrals who feel justifiably resentful as their own dreams of success fade into a fight for Premier League survival. When the private equity firm PAI Capital were causing waves in pre-season, I never took them seriously because it was transparent that a proposed takeover was primarily a property deal and the current custodians weren't going to touch it with a barge pole. The imminent investment from Daniel Křetínský, on the other hand, appears far more welcome. The Icelandic moguls proved that investment can be a mirage but, as a majority shareholder of Sparta Prague, Křetínský's joining the board looks more considered and will hopefully be an extension of our lucrative Czech connections.

There will surely be a downturn between now and the end of the season but a calendar year of steady growth on and off the pitch gives faith that it will be a blip rather than a downward spiral. Today's victory has only cemented this new-found status and belief. Yes, we've beaten the big boys plenty of times before, it was the West Ham Way to raise our game when least expected, an anomaly on a losing streak, whereas the bossing of Liverpool – inflicting the first defeat of the season on a team that strolled past the champions of Spain in midweek – is just the latest post on an upward trajectory. That the stadium was rocking and the pundits commented on the hair-raising noise shows that the fans are finally enjoying where we're at, further strengthening those foundations.

'Massive' still carries a hint of ironic self-deprecation but no one could accuse West Ham of being a small club anymore.

Blipping Good

1 December 2021

[Wolves 1-0 West Ham]

[Man City 2-1 West Ham]

Consecutive defeats for the first time since April. Let's put this blip into perspective:

- We've lost two in a row and we're *still* in the top four!
- For a West Ham fan, going half a year without suffering two defeats on the spin is almost unheard of. We're more accustomed to season-long blips.
- Both defeats came away to teams currently in the top six.
- We remain competitive and still haven't lost by more than a single goal all season. Although we didn't create much, we were in with a chance of getting something from the Manchester City match for 90 minutes, which is more than most teams manage.
- We'll lose more matches. We're fighting for a European place, not the title. The 'Invincibles' level or even Fergie's title-challenging credentials of 'six losses and you're out' remain a distant dream.

- If we enter 2022 in the top six, in the semi-finals of the League Cup (one round away) and safely through to the European knockout rounds (guaranteed with a match to spare) then that would be dreamland as far as I'm concerned.

Now bring on Brighton and, fingers crossed, an end to this blip!

[West Ham 1-1 Brighton, last-minute Maupay equaliser]

Planting the Claret-and-Blue Flag

5 December 2021

[West Ham 3-2 Chelsea]

- 48 matches without defeat when leading at half-time.
- No more than one goal conceded to any opponent this season, including Juventus x 2 and Liverpool with ten men.

They're some decent stats we've just consigned to the Chelsea history books. And an unverified one of our own:

- 40 matches without losing by more than a single goal (the longest run in Europe's top five leagues, including cup competitions).

In classic West Ham fashion, the measure of achievement depends on how many we've lost by! But it also reveals a consistency and competitiveness that's uncharacteristically West Ham. And this is how the current top four mini-league would look:

	P	*W*	*D*	*L*	*Pts*	*GF*	*GA*
Man City	3	2	1	0	**7**	5	3
West Ham	3	2	0	1	**6**	7	5
Liverpool	3	0	2	1	**2**	5	6
Chelsea	3	0	1	2	**1**	3	5

Moreover, we've knocked both Manchester teams out of the League Cup. What's obvious is that we're mixing it! Although formations and tactics show the opposition respect, we don't look awed by anyone. It still feels strange to be looking up rather than down (although eyes definitely remain more on European berths than a title challenge) but the upward trend brought by Moyes's second coming has me believing for the first time that we're serious Champions League contenders.

Of course, things can quickly unravel. The injuries to Zouma and Johnson, added to Ogbonna and Cresswell, stretch a depleted defence worryingly thin. Yet, for all their knockers, Diop, Dawson and Masuaku oversaw a two-goal turnaround against the reigning European champions. As Masuaku's freak winner showed, you never know what might happen!

The Backroom Disciples

18 December 2021

What started as satirical false idolatry fast became genuine faith and, although there remain some disbelievers, the second coming of the Moyesiah has been nothing short of miraculous. Even in light of failing the Gunners test [Arsenal 2-0 West Ham], hearing him preach about maintaining standards rather than seek to blame the satanic forces of officialdom and gamesmanship was in fact rather pacifying; let's not worry about Arsenal going fourth, let's concentrate on ourselves.

Everyone now is singing from the same hymn sheet, bar the odd bum note. Credit for the camaraderie can't, though, go to one man alone. While it follows that the manager/head coach sets the culture, it's his followers who instil it. Hence, when Moyes was isolating with Covid last year, Alan Irvine stepped into the breach and we played better than ever. Irvine has since moved into a technical advisory role, replaced by Billy McKinlay, with Paul Nevin, Kevin Nolan and Stuart Pearce as first-team coaches. It's rare, if not unique, among Premier League clubs for a manager to have five others with managerial experience serving alongside him. Granted, aside from Pearce, none of them have managed at a high level, yet it's still unusual in the egotistical world of football for a manager to welcome assistants with managerial ambitions, placing a potential Judas in the midst (Billy Bonds and, ahem, Harry Redknapp know the score). Maybe McKinlay, Nevin and Nolan have already had their fingers burned – Pearce certainly has during his time with Manchester City, England U21s and Nottingham Forest – and are happy to let the Moyesiah take the limelight while they reap the fruits of coaching at the top level without bearing the burden said limelight brings. Either way, the collective seems to be operating smoothly as a brains trust.

Credit too to the medical team. They may not be capable of bringing anyone back from the dead, and the defence are currently falling apart one by one, but the settled team of the past two seasons (we're the least changed of any team, although some regard that as a managerial weakness) is only possible with good care. It also suggests that where, in the past, players were happy if a little niggle took them out of the firing line, the culture in the current squad is more martyrdom: Moyes might not walk on water but his players it seems would walk over hot coals for him.

This Christmas, should the surrender of fourth spot signal a downward spiral, there may be a temptation to crucify the wise man at the helm. At least, unlike with Jesus, the disciples seem to have his back. And remember, this is the season of goodwill; if there has to be a crucifixion, it traditionally takes place at Easter.

The Shopping List Game

26 December 2021

Everyone's strapped for cash in the new year and Boxing Day sales aren't what they used to be, yet January also brings the promise of new beginnings and rejuvenation. Where previous transfer windows have offered hope of salvation, this time it's imperative that we invest if we're to fulfil the potential of a promising year. Dreams of silverware in the League Cup were agonisingly dashed by Spurs [Tottenham 2-1 West Ham], although a semi-final line-up of the North London rivals plus Chelsea and Liverpool suggests that even a Europa League containing the fallen giants of Barcelona might be more winnable. And after an injury-ravaged and out-of-form December, Champions League qualification once more looks to be a pipe dream, but cementing our place on the Europa League stage and as the club most likely to break the top-six stranglehold looks eminently achievable and places us in a strong position to attract fresh blood. So, to the biannual shopping list game. Because it's fun spending other people's money!

Whether Daniel Křetínský's stockholding will bring the desired windfall remains to be seen. The expectation of having owners with a combined net worth of $5.6bn is that we're no longer shopping in the bargain basement.

On the other hand, that estimated wealth only ranks ninth on the Premier League rich list, some way short of Newcastle's $430bn and also behind Barnsley ($9.1bn), Fulham ($7.9bn), QPR ($15.5bn) and Stoke ($9.4bn). The question isn't so much how rich but how philanthropic the owners are. Even then, financial fair play means that investment is, to some extent, restricted to what's sustainable, which is why we'd have always had to outgrow Upton Park to compete at the next level. We're not yet shopping in Waitrose but Sainsbury's would be a fitting analogy given that it's one of Křetínský's prime assets.

So, what should we spend our money on? Given that funds aren't limitless, let's sort the priorities first ... central defender or centre-forward?

Centre-Forward

Antonio's strength and mobility is central to our style of play but it also places an undue burden on him to be in beast mode every match. When he's off-colour or injured, despite Bowen's best efforts to compensate, we look one-dimensional. So a centre-forward is an absolute must. GSB's desire for a marquee signing has been supplanted by Moyes's expediency; while the gaffer's reluctance to blow the budget and his willingness to wait for the right player are both admirable, we definitely do need an extra body, or two.

Given the requirement to replicate Antonio's skillset, my money would be on Adam Hložek (£15–20m) and Daryl Dike (£15m). Both youngsters are raw but adaptable and, unlike our first choice, have time on their side to smooth out rough edges. Both can play up top or run the channels so they and Antonio could even form a powerful and pacy front three! Spending big money on young, relatively untested players is always a gamble but at £40m for Haller the quoted prices are no longer eye-watering and they have the potential to be worth an awful lot more. Křetínský's ties with Sparta Prague should smooth a move for the Czech hotshot, while US international Dike (who should have been snapped up by someone after ripping up the EFL in his half-season with Barnsley) has Hammers connections as the cousin of Emmanuel Emenike.

Italian international Andrea Belotti is perhaps a more natural and proven No. 9 and is apparently available at a cut-price £10m due to his refusal to sign a new contract at Torino. Having just turned 28, he definitely has a good few years in him. Similarly, Divock Origi has only six months remaining on his Liverpool contract, is the regular scorer of priceless goals and must surely be desperate to be more than a bit-part player as he enters his prime. Then there's another contract rebel, Arsenal's Eddie Nketiah. The travails of Dominic Solanke and Rhian Brewster show that U21 brilliance doesn't necessarily translate to senior football but Nketiah has just hit a hat-trick in the quarter-finals of the Carabao Cup and has fine pedigree; his problem is that he's not as good as Gabriel Martinelli but he is, impartially speaking, a better prospect than Sonny Perkins. Any one of these five would be an exciting addition. Given their very reasonable prices, our lack of depth in this position and the fact that there's no such thing as a sure thing, any two of the five would be better still.

Central Defender

This looked like a position of strength after Kurt Zouma finally signed. While Diop and Dawson have done themselves justice in both cups, they have at times looked decidedly second-string in the league. Injuries are indiscriminate and to have lost our two best centre-backs at the same time has been a hammer blow. To have five senior centre-backs seems like overkill but reinforcements are undoubtedly necessary if we're to maintain a European push. And, as with centre-forwards, let's strike while the iron's hot and we're in a position to attract quality at economical prices. Burnley's James Tarkowski has been linked for a while now; Leicester seemed a more likely destination last summer but they have even more central defenders (both fit and injured) than we do. Another contract rebel, he's been reliable for many years and would be a snip at £10m if Burnley, mired in a relegation fight, can be persuaded to let him go.

Perhaps more judicious would be a loan move with an option to buy for Nathan Aké. He might not have made the grade at Manchester City but if Pep Guardiola thinks you're worth £40m then it's safe to say you're a decent player. Given Ogbonna's season-long absence (and age), being left-sided is especially advantageous. Then there's Liverpool's fifth-choice central defender, Nathaniel Phillips, who proved his worth during their own injury crisis and, like Origi, would surely benefit from regular football. And Duje Ćaleta-Car offers another interesting option; we've certainly done good business with Marseille before and a Croatian compatriot might bring out the best in Nikola Vlašić à la Souček and Coufal.

As with the centre-forwards, any one of these would be welcome and, assuming a reasonable degree of success, would likely usher Issa Diop out of the door next summer, leaving academy prospects (Jamal Baptiste, Aji Alese, etc.)

to provide emergency back-up. The young Frenchman has all the physical attributes but appears to lack concentration and leadership, which is all the more disappointing given that he captained Toulouse.

Aldi Special Buys

The things you don't really need and may raise a few eyebrows, but what the hell! Jesse Lingard was last year's and, although he was returned, we'd take him off Manchester United's shelf again if only he'd make up his mind about whether he wants to be a January special buy, a summer freebie or to remain a benchwarmer at Old Trafford. Dele Alli could be the 2022 version, although it's doubtful Spurs would let a one-time wunderkind leave for a team vying for the same league position. Eden Hazard is surplus to requirements at Real Madrid. A couple of years ago, the sight of him in claret and blue would have been unthinkable; now, overpaying for an injury-plagued virtuoso seems about right. Perhaps most intriguing is Adnan Januzaj, who David Moyes got a tune out of at Manchester United and has since become a forgotten man but is still only 26 and playing Europa League football with Real Sociedad. More defensively, Everton's Lucas Digne has been cast aside by Rafa Benítez, the reasons for which may set alarm bells ringing, but he'd certainly be an upgrade on Arthur Masuaku and stiff competition for Aaron Cresswell.

There's general consensus over what's on the shopping list, even if the brand names differ. To further prove that the club culture is evolving, it would be great to break from bad business habits and get any acquisitions bagged up early rather than leaving it all till the last minute. There's a New Year's resolution for Messrs Gold, Sullivan and Křetínský!

Plenty Still to Play For

23 January 2022

Football's been an absolute bastard this past week.

Sunday – a frustratingly disappointing loss to Leeds [West Ham 2-3 Leeds] when we should have snatched a draw from the jaws of defeat with the last-gasp sitter that the in-form Bowen inexplicably tried to shoulder rather than head.

Wednesday – 90th-minute check shows Leicester are doing us a favour by beating Spurs 2-1, just five minutes of added time to see out. 95th minute, bugger. 96th minute, double bugger. [Leicester 2-3 Tottenham]

Saturday – sucker-punched at Old Trafford with the final kick of the match when the build-up looked offside to the naked eye. [Man Utd 1-0 West Ham]

Still, if anyone can shoulder this sort of shit, it's Hammers fans. If this is what counts for failure – still fifth in the league (albeit several teams below with games in hand) and two cup runs filled with potential – then, frankly, we're laughing. The key word, though, is *potential.* After a bright 18 months, faded ambitions and dashed dreams is what long-time West Ham supporters have come to expect, but it isn't what we should accept in the modern era of 60,000 attendances. January is never the easiest time to do transfer business, especially with Covid continuing to dent football finances and the wider economy, but the owners risk taking us back to square one if they don't use this window to build on the good work Moyes and the boys have already put in.

The Lingard saga may be tiresome but there's no doubting his energy would be welcome. And Liverpool's Nat Phillips and Divock Origi, surplus to requirements at Anfield, would strengthen our options at both ends of the pitch. With the possibility of getting all three for approximately the same price as Vlašić, then we just need to get it done. Then, just maybe, this season will be one that doesn't fade and die.

Champions League? You're Having a Laugh!

31 January 2022

As the minutes tick down towards 11pm, the silence from East London is deafening. And I say to our board, who've received ample understanding and support from me in the past, enjoy the peace while it lasts because the murmurs of discontent will quickly turn to full-blown demonstrations unless Moyes continues to perform miracles with a depleted defence and no natural striker.

On 1 January, the wish list was fairly simple: cover for Ogbonna/Zouma to shore up a leaky defence, and support for a flagging Antonio. One centre-back, one centre-forward. They didn't need to be show-off signings, merely steady pros to plug gaps and give us a fighting chance to go deep into European competition and maintain the push to be back there next year. Lingard and another left-back might also have been nice but fans weren't being greedy.

And forget 1 January, the shopping list could have been written months previously. It beggars belief that multiple targets haven't long been identified, so why the stasis until late-January and then a scattergun approach of unrealistic £50m bids for Leeds duo Raphinha and Kalvin Phillips and a £45m bid for Benfica's Darwin

Núñez, who's currently on the other side of the Atlantic with Uruguay, making any deal logistically impossible?! It reeks of Sullivan's classic 'we tried' shtick, and while I've sympathised with some of his past ambitious failures, when we're actually in a position to attract the calibre of player who should be playing European football, such bogus bids smack of lies and falsehoods. We were promised that we'd be challenging for Champions League football and, with a reasonable investment, we probably would be.

I'm not one of those who thinks that tens of millions of pounds is a trifling amount and I fully endorse frugality. But let's look at the destination of some of our reported targets ... Nat Phillips has today gone on loan to Bournemouth for fuck's sake. Someone who's given man-of-the-match performances in the Champions League has stepped down to the Championship for playing time when we could surely have guaranteed him more minutes than he's had at Anfield, and all for a small loan fee. His team-mate Origi looks to be staying where he is until he becomes a free agent in the summer, and the lack of interest in someone who's scored in the Champions League Final and is a semi-regular in FIFA's number-one-ranked national team truly mystifies me. Meanwhile, Lingard remains at Old Trafford, primarily because Manchester United wouldn't sell to a Champions League rival. If we can take any comfort, it's that our 'Champions League rivals' United and Arsenal have been equally inactive. And optimists might now anticipate a bonanza summer of free signings such as Origi, Lingard and Sam Johnstone from West Brom, except that the squad needs strengthening now if we're not to miss out on an opportunity to compete with the top four.

That lack of genuine ambition is the most damning indictment. Newly flush Newcastle have unsurprisingly outspent everyone to try to survive in the Premier League; should they do so, they'll keep strengthening and, although success isn't always transfer-based, will be expected to be competing at the top before too long. Comparable-sized clubs such as Aston Villa and Everton have also invested heavily again. Indeed, in between spending more than £30m for two full-backs in the first few days of the transfer window, Everton have managed to sack Rafa Benítez, make a meal of Frank Lampard's appointment and still get in Donny van de Beek and possibly Dele Alli in the few hours of the transfer window that remained! And we've somehow failed to sign Duje Ćaleta-Car, who we've been eyeing up for over a year, due to haggling over the payment structure of a £15m deal.

When Sue Gray dropped her preliminary report on Downing Street parties around midday, it seemed contrived to distract me from our institutional transfer failings. And I genuinely don't know whose dithering and deceit I'm angrier about right now: Boris's or Dave's.

Cup Upset

5 February 2022

[Kidderminster 1-2 West Ham (AET)]

Has such a dramatic victory ever been so deeply unsatisfying? Presenter Mark Chapman's acute observation that it was possibly the cruellest match he'd witnessed would have been seconded by every watching neutral. The magic of the cup is alive and kicking and so, just about, are we! Unbelievably, we've never actually lost to non-league opposition, although we've seen enough shitshows against the likes of Farnborough (1992), Grimsby (1996), Wrexham (1997), Wigan (2018) and AFC Wimbledon (2019). This would have topped the lot. In fact, the 113 league places between the clubs would have made it the biggest shock in FA Cup history. And, had Kidderminster prevailed, we could have had no complaints. Some of our players earn more in a week than theirs will in a whole career, yet the 120 minutes showed how fine the line is between those who make it and those who don't. Thank the football gods for that all-important injury time!

A mortifying defeat, on the back of a demoralising January, had the potential to cast a dark shadow over the rest of the season. Instead, despite the abject performance, there are positives to take if you look hard enough. For one, those late, late goals were reminiscent of Fergie's Manchester United; it's not often West Ham manage to pull out undeserved victories in that manner so maybe there's change afoot. Second, Declan Rice's drive and passion didn't look like somebody whose mind is on his next club. And the class he showed in visiting the Harriers' changing room afterwards shows he knows that football is about more than just collecting medals and money.

Make no mistake, though, Rice was the only real difference between the teams and if the first half was a harbinger of life post-Dec then we'll be watching through our fingers if anyone stumps up the nine-figure fee that he further justified with his fancy footwork in the 91st minute. Others won't be missed. No one plays professional football, never mind Premier League, without having some talent, so where does it go? I cling to the hope that Yarmolenko will produce a moment of magic or Diop a dominant performance but their balance sheets are firmly in the red. Kidderminster centre-back Matt Preston, who was being named man of the match at the fateful moment Rice struck, must wonder how he's dropped out of league football while his opposite number – who again resembled Bambi on ice for the 45 minutes we were all subjected to – gets linked with the world's richest football club!

29 Million Lives

8 February 2022

If it had been Issa Diop, he'd have been sacked, or suspended at least. Such is the cold hard business of football. David Moyes intimated as much when he justified Zouma's selection [West Ham 1-0 Watford] with the dispassionate statement that 'he's one of our better players'. His balance sheet was firmly in the black but is now deep in the red.

First things first, Zouma's actions were despicable. I've brought myself to watch the video of him abusing his pets and it's sickening. I wish that he wasn't a West Ham player. Which is a different thing from saying he should be sacked, as many outsiders and even a few insiders are calling for. In the court of social media, the outrage is audible, but is it proportionate?

Should he be prosecuted and face jail time – which is a very real possibility – then dismissal is vindicated on the basis that he can no longer fulfil his contract of employment. In the meantime, gratifying as it might be for West Ham to take the moral high ground – especially when owners, players and fans of all stripes seem intent on dragging the game through the mud – few clubs can afford to willingly write off an asset that cost them close to £30m only six months previously. And it's not just his face value, it's what he brings to the team – we'd also be writing off any real chance of Champions League qualification or FA Cup/Europa League success, which is punishing the team and the fans more than it is the perpetrator. Because, if we were to sack him, it's fantasy to think that another club won't offer him a contract, especially once the furore's died down. It would be Di Canio Mk II, only with West Ham's role reversed from beneficiaries to losers.

Moreover, I'm inherently uncomfortable with the idea of employers as moral arbiters. There has to be some distinction between working and private life, even if it is blurred by the ubiquity of social media and footballers' dubious position as role models. Zouma will rightly forfeit all personal endorsements, as well as facing the heaviest possible fine – presumably donated to animal charities – for bringing the club into disrepute. In general though, it's not an employer's place to pass judgement on anything bar an employee's work and to do otherwise opens a whole can of worms. Let he who is without sin cast the first stone and all that.

I don't want to go too far in defending Kurt because what he did is basically indefensible but I'd also stress the importance of being kind and the significance of second chances. We all make mistakes, although most lapses of judgement are neither criminal nor quite so emotive. It's already been suggested that he, and hopefully his brother, will be required to undertake an RSPCA education course and remarked that no adult should require teaching that it's not funny to mistreat a family pet. Nevertheless, you have to question the root of such behaviour and the fact that one Zouma thought it okay to assault his cat while the other thought it entertaining to film and share suggests a faulty wiring in their own family history. There's no justification in the immediate context of the video but, given that violent behaviour is typically learned, there may be reasons to sympathise in a much wider context.

Playing Zouma tonight, in a victory that seemed a mere sideshow to the viral footage of an idiot kicking his cat (not to mention the unfortunate overshadowing of Isla Caton's memorial), seemed imprudent but becomes logical on the insistence that footballing decisions are kept separate from disciplinary ones. There's also an argument that making him face the hostility at its hottest is more of a sanction than allowing him to sit it out while the controversy fades. BT commentator Ian Darke referred to him as the 'pantomime villain' of the evening. Heinous as his behaviour was, and deserving of serious punishment of some kind, there will be another cause célèbre along within a week. There's a certain amount of wisdom in taking a leaf out of our prime minister's playbook and shamelessly riding it out, much as it shames me to say it. Like Boris, West Ham appear almost hell-bent on implosion in 2022 but, please, no more parties or feline felonies. Let's get back to business and stop the stupidity.

Stormy Weather

25 February 2022

Delayed by Storm Eunice, I had to rise at 4am last Saturday to subject myself to West Ham versus Newcastle [1-1]. My first match at the London Stadium in a matter of years, it served as a reminder why a West Ham season ticket never particularly appealed, even when I lived minutes and not miles away.

Watching West Ham is rarely fun, even if much of the past two seasons has been far better than we're accustomed to. Recently, everyone giving minimum 7/10 performances has reverted to only a couple giving a good rather than mediocre showing (credit Bowen and Dawson). Another flat match raised the chicken and egg enigma of spectating: is it the fans' duty to inspire the players or vice versa? In fairness, it's probably reciprocal. Some of the drawbacks of the London Stadium were personally evident to me for the first time as every other match I've attended has generated a good atmosphere. With little to get excited about, the silence is louder in a vast arena. And with big stadiums come bigger expectations: a draw with relegation contenders is no longer an acceptable point.

This weekend comes a six-pointer [West Ham 1-0 Wolves] that will hopefully get things going again. Despite the recent lack of quality, there's certainly something to be said for picking up points when not playing well. And competing for European places rather than Championship ones. Newcastle and Wolves are among the in-form teams right now but I'd still rather be in our position than either of theirs. Realistically, I'm looking at finishing top seven (enough to secure a European berth assuming both domestic cup winners come from the top six, which they usually do) rather than top four. A win on Sunday will put some daylight between us and Wolves, who are the only other team pushing the standard big six this season.

But, of course, it's not just about making up the numbers. Having reached the Europa League knockout stages, we're in it to win it. Should that happen, sod seventh! Six-times winners Sevilla weren't the ideal draw.

That said, there are no easy matches at this stage and we often perform better in hope than in expectation. No one has made mugs of us in quite some time so we should still be in the tie after our visit to Estadio Ramón Sánchez-Pizjuán, then we'll really see what sort of atmosphere can be generated at the London Stadium. As hosts of the final on 18 May, Sevilla will be the toughest opponents imaginable but, should we overcome them, we'll definitely fancy a return trip in a few months.

One way or another, there are more storms to come this season. Not least in the geopolitics that could yet stop European football. Out of Covid and into war … it puts a bore draw with the Geordies into perspective.

Limping Through Spring

4 March 2022

Spring. A time of renewal. Starting over. Fresh hopes. Or not.

In West Ham's case it symbolises the end. Out of the FA Cup for another year, defeated by Southampton's reserves [Southampton 3-1 West Ham, FA Cup fifth round], who were simply brighter and more energised than our first team. There are 11 or 12 heroes in claret and blue this season, but nothing in reserve. A disappointing FA Cup exit reinforces the feeling that we made our bed in January; when we had momentum, the failure to build on it has stripped us of all impetus. The effort is still there, we didn't play badly at St Mary's, but the spark has gone.

To even have our sights still on fourth is an achievement but realistically I'd settle for sixth or seventh as the season threatens to peter out. To that end, Sunday's narrow win versus Wolves was massive. We're not playing particularly well right now but we're still picking up points. Just a couple more months to go to that summer break …

Heaven-Sent

13 March 2022

[West Ham 2-1 Aston Villa]

Plenty of events have placed football in perspective in recent years. Yet sport maintains an unerring ability to transcend national and personal disasters.

When Andriy Yarmolenko, one of the most celebrated players in Ukraine's history, was granted compassionate leave, the insensitive remarked that he wouldn't be missed. In fairness, based on the past year and a half, such observations weren't inaccurate. Inside-forward is the one position where we actually are well stocked and Yarmo's inability to live up to his status as the club's top earner has made him less popular than Bowen, Lanzini, Pablo, Benni and even Vlašić, who's yet to produce one of those few special moments that Yarmolenko has treated us to.

Nevertheless, there couldn't possibly have been a more popular goalscorer today. Sometimes it's written in the stars. The only thing that could have been more apt is if it was a winner against the roubles of Chelsea, but then he gave us one of them two years ago. If he were to never kick another ball for us – and chances are likely to be limited before his contract expires in the summer – these are moments that will live long in the memory.

Bring On Barça!

18 March 2022

[Europa League last-16, second leg: West Ham 2-0 Sevilla (AET, 2-1 agg.)]

Having dispatched Sevilla, perennial winners of this tournament and the team of the current highest standing, we shouldn't be scared of anyone. Only, I'm more scared of Braga than I am of Barcelona. It would be classic West Ham to beat the best and then lose to relative nonentities. Witness knocking Manchester City out of the League Cup only to fall to Spurs in a subsequent round! Therefore, Lyon and Barcelona represent a decent route back to Seville for the final.

The downside is that the home legs were drawn first, so the cauldron of noise created last night won't be quite so climactic. Never again let it be said that the London Stadium lacks atmosphere. It was on the promise of nights like this that we made the move, so the norm must now become both regular European football and cacophonous vocal support.

My biggest fear, more than any potential opponent, is that the first legs will prove damp squibs. European football has a reputation for cagey affairs but we need to be brave and play on the front foot to maximise home advantage. Having a small deficit to overturn against Sevilla suited the mindset that's seen us come from behind to pick up more points than anyone else in the Premier League this season. We're less comfortable defending leads, even healthy ones! The most successful team I ever played in had a nil-nil mantra, the secret being to maintain an equilibrium and play our own game. Moyes has undoubtedly got us on a more even keel than I've ever known but we do still have a tendency to invite pressure when protecting a narrow lead, which could be asking for trouble at Camp Nou (no disrespect intended to Eintracht Frankfurt who, until Barça's recent revival, I probably would have fancied to win their quarter-final).

If fan performance last night was 10/10, team performance was probably only about 7.5, with a lot of sloppy play compensated for by sheer heart and desire. There's more to come, and Sunday's match against Spurs [Tottenham 3-1 West Ham] represents their cup final rather than ours this year. Like I said, bring on Barça.

Who's the Biggest W*nker?

8 April 2022

[Europa League quarter-final, first leg: West Ham 1-1 Lyon]

Teams we've failed to beat at home this season include Crystal Palace, Southampton, Newcastle, Brighton and Brentford. Ergo, a draw with Olympique Lyon, 2020 Champions League semi-finalists, was never going to be a disreputable result. That it was achieved with a referee who made Mike Dean look like Pierluigi Collina actually makes it quite a remarkable result.

Cresswell's soft sending-off was of course the turning point. Felix Zwayer's vexing decision to reach for the red was reminiscent of Keith Hackett all those years ago when Tony Gale tugged back Gary Crosby. The vital difference is that this time we didn't fold. In fact, I'd go so far as to say it galvanised both players and fans in a match that looked as if it was meandering towards a draw anyway. And, having shown that Lyon's suspect backline can be breached with 10 men, going to France with 11 shouldn't be a daunting prospect. The red card altered the narrative so that their supporters, used to victory, would have expected as much. Instead, a draw perpetuates the disaffection around the Parc Olympique Lyonnais in what's an underwhelming season where all hopes rest on the Europa League. If things don't go their way early on then expect the hostility from the stands to be directed towards the home team rather than the away.

The game will likely be settled on small margins, so let's hope for a better ref! The sending-off was derisory but Cresswell unfortunately gave him a decision to make and there's enough subjectivity in such a call that there was little hope of it being overturned. Zwayer has history – a ban for match-fixing in 2005 and a performance so scandalous in this season's Dortmund vs Munich match it resulted in Jude Bellingham's irate post-match complaints being investigated by police! Moyes was justified in bringing up the 'foul' on Bowen in the build-up to Cresswell's 'foul', not because of any realistic expectation that play would be taken that far back but because it further highlights the dubious decision-making. Most inexplicable were Bowen's farcical booking and stopping play for Lyon's play-acting. And the Oscar goes to Moussa Dembele, whose sly wink said it all.

Runners and Riders

11 April 2022

On the weekend of the Grand National, when a 50/1 shot ridden by a retiring amateur jockey reminded us of sport's capriciousness, West Ham failed to take advantage of Wolves, Manchester United and Arsenal's earlier falls, instead resembling a mare that's been flogged to death by limping to defeat at Brentford [2-0].

Although not quite ready to be put down, Antonio isn't the thoroughbred of early season. He has, however, run the football equivalent of 30 furlongs. For someone with dodgy hamstrings to have been used so relentlessly, we ought really to marvel at his resilience rather than bemoan his form. Like Atlas, he's shouldered our offence all season long because there's nobody else to take the weight. Which begs serious questions of the trainer and owners …

With the teams around us losing – bar Spurs, who look by far the freshest and are reaping the benefit of a change of personnel and the January investment in Bentancur and Kulusevski – we had a free hit in the race for European football. With Lyon looming, it would have been sensible to rest the hardest-worked members of the squad, such as Souček and Antonio. Clearly, Moyes doesn't trust the likes of Diop, Masuaku, Král and, most damningly, his own big-money acquisition, Vlašić.

Given the fretting over Thursday–Sunday fixtures, the possibility of standing sixth and Europa League semi-finalists at Easter represents a Herculean effort from the tried and trusted regulars. With five subs coming into effect next season though, it's going to be even more of a squad game, weighted in favour of the big spenders. So, will we do a Noble Yeats or are we going the way of Discorama and Eclair Surf, the two tragic fatalities of Saturday's race? I see three possible outcomes …

50/1 Fairy Tale

Winning the Europa League is the outside bet that will catapult us to another level. Even with minimal investment, the glory and the Champions League football it secures for next season would attract the many free agents coming on to the market (Lingard, Origi, Nketiah, Belotti, etc., even if the likes of Mbappé and Pogba remain in another galaxy). Proper investment could see us surpass the bottom half of the big six.

10/1 As You Were

Noble defeat to Lyon or Barcelona and a sixth- or seventh-place finish keeps things ticking over. Rice might be persuaded to stay for another season and a couple of decent summer purchases keeps the faithful believing that there are more majestic European nights on the horizon, but next season looks another slog for a thinly stretched squad.

1/2 Bubbles

Finish eighth in what's effectively now an eight-horse race, narrowly missing out on European football. Rice is allowed to leave for £100m, which is reinvested in half a dozen squad players. Lingard joins Newcastle. They, a similarly well-backed Aston Villa, a flourishing Crystal Palace and a resurgent Leicester and Everton push us into the bottom half of the table, anxiously looking over our shoulder as Bowen, Souček and others wonder where they'll be plying their trade in 2023/24. The 33-year-old Antonio is still our sole centre-forward.

Good Friday

15 April 2022

[Europa League quarter-final, second leg: Lyon 0-3 West Ham (1-4 agg.)]

It's a worry when West Ham have the power to make or break your Easter weekend! I didn't breathe easy until about the 85th minute last night but Lyon never really looked likely to stage a resurrection. It was a textbook Hammers performance against ideal opponents for Moyes's style of play; content to keep possession but without much thrust, they were easily suffocated and picked off. It could have been different if Ekambi's early drive had hit the post and gone in, but even if Lyon had taken the lead I'd have fancied us to cause them problems. As it was, Big Daws enhanced his cult-hero status by resembling a cross between Bobby Moore and Stuart Pearce, while Antonio did everything but score and all the others looked incredibly composed for what was probably the biggest match most of them have ever played.

On the eve of the match, I described it to the kids as one of the top-ten most important of my lifetime, which may sound a tad hyperbolic for a quarter-final but it's rare that we get this close to silverware. Ignoring the play-offs and relegation six-pointers, of which we've had so many that I've lost count, the only matches I could think of that topped it were the 2006 FA Cup final/semi-final and the 1991 semi (plus Italia '90, Euro '96, Russia 2018 and Wembley 2021 from an England viewpoint). Apologies to the boys of '86 but that's just beyond my memory's reach.

Now we face Frankfurt in an even bigger tie. That it's a rematch of our last European semi-final 46 years ago seems a favourable omen given that we prospered 4-3 on that occasion, albeit with the home/away legs reversed. Like Lyon, they currently flounder in mid-table but a team that conquered even a below-par Barcelona can't be underestimated. That they took 30,000 fans to Camp Nou indicates that a Europa League run means as much to their fanbase as to our own, whereas for Barça it was only ever a consolation prize. That arguably makes Frankfurt more formidable opponents and the Waldstadion will be an intimidating place to visit in the second leg. Then again, the Lyon crowd created a raucous atmosphere and it was water off a duck's back to our lads, with even stand-in Diop displaying the elegance of a swan.

I've seen headlines already that suggest it will be a failure if we don't now win the trophy but it will still be a fairy tale if Noble and Rice jointly lift it on 18 May. The appeal of a glamour tie with Barcelona – besides a trip to Catalonia, which I couldn't afford (I wasn't even able to get tickets to London for the Lyon first leg after all 60,000 were snapped up before reaching general sale) – was that there's zero shame in the claret and blues losing to *La Blaugrana*, whereas everybody left in the competition is eminently beatable. Which isn't the same as saying we will or should beat them, just that we very well could. It's easy to get dizzy with the idea of a story-book ending for Mr West Ham, yet we need to maintain the humility he himself shows in the well-received image sweeping the changing room floor after possibly the most momentous victory of his career. No airs and graces, just quietly setting the standards for others to follow.

Neither our captain nor manager are perfect, and I was among those bemoaning Moyes's failure to rest key players in the understandably flat showing against Brentford. Needless to say, all is forgiven today. Will the Europa League take precedence now? Well, it's dangerous to put all your eggs in one basket. The gaffer's asked a lot of the players but he's also made clear that every competition is important and that standards can't be allowed to slip. Therefore, expect to see most of Thursday's heroes take to the pitch against Burnley on Easter Sunday. I'm not particularly religious but I'd happily do another 40 days of Lent to keep the big man* looking out for us.

* God, not Dawson. Craig is a mere mortal, although he's doing a good impression of a miracle performer. Loving the Ballon D'awson pun!

Purist Versus Pragmatist

17 April 2022

On the one hand, I really wanted to see Crystal Palace overcome the odds and win the FA Cup for the first time in their history. On the other, I really don't want a team below us taking up a valuable European place.

Chelsea looked half-asleep in the Wembley sunshine, still smarting from their gallant midweek failure in Madrid. Because who cares about an FA Cup semi-final having just missed out on a Champions League one? Answer: Crystal Palace and at least 86 of the other 92 clubs in the Football League.

It's almost taken for granted that seventh place in the Premier League equals European football but that's only because the cup competitions are monopolised by those who occupy the places above. Yet how little they mean to the fans was revealed by an Easter Day conversation with the Liverpool-supporting brother-in-law, who neglected to watch the previous day's victory over arch-rivals Manchester City in the other semi-final. And on the prospect of an unprecedented quadruple: 'We might not win anything.'

Er, you've already won the League Cup, less than two months ago! So easy to forget, especially when it was a dress-rehearsal against the same opponents they'll face in next month's FA Cup … these matches just blend into one another for Liverpool, Chelsea and Manchester City fans.

At least Arsenal, Spurs and Manchester United are trying to make things more interesting in the race for fourth. For two weekends in a row they've unexpectedly dropped points. Had we managed to beat either Brentford or Burnley [1-1] then we'd be right in the mix. Burnley even handicapped themselves by inexplicably sacking one of their greatest-ever managers less than 48 hours before visiting the London Stadium. Still, it's hard to feel too down with a draw that keeps us in the driving seat for seventh – and that last European qualifying place – when it was a 3-0 defeat to the same opponents four seasons ago that saw large-scale protests and recriminations.

Settling for seventh is actually galling when January investment could have propelled us to fourth but there are still 85 out of 92 Football League clubs who would swap places with us. As much as I want to win things, I rather dread the day that it's taken for granted. A Spuds-supporting friend had subjected his excited young son to yesterday's late loss to Brighton and, while laughing at their misfortune, the rest of us also sympathised with the football-mad six-year-old's tears and tribulations. 'He was inconsolable from the goal until the final whistle. Proper weeping!! It's a rite of passage though, innit?' Failure is character-building. Manchester City and Chelsea fans born 50 years ago are generally better human beings than those born 15 years ago. They say it's the hope that kills you but it's also the hope that keeps things interesting. It's the expectation that truly numbs and kills … give me the belief that things are winnable, prove it once in a (claret and) blue moon and I'll be happy.

Declan Rice Appreciation Post

19 April 2022

Like somebody in a relationship that they think is too good to be true and refuses to get carried away for fear that it will all come crashing down around them, I don't like to big-up Declan Rice too much. The world and his wife can see that Dec could do better, the man himself knows it, but he's not an arrogant c*** so the main hope is that he'll treat us well a little while yet and it will all end on good terms. And who knows … the way in which he kissed the badge after scoring against Lyon suggested his heart really does belong with us, but football fans have been burned enough times to know not to read too much into these spur-of-the-moment romantic gestures!

No one player defines the club but if we could pick 'the one' then it would definitely be Declan. My wife likes to categorise footballers into 'nice young men' and 'nasty pieces of work'. Dec has always fallen into the former but he also has just enough devil in him – that ruthless will to win is what makes him the player he is, especially after being released by Chelsea at 14, and it's why there can be no resting on our laurels if we're to have any hope of keeping him. We need to match the self-improvement that's seen him go from defensive shield to penetrative runner, making more ground than any other player in the Premier League this season. In the wake of our injury crisis – Diop reportedly being the third centre-back to be ruled out for the season – there's talk of Rice moving backwards but my feeling is that such a tactic would indeed be regressive. It's previously been said that he's both the best midfielder and the best defender we have – the same could possibly be said of England right now – but since cloning is sadly not an option, I'd keep him in a more advanced position where he can have more influence on the game. And it's not like we're spoilt for choice with midfield replacements either! Dec is our engine, a Rolls-Royce of a footballer, surrounded by Ford Escorts.

There have been rare moments when Rice has gone off the boil (pun totally intended, sorry) or looked despondent following a defeat, with supposed body language experts claiming on clickbait articles that he's agitating for a move. Well, as Moyes keeps politely stating to the press pimps, he's ours contractually until 2025 so others can cast envious glances but we want to build around him. Fail to do so and fans won't begrudge him a trophy-laden career elsewhere. If Manchester City or Liverpool made an offer then it would be understandable if his head was turned. But Manchester United at present look further from silverware than us and, under their current embargo, his first love Chelsea can't even buy a bag of rice, never mind the player.

Make good on the vows about squad investment, flash a trophy in front of him and I have faith that he'll put pen to paper and commit the best part of his career to his second love. Or am I just a love-drunk fool?

They Don't Think It's All Over

29 April 2022

[Europa League semi-final, first leg: West Ham 1-2 Eintracht Frankfurt]

After a dispiriting evening, it was some solace to hear the players sounding more confident than I feel. More heroics will be required in Frankfurt but then that's kind of been the theme of our Europa League knockout adventures. Overturning the deficit against Sevilla, overcoming a numerical disadvantage against Lyon …

We made life particularly hard for ourselves by giving their centre-forward the freedom of the 18-yard box to turn and float in a cross to test whether Fornals was awake in the first 50 seconds. He wasn't. That unfortunately played into their hands as, like a mirror image of ourselves, Eintracht Frankfurt are most comfortable without the ball and playing on the counter-attack, which made it all the more frustrating that we allowed them to waltz through again at 1-1 without applying any serious pressure.

I don't expect home advantage to change the pattern of play, which gives hope that we can stage a repeat of the last round if we're at our sharpest. Basically, it's a case of who takes their chances. Had Areola not got a strong outstretched hand to the ball in the second leg against Sevilla then this might all be moot. Similarly, Lyon seems a breeze in retrospect but it's easy to forget they hit the post with the tie level. Last night it was 3-1 on striking the woodwork and, had any one of them gone in, the second leg would look quite different. Bowen's insane injury-time bicycle kick in particular would have changed the complexion of the tie. How many times do they cannon off the bar and go in off the keeper? Luck deserted us in that second.

Except for the absolute best, every club relies heavily on Lady Luck in their quest for silverware, whether it's a favourable draw or a kind deflection. We need to be flawless in Frankfurt, but we also need to find fortune.

Architects of Our Own Downfall

5 May 2022

[Europa League semi-final, second leg: Eintracht Frankfurt 1-0 West Ham (3-1 agg.)]

Flawless? Far from it. Fortunate? About as lucky as a punter who's staked their life savings on Sad Ken. Still, you make your own luck, at least to some extent. The semi-final was shaped by a lethargic first minute in London and a killer red card in Frankfurt. I've no wish to vilify Cresswell because he's been a fine servant to the club but identical red cards in consecutive knockout stages severely blot his copybook. His flailing limbs as he was caught the wrong side of Hauge personified the latter part of our season: tired, disjointed, wayward.

Despite Moyes's obvious anger (lashing out at a ball boy is never a good look even if it's understandable), there can be few complaints about VAR upgrading yellow to red. There's a case that their man never had the ball under control and deliberately unbalanced Cress but if the boot had been on the other foot we'd have been howling for a dismissal. The biggest complaint is that a single reckless moment stole from us any realistic opportunity to progress. What could have been if it had stayed 11 vs 11 ...?

It's pointless getting hung up on 'what ifs' but *what if* the board had shown the ambition to capitalise on the promising position we were in in January? I've often been a GSB apologist, primarily because I don't think they're the bogeymen that they're often made out to be. The journey under them has undoubtedly been flawed but, if you compare where we are now with where we were when they took over, it would be hard to conclude that they've done a bad job. That said, a fair amount of the progress seems to have happened by luck (ironically enough) rather than sound judgement, and they must be the only fans who didn't recognise the urgent need for squad reinforcement if we were to maintain that Champions League challenge that they imprudently promised all those years ago. Are they simply biding their time before the sell-on clauses relating to the stadium expire in 2023? Hints that UK Athletics is ready to desert the London Stadium point to an interesting few years ahead.

So, congratulations to Frankfurt. They were nothing special but they deserved it over both legs. And congratulations to Rangers. Were they the best two teams in the competition? Not by a long shot – both would struggle to finish in the top half of the Premier League – but it's a final match-up that substantiates that prerequisite of performances plus providence. Seville will be quite something on 18 May and I'm gutted not to be part of it. Credit to the vast majority of fans who've followed our European adventures with distinction, and special mention to the few I know who had erroneously booked to be in Barcelona tonight and will no doubt be cancelling or transferring more flights to Spain tomorrow. As galling as the German celebrations were, their support was immense and they've been waiting almost as long as we have for a European final, albeit with a lot more domestic glory in the meantime. This century alone, Middlesbrough and Fulham have reached Europa League finals while Portsmouth, Wigan, Leicester, Blackburn, Birmingham and Swansea have all won domestic honours. The abiding reaction is the guttural plea, *when does it get to be our turn*?

Our final now is Sunday's match against relegated Norwich to make sure we're back in European competition next season. Given the remaining fixtures, three points should be enough to secure seventh, best of the rest, top of the league outside of the big f***ing six, who look set to monopolise the top half-dozen positions for the third time in five seasons, as well as tightening their stranglehold on the Champions League coffers with the proposed backdoor pass for the clubs with the best coefficient ranking. Newcastle's ability to disrupt the hierarchy is welcome even if it does threaten to knock us further down the pecking order. Oh well. To parrot our social media admins, 'We go again.'

A champagne season kept its fizz long after Christmas but went flat in the spring. One day we'll get to tell the story of when the corks popped in the summer and the joy bubbled over. All I ask is for one little bubble to stay airborne. To quote from one of the lesser-known verses:

> Happiness new seemed so near me,
> Happiness come forth and heal me.
> I'm forever blowing bubbles …

Acknowledgements

THANKS TO my parents for letting me go my own way, to my children for providing some perspective, and to my wife for being an occasional football widow.

Special thanks to season ticket holders Richard Porter, Michael Rowland and Kim Sibthorpe for supplying images. Impostor syndrome took hold while compiling this book; who am I to narrate these times? It's only that I happened to write down what was in my head, and I hope the contents authenticate my commitment, but a picture speaks a thousand words and those who were actually there – week in, week out, home and away – are the lifeblood of the club.

Thanks also to the WHUFC communications team for permission to use official club photos.

Finally, thank you to Pitch Publishing's editorial and design teams for making sense of my ramblings and setting them to print. Hopefully enough people will buy it to justify a sequel on the momentous occasion of West Ham actually winning something.

* For bonus material and further reading, please visit **www.chesterhammers.wordpress.com** *